ing

cate

PCCS BOOKS
Ross-on-Wye

First Published in 1995
Reprinted in 1996
Reprinted 1999

PCCS Books Ltd
Llangarron
Ross-on-Wye
Herefordshire
HR9 6PT
UK

Next Steps in Counselling - A Students' Companion for Certificate and Counselling Skills Courses

ISBN 1 898059 06 3

Cover design by Peter Kneebone
Printed by Redwood Books, Trowbridge, Wilts.

Contents

Chapter 1: **Introductions**   1

Section I - *Thinking about Helping*   13
Chapter 2: **Extending Our Thinking About Human Problems**   15
Chapter 3: **What is Helping?**   25
Chapter 4: **Defining the Counselling Approach**   33
Chapter 5: **The Core Conditions**   41
Chapter 6: **The Core Conditions Plus?**   59

Section II - *Theoretical Interlude*   67
Chapter 7: **Theoretical Interlude**   69

Section III - *Practising Counselling Skills*   93
Chapter 8: **Setting Up and Getting Started**   95
Chapter 9: **Listening and Exploring**   107
Chapter 10: **To Question or Not to Question?**   123
Chapter 11: **New Perspectives**   133
Chapter 12: **Challenge**   143
Chapter 13: **Action and Ending**   147
Helping Skills in Action: Karen's Story   155

Section IV - *Counselling Skills Issues and Settings*   163
Chapter 14: **Counselling Skills for Difficult Situations**   165
Chapter 15: **Ethics for Counselling Skills**   185
Chapter 16: **Helper Support**   195

Endpiece   207

References   213

Further Reading   214

Index   215

Acknowledgements

The authors and PCCS would like to thank the following publishers and authors for their kind permission to use extracts from the copyright material listed below.

British Association for Counselling, (1998) *Code of Ethics and Practice: Guidelines for those using Counselling Skills in their work,* Rugby: BAC.
Carkhuff, R.R. (1969), *Helping and Human Relations,* Holt, Rinehart and Winston.
Mearns, D. and Thorne, B. (1988) *Person-Centred Counselling in Action,* London: Sage.
McLeod, J. (1993) *An Introduction to Counselling,* Milton Keynes: Open University Press.
Rogers, C.R. (1951) *Client-Centered Therapy,* London: Constable.

Introductions

1

Many textbooks start with an *Introduction* which often seems a bit dull, going through the motions of saying why the book was written and how to get the best use out of it and thank you to all sorts of people the reader has never heard of. We don't want to start like that this time, although there are some thanks to be recorded and some of what we say in this first bit will tell you about why the book was written and how you might use it. We want to start in much the same way we would start with you in a face-to-face group, with *real introductions* and some exploration of the *ground rules*.

We will introduce you to ourselves, and to some of the illustrative characters whom we have invented to populate the vignettes in the book. We hope it helps you to make sense of our approach, our style and our choice of content.

Activity
Before you read any further please think (and make some notes if it helps) about the following:
- *If we were meeting at the beginning of a course, what would you tell us - and your fellow students - about yourself?*
- *What would you like to know about us and them?*
- *How do you feel doing this sort of exercise?*

You will have noticed from the spine that *'Next Steps'* has two authors and although we have tried to let the book have its own 'voice' there will also be times when we want to write as individuals, so it seems appropriate to introduce each other. To avoid too much repetition, it's worth noting first that we have some things in common. (That now includes this book and its history.)

Both of us are English, largely able-bodied, white, male, vegetarian, divorced and now living in other stable heterosexual relationships with family commitments We both have academic backgrounds in Psychology and although our career paths have been very different, we both have long histories in the world of counselling. We have been acquainted through the counselling conference network, that many practitioners and academics inhabit, for many years but have only got to know each other well since Pete accepted an invitation to be the external examiner for the professional post-graduate diploma course for which Alan has responsibility at Nottingham Trent University. Alan (initially with other Trent colleagues Ann Morley and Richard Broadley) had been struggling with some bits of this text for some time and when Pete moved out of his college work and into full-time writing and publishing, it was agreed that what had already been started could form the basis for a text to be written by us which would be part of the *'Steps'* series that was being planned by PCCS.

Part of the motivation for me, Alan, in wanting to get into joint authorship, which is rather demanding, is getting to know Pete better. At the moment it feels like working together is stimulating and satisfying from the point of view of the writing itself and it has also enabled us to become friends. I hope it still feels like that when we get to the end.

Alan introducing Pete

In the earlier text in this series (the Students' Companion for Basic Introductory Courses called *'First Steps in Counselling'* which Pete wrote) he introduced himself, talking a bit about his partner, their children and his start in counselling as an undergraduate, working on a drop-in, phone-in youth counselling project (Off the Record in Newcastle-upon-Tyne in about 1972). Pete also said a bit about his move out of college teaching and management to working with Maggie, his wife, at their own writing publishing and training enterprise, and the effect this was having on his sense of what was work and what wasn't. He did not say, because he is far too modest, that he is one of the most experienced and respected trainers of counsellors in the country having set up and helped to run a whole raft of courses in counselling (including certificate and professional diploma courses which have been highly acclaimed). Before that he had an innovatory career in teaching and examining Psychology GCEs and after it he got swept into higher management, before he decided that that was not the best use of his talents and was reorganised into the, for him, happy state of redundancy.

Pete seems to me to be genuinely enterprising (witness the risk and hard work undertaken to get PCCS on the road), but, perhaps surprisingly, does not seem to be motivated much by money or power. He says he is doing all these things because he thinks it might be valuable and more importantly because it looks like it could be good fun. Pete cares a lot about people, and about issues like standards in training, but I think one of the fundamental criteria for him when trying to decide whether something is worth expending energy on is will it be a whizz? If it might be, then it's in with a chance. It's difficult to put this over, Pete seems to have found a great balance between being earnestly committed and taking nothing too seriously. He is really good to be with, quick witted, inventive and warm, he's supportive and encouraging, and really very engaging, but I can't go on because I keep sensing his rather whimsical smile as he reads this!

I think Pete's lightness of touch has had a significant effect on my writing. In a face to face teaching situation I can be inventive and quite lively, but my style in writing (and I haven't done that much) tended to be academic and a bit ponderous. I hope that I've escaped that here without creating a false mateyness that would just trivialise and patronise.

Pete introducing Alan

Each time I do an exercise in which I have to introduce myself or someone else I seem to get less and less spontaneous. The activity of writing itself tends to destroy spontaneity, but I would like to try to recapture mine right now and try not to be influenced by Alan's style or what he has written about me.

We met several years ago at various conferences and workshops on the counselling/training network, although we didn't really *meet* until we spent an evening together in the bar at a BAC conference a few years ago. Since then I have got to know Alan in a number of professional and some more personal settings.

Alan works at Nottingham Trent University where he is Principal Lecturer in Counselling & Psychotherapy and he also has a thriving private practice as a counsellor and supervisor of counsellors in Nottingham. Alan is a natural teacher and facilitator. He may have had to learn the skills at some time, but has a certain easy presence in front of a group that seems so much a natural part of himself which I admire. I look forward to him bringing that part of himself to our working together on this book.

In addition to his varied work in Nottingham, he also finds time to serve the wider community of counsellors and therapists through his work with BAC where he is currently Chair of the Individual Accreditation Group. He is also a member of the Committee for the British Psychological Society Division of Counselling Psychology.

What I like most about Alan is that he is a principled and thoughtful person with an enthusiasm for counselling and personal development. I like the passion with which he holds his views and his readiness to share this with anyone. We have really good fiery discussions over the issues on which we do not agree, yet he always seems to keep an open mind in the heat of it all.

With his high-powered counselling and psychology connections, you might think that he could be aloof or distant. You would be wrong. As well as being down-to-earth, Alan Frankland is a kind, colourful, big man; not larger than life, but just the right size for life in every sense and as such he stands out in the crowd. I think he is great company.

Alan and Pete introducing this book
One of the things that makes many textbooks about counselling and therapy come to life are the chunks of case material that they contain, in other words the sense of other people, other lives, that the authors get across to us to make and illustrate their points. This book is intended as a Companion for Counselling Skills/Certificate courses, not for courses aiming at professional counsellor training, so it seemed to us that we should not be illustrating every point with material drawn from formal counselling situations, because many of you who use this text are not aiming to be counsellors or therapists. If it is your intention to use some of the counselling skills approach in your current work or in other helping relationships, and we always use examples from formal counselling work, then there would be a mismatch.

It is also our intention to add skills to your repertoire, not take any away. By this we hope that counselling skills could always be an additional option in any helping situation, not a replacement for other professional skills. Whatever professional helping skills you have already such as those associated with for example, nursing or teaching, we would wish you to keep and develop. Further skills we will be hoping to develop are the ability to know when counselling skills might be useful and when they might not, and to be clear about the difference between using counselling skills and being a counsellor.

It seems to us that relatively few people want, or need, or get offered, formal counselling help as they make their way through life, but millions have the need for some kind of help that could be (and sometimes already is) enhanced by a counselling approach. We want to draw examples from this range of experiences and not primarily from therapy. If we are not using actual case histories, how are we to populate the book, to give it life in the way that such studies might otherwise have done? We have settled on two strategies.

In the first place, we are inviting you to be in the book with us. In many of the chapters we introduce activities and exercises (as you have already seen both in this book and in *'First Steps'*) which we ask you to use a pen and paper on your own or maybe with a friend or fellow student to join in with. We might get you to list some of your own thoughts, capturing and categorising some of your own feelings and responses, discussing in an internal dialogue or actually with colleagues some of the issues raised by these activities. Often we will include some of our personal responses, not as 'right' answers in any way, but as grist to the mill in coming to an understanding of human processes. At other places too, you will find bits of our own lives and experiences where they can serve to clarify or illustrate a point.

Secondly, we have introduced a cast of characters in situations drawn from life. These are not portraits of particular friends, relatives or clients loosely disguised, but portraits that we hope have a truth and reality even though they are of fictional people in fictional lives. Unless you read nothing but textbooks and biographies, and only ever use T.V. for news and current affairs you know that such characters (given a bit of generosity from the reader or viewer) come to life and can be as real as the actual Neighbours on your Street, at Home and Away.

Introducing the people in our vignettes

Ashley, coming up to sixteen, a pupil at Marketon Comprehensive, a school which may have to go some way to respond to him appropriately.

Beth, a married woman in her early fifties, with grown up children and a demanding job.

Charlie, middle aged, divorced, living in a pit village which doesn't have a pit any more.

Devina, late thirties, of Mauritian origin, originally came to England to train as nurse twenty years ago, now working as a counsellor for a G.P. practice, and as a college lecturer, and as a mother to three young people.

Frank, the name we have given to an unhappy single guy who first appears in some of Carl Rogers' work (Rogers 1951).

Georgie isn't very bright or very happy - but when this young man does smile he could break your heart.

Helen is just a baby when we first meet her. Not everything she learns from her parents Ian and Jane is really that beneficial, but 'with a little help from her friends'...

Karen is a confident professional woman, then one day an articulated lorry pushes her off the motorway.

We have given our characters problems and issues to carry, some of them feel the weight of that most of the time, although in others, as with you and I, the stresses we have as a result of our life circumstances and the kind of society we live in, only weigh on us some of the time. The rest of the time, like everyone else, they seek to make the best of what they've got; trying to grow, to be happy, to laugh, to be loved, to be in relationships, to care for others and to be cared for, to work because they need to and for the pleasures it can bring: in short to be members of British society at the end of the twentieth century.

Of course there is a chance that our skills are not up to animating these people and their dialogue beyond cardboard-cutout characters, (otherwise we'd be soaps script writers and not counselling trainers!).

Groundrules

As we have mentioned above, we would like you to be in this book with us, which means that you must find it comfortable enough to get into and learn through. If the book were a course, as tutors rather than authors we would spend some time early in the course asking you what kind of environment you need in order to feel comfortable and safe enough to take the risks necessary if we are to learn about ourselves and counselling. This is sometimes referred to as negotiating groundrules.

We can't exactly negotiate groundrules for this book with you, but we can tell you how we have gone about creating the learning environment of the book, and we can suggest that you ask yourself some simple questions about your own preferences for a safe learning environment.

Activity
What do you need in order to create a safe learning environment for yourself?
• What sort of balance between support and challenge? (see 'First Steps in Counselling' p.31)
• What about confidentiality?
• What about issues of equal opportunity and oppression?
• What level of commitment to learning do you want from others, e.g. attendance and punctuality?
• What quality of feedback do you think will help you learn best?
• What other 'learning environment issues' are important to you?

For our part, we have tried conscientiously with the characters, the vignettes, and with the rest of the text to avoid stereotyped and oppressive imagery. This has been one of *our* ground rules as authors, but like everyone else writing in English at this time we have struggled with the fact that gendered pronouns like 'he' and 'his' inevitably put readers in mind of males. We have used a number of devices to deal with this, sometimes using 'he', sometimes 'she' to mean both, sometimes using the third person plural because its not gendered, although it may not always be grammatically quite in order.

We have tried to ensure that needy/disadvantaged and provider/carer roles are reasonably distributed and to ensure that problems are not unreasonably attributed to age or gender, to race or sexual preference, to religious beliefs or physical abilities. We have taken the fairly pragmatic view that being oppressed implies no blame but it certainly can produce problems in living for the individuals concerned. We hope that, like real people, our characters will sometimes surprise you.

In a live group we might hope to see the emergence of a ground rule that acknowledges the reality of oppression, a ground rule that encourages all participants to challenge oppressive behaviour in themselves and in others, but acknowledges that learning is about reaching out for what you don't know so that it is inevitable that learners (and to some degree we are all learners) will make mistakes, and that it is desirable that they should do so, otherwise they cannot continue to learn. We have applied this rule to ourselves, and hope that you will too, as you

think about the material here and on your course. Part of learning comes through feedback and we would be glad to hear from you if you have thoughts on these issues, or anything else in this book.

How this book works
Learning about counselling skills involves three main strands or broad topics:
  • Theory
  • Skills
  • Personal development or personal growth.

Some courses in counselling skills may be divided up into these topics with a certain amount of time devoted to each, whilst some present sessions in which the student is expected to unravel the 'cloth' into the individual strands. Books may be organised in these ways too, with some containing sections on

---

Why is it important to get your learning environment *right* when learning counselling?

We think we have presented the ideas in this book in a logical order, more or less proceeding from first principles to detailed analysis of skills and some thoughts about counselling in practice, but there's more to it than that. Both counselling and learning are processes of change. In a counselling setting, the change sought would be positive, safe yet challenging, self-motivated and self-directed. In a learning setting, especially one in which the learning is about counselling skills, we would also want the change process to be positive, safe yet challenging, self-motivated and self-directed.

It is vitally important that you, the learner, have a big hand in the creation and maintenance of your learning environment so that you can direct your learning in a positive, challenging way. This means having a say in how it is set up, i.e. to be non-oppressive, safe and confidential, yet stimulating and challenging and all the other things that you want it to be. It is up to you to negotiate these things.

skills and theory. You can see from the contents page that *this* book is organised in four main sections:

1. Thinking About Helping.
2. Theoretical Interlude.
3. Practising Counselling Skills.
4. Counselling Skills Issues and Settings

There are two important points we would like to make about this book:

• Firstly, we don't just start Chapter 2 and let you get on with it. There's plenty of opportunity to review your learning as we go along and of course, the vast majority of readers will be students on a counselling skills course where you will get information, direction and support from your course tutors and from your fellow students.

• Secondly, one of the strands of learning listed above (personal development) is missing from the contents page. This is deliberate. We think it is important at this stage for you to follow your own path of personal growth, and determine what it is that you wish to learn about counselling skills, so we have put *this* book together so that at different times we are:

• giving information in some parts (e.g. theory and topics such as support and supervision),

• asking you to get involved via exercises or looking at you own experiences in others (e.g. in skills development),

• expecting you to plot your own course of learning through the book on other issues (e.g. personal development, oppression and boundary issues in your counselling skills practice),

• and also suggesting that you keep a record of your learning or journey through the book in the form of a personal or learning journal.

The book is organised into four major sections, *Thinking About Helping, Counselling Theory, Skills Practise* and *Issues and Settings,* whilst there are the *vignettes* running through all three sections. We hope it doesn't get too confusing, but we do expect that you will have to flick back and forth through the pages to 'chase' certain themes. At the same time, some people will wish to start at page 1 and read the book all the way through to the end, just like reading a novel. We hope we've written a book that's interesting enough to do this with too.

To help show you how you might plot your course or plan your learning pathway through the book we have drawn what we call a **Learning Grid** on the following two pages, in which you can locate and follow some of the major themes in the book for yourself. These themes are not clearly marked like a wildlife trail through a country park. They're there to be *discovered*, but we've given you what we hope are helpful map references. There are plenty of possible themes that you might be interested in that we've deliberately not included (the Grid isn't intended to be exhaustive), and you will have to do the searching yourself, which means you will hopefully get the pleasure of making your own discoveries.

We have included as an example of how it might be done, *Boundaries of counselling skills and other helping relationships.* We have given a few signposts for *Issues of power and oppression,* leaving you to complete it in your own way. We have left *personal growth possibilities* blank, because we don't know what your personal growth possibilities might be.

Learning

	Section I *Thinking About Helping*	Section II *Theoretical Interlude*
Boundaries of counselling skills and other helping relationships.	Chapters 2, 3, & 4 (all of them) Chapter 5, pp 53, 54, 55 Chapter 6, pp 59, 64	Chapter 7, pp 72, 73, 77, 78, 82, 83
Issues of oppression and power.	Chapter 2, pp 17,18, 19, 20, 21, 22 Chapter 3, pp 27, 29	
Personal growth possibilities.		

Grid

Section III *Practising Counselling Skills*	Section IV *Counselling Skills Issues and Settings*	
Helping Skills in Action: Karen's Story, pp 155-162	Chapter 14, pp 167, 171, 176 Chapter 15 (all of it). Chapter 16, pp 195, 196, 202, 203	Boundaries of counselling skills and other helping relationships.
	Chapter 14, pp 175, 176 Chapter 15, pp 186, 187	Issues of oppression and power.
		Personal growth possibilities.

Making a record of your learning

In *First Steps in Counselling* it was suggested that students or trainees might like to keep a personal journal during their introductory course to help monitor their process of learning and personal development. As you proceed through the various stages of your counselling skills training (and counsellor training, if that's what you decide to do) it becomes progressively more important to keep a record of your learning and development.

Since this book is written for people at the stage of learning about, and developing, counselling skills, we thought it would be useful to take a moment to consider just what kind of recording and monitoring of your experiences would be helpful to you. We have already asked you to think about what groundrules you want in order for your learning environment to feel safe. Now we'll do the same thing with the focus on recording your learning and development.

Activity
• *Think back to other occasions when you have wanted to learn things.*
  • *What kind of record did you keep then, notes, diagrams, quotes from books?*
• *Learning about counselling is different from some other subjects because for much of the time you will be learning about yourself.*
  • *What ways of recording learning would be best for counselling? (You could brainstorm ideas with fellow trainees.)*

In addition to the ideas you have come up with we would like to offer one or two suggestions based on our experiences as both learners and trainers.

Personal Journal: recommended by the majority of counselling skills or certificate courses. Your course tutors may have some requirements as regards the headings you can use. A personal journal can be kept just like a diary, without any structure other than dates and possibly times for each entry. You may, however like to differentiate between course times and other times, or even have separate pages or parts of each page for personal learning, skills learning, group issues, aims and goals, assignments or whatever. A personal journal, course requirements aside, can be as flexible as your imagination will allow.

If you do decide to split your personal learning journal up into sections, it might be helpful to ask yourself some of the following questions:
  • What do I want to learn this week/month/year?
  • What have I learned/discovered this week/ month/ year?
  • How did I learn/discover these things?
  • How do I feel about the things that I have discovered?
  • How do I feel about my learning process?
  • What is going on for me on the course?
  • How do I feel about course-related or group-related issues?

There will probably be other questions you can ask yourself and other themes in your learning and development that you will want to explore.

Reading Log: It might be helpful to keep a record of books, articles and newspaper cuttings that you read during your counselling skills training. Indeed, the title, author, publisher and date published of *any* published material or media (TV and radio programmes too) connected to counselling could be entered in your reading log. You might find it useful to write down both a brief summary of the book or article along with any quotes plus the page references, and in the case of magazine and newspaper articles, you could even keep the cuttings.

As you progress through your training, there will be many occasions when you need to remember that particular 'perfect' quote or make reference to that brilliant book...if only you had kept a record! Essays and other assignments are also made much easier with an up-to-date reading log.

Skills Directory: Keeping a list of counselling skills that you have come across during your reading and training can be an extremely useful reference for the future. A suggested structure for such a 'directory' could be as simple as:
  • naming and defining each skill,
  • noting in which theoretical approach it originated,
  • suggesting when it might be appropriate to use the skill, and
  • an illustration of what the consequences of using it might be.

There are many ways you could choose to 'catalogue' counselling skills, including offering your own views and comments on the skills you discover in the literature and your feelings on trying to acquire them in practice.

Chapter Summary

Introductions

In helping relationships that use counselling skills it is important to get things right from the very first moment of the relationship. The same is true when it comes to *learning* about counselling skills. The environment in which we learn has to be just right. We have tried to do this in this first chapter:

1. On counselling skills courses it is important that we get to know the people we will be working with, both fellow students and tutors. Alan and Pete introduced each other to give some idea of who they are and how their relationship might affect their work as authors.
2. This book will develop ideas about counselling skills through the use of characters in vignettes. The characters are; Ashley, Beth, Charlie, Devina, Frank, Georgie, Helen and Karen.
3. In face-to-face learning groups, *groundrules* are important. We wanted to let you, the reader, know something about our groundrules for writing..
4. Some topics such as the boundaries of helping relationships, power and oppression and personal growth do not appear as discrete chapters in the book. A *learning grid* is included to help you trace your learning pathways through the book on these and other issues.
5. Making a concrete or permanent(ish) record of your learning in counselling skills is encouraged by most tutors. We suggest a *personal journal, reading log* and *skills directory* to give you some ideas.

Section I
Thinking About Helping

Extending Our Thinking About Human Problems
Page 15

What is Helping?
Page 25

Defining the Counselling Approach
Page 33

The Core Conditions
Page 41
Empathy; page 41, Respect; page 46, Congruence; page 50.

The Core Conditions Plus ?
Page 59

Vignettes

Ashley: 19, 21, 22, 29, 63.
Beth: 20, 21, 22, 26, 51.
Charlie: 19, 21, 22, 36.
Devina: 33.
Georgie: 47, 53.
Helen: 49.

Extending Our Thinking About Human Problems

2

When we don't have our 'helping hats' on it is sometimes easy, and even pleasurable, to analyse and categorise people; and to say,

> *'You know what her problem is...she's been spoilt,'* or, *'He's a bully,'* or, *'No wonder he's like that, he's been henpecked.'*

This unidimensional way of dealing with people and their issues is reinforced all around us. The tabloid newspapers are full of snapshot personal details and commentaries on the Royals, and other Rich & Famous, and the Less Well-Off and Not-So-Famous. The T.V. ratings are topped by soaps, where luckily the characters are not always presented as flat cardboard cut-outs, but even so we are still encouraged to make judgements about their personalities and their lives, and are 'invited' to sort them out.

But as helpers we have to develop a way of relating to others and approaching their problems that does not see them as simple, 'categorisable' beings who can be dismissed in a single, neat judgement, but which allows space for the richness of the individual and the multidimensional nature of their lives, whilst acknowledging and reflecting the fallibility of us all.

This chapter was very difficult to write because it could be seen as encouraging you to put people into boxes; to look at them and their lives and to say,

> *'Ah yes, I know what's wrong with them.'*

We do **not** want to give that impression. We believe that that way of working is limiting and disrespectful and does not have a rightful place in a counselling approach to helping.

However it is necessary (and this is where our dilemma crystallises) that those who are helping others should be aware of all the complex factors affecting the individual.

'No man is an island' is a truism that has a particular meaning to helpers. Individuals live in the real world and that real world rubs off on us, knocks corners off us and moulds us into particular shapes and sizes. As people using counselling skills we should be on the look-out for these real-world forces so that we can appreciate their size and power. Not so that we can reduce people's problems but so that we can be ready with some understanding. We will not know a person's particular response to those forces because they will all be different, but we will better prepared for the issue should it arise.

We hope this opening chapter helps you understand this dilemma - striking a balance between seeing the person on the one hand and at the same time the wider issues that affect their lives on the other. Encouraging a flexible, informed way of thinking about human problems does have its challenges. If the chapter seems to stray across the line, then this simply reflects the nature of the dilemma.

We believe that helpers need to move away from simplistic unidimensional ways of thinking about problems, so this chapter aims to be an extended exercise in 'interactive' multidimensional thinking. It is rather like thinking aerobics - the start of a fitness programme for the mind to get us warmed up and flexible for the really hard work later on. We are inviting you to see how complex problems really can be, and how we need to develop ways of understanding that do justice to this complexity.

We also aim to base the evidence in our experience as much as possible, and throughout the chapter we try to develop examples of common problems that may touch any of us in various ways at various times.

Being Person-Centred in outlook can be unidimensional if it is taken as an excuse to ignore the world and see everything as an individual problem. We neither wish to turn our backs on the world to concentrate on the individual, nor to ignore the individual by disrespectfully pigeonholing them.

I started out on this chapter by trying to list a number of situations where I felt I needed help, where I had a problem, or where others seemed to be indicating to me that they had a problem in getting through their lives. I did it as a kind of brainstorming activity, the problems did not have to be of any particular type or importance.

> *Activity*
> *You could try this brainstorming activity too. Getting involved might help you understand the issues better.*
> • *Make a list of your own problems.*

My initial list included items about:

- cutting my finger when cleaning out a drain,
- deciding whether to buy a house,
- the fan-belt on my van breaking,
- feeling unreal when I heard that my Mother had died,
- being out of breath and out of my depth in rough water,
- wondering whether I could sustain the tension of a love affair,
- feeling powerless in the face of changes at work, and the behaviour of a manager towards me,
- not being able to lift an awkwardly shaped trunk on my own,
- not being able to find a diagram I needed to illustrate a lecture,
- being conscious of feeling overweight.

I then thought about other people's problems in living that I have some involvement with and I added:

- being asked for extra time to complete an assignment,
- caring for a little girl after her father had been killed,
- telephone calls from a friend having a hard time on a course,
- being sent photographs of a knife slicing an apple,
- other, more direct, requests for help from my counselling clients,
- a member of my family wondering aloud about how to get back from a late film,

• being aware of a black colleague denied an opportunity for a career development,
• the raggedy man who shouts a request for money for a cup of tea sometimes when I walk to work.

Activity
• *How you would sort your list into different types of problem?*
• *How many different categories of problem can you see in your list?*
• *Make a note of your categories*

As I was categorising these problems it seemed to me that some were essentially **practical** and that others were more **personal**, although I noticed that even the most practical had a personal dimension and vice versa, e.g.:
• The RAC man who came to replace my fan-belt had to deal with my anxiety as well as the practical issues of getting me going again.
• The care I offered to the young person traumatically bereaved was not just love and some kind of security, but at times day-to-day care, food, clean clothes and trips to the zoo.

Even if you might have made a somewhat different classification of these needs, I am pretty sure that this practical/personal division will also make some sense to you. Even this very basic classification of people's needs into personal and practical demonstrates that people, their needs and our ways of understanding how we can help are not unidimensional. We can see straight away that people and their needs are complex, multidimensional and

multifaceted. Our ways of thinking must be so too if we are to understand their needs in all their richness.

To start with, it is probably worth making the point that not all personal difficulties are purely individual difficulties. It is often said that human beings are fundamentally social beings, so their difficulties will have a social dimension, either in relation to the wider society, or to do with their immediate social environment. It is even probable that the majority of those problems we see as *wholly* individual will have had their roots in social experience of some kind. This is part of the reason why problems are helped through essentially social or interpersonal relationships.

There are a number of personal difficulties which we experience in relation to Society, or the broad national structure(s) and culture(s) in which we grow up and live our lives. These difficulties sometimes have to do with *systems* operating within our societies like Education, Work or Employment and the Economic system, the Legal System etc. They could be called *Systemic Issues*

When someone is caught in the middle of a systemic issue, we may think of many ways to help them resolve the problem and ease their distress:
• At one extreme, we might think that the answer lies in reforming the system.
• At the other extreme we might think that the individual themselves has to change.

It is clearly not the case that an individual's difficulties with one or more of these systems can *only* be resolved by reforming the system itself, but too often helpers seem to err in the opposite direction in believing that problems with systems are actually just personal issues of maladjustment that can *only* be resolved within the individual.

For some people, being able to operate effectively within systems, and being able to challenge them effectively, is made more difficult because of beliefs and values which operate in the society to suggest that such individuals cannot or should not succeed because their success could be seen as a threat to the society..

These forces can be summarised under the general label of *Issues of Oppression*. Whilst there are a variety of forms and foci of oppression which affect different people in different ways it is clearly a major force in the personal lives of many individuals, and we need to develop some understanding of the issues involved if we are to be effective helpers because otherwise we risk seeing all personal problems as merely individual problems, and end up reinforcing the problem rather than helping to resolve or ameliorate it.

One way of understanding our interactions with the wider systems of society and the issues of oppression is to ask questions about the power that individuals have (or experience themselves as having) to influence the path of their own lives. It is clear from our own experience, let alone numerous political, sociological and psychological studies, that people feel uncomfortable and unhappy when they experience themselves as relatively powerless.

The illustrations on the following pages should help to clarify these concepts. These are fragments of stories about peoples lives and the sort of help they can expect to get in everyday situations. The help given in these illustrations is not there as a model of good practice, but as a focal point for discussion. None of the characters is real.

Note *We have used the same conventions throughout the vignettes;*

• This typeface is storyline or conversation.

• *This typeface is commentary on the story.*

Some characters appear just the once, whilst others are followed through the book. You will find the pages on which the vignettes appear, listed on the reverse of each 'Section' title page.

Ashley

Ashley is a tall, attractive, intelligent teenager with a big grin and a fast line in backchat who is seen as disruptive in class and sometimes is aggressive towards female teachers. He has been bunking off from classes in his successful market town school for several days this term. He and his parents approach the year head asking for assistance to avoid the exclusion ruling that seems imminent. To the year head, and maybe even to Ashley and his parents, the problems will seem to be both personal and individual. Other people in his class get on with their teachers and there is a polite but friendly atmosphere in his group. Ashley seems to lack self-discipline and is seen as unwilling to develop his assumed strengths in music and basketball.

All this may be true, as is Ashley's parents' acknowledgement that he has not really settled since his paternal grandmother died and the family moved away from the city to live in Marketon, his mother's birthplace. But is it enough to only understand the problem in these individual terms?

If we add the information that Ashley's father came to England from Jamaica in the late 50s it immediately becomes clear that this is not just an individual issue; that stereotypes may be operating (his teachers expect him to be good at music and sport), but issues of oppression will need attention as much as issues of grieving. The apparent failure to interact positively with the educational system, and the risk of negative interactions with the legal system in bunking off and aggression to teachers is not simply an individual idiosyncrasy but a personal response to a wider oppression issue.

If Ashley and his family are to sort this out they might need to develop some sense of their power to make things different, and to deal with the whole range of the issues from the personal grief to the (possibly unintended but nevertheless real) oppression of the expectations placed on the only black teenager in a school that has not yet thought its way through these important questions.

Charlie

The roots of Charlie's problem seem simple by comparison. He is in his mid-forties and has not worked now for several years. His redundancy money is long gone and he is depressed. This is clearly a Systemic Issue, to do with redundancy and unemployment in an industry that is past its peak in a slowing economic climate. Charlie has a personal problem but its causes are clearly not just individual. Even when Charlie gets charged with petty offences the probation report makes much of the depression that is common to the long-term unemployed in financially depressed areas when men feel disenfranchised from the economic and social system.

And no doubt there is truth in this, but there is another side to this too. Charlie's ex-workmate Zack was made redundant on the same day, and he's not depressed and offending. He has been no more fortunate in finding work than Charlie, and he and his wife had a really hard time adjusting to him being at home all day and not having the big money they were used to, but Zack has come through the depressed stage, he has got involved with the local community centre, helps to run the youth league team and is trying to learn the trombone to revive the town band. Zack is no brighter than Charlie, but seems 'luckier' and has begun to make a new life.

If there are such marked differences in response to systemic issues can they really be an adequate explanation ?

Beth

Beth has worked reliably for the same organisation for fourteen years, since she returned to work at 38 after her daughter went off to university and her son started an engineering job. Now at 52 she has, apparently suddenly, begun to make important errors in her work, she seems to be distracted and offhand with colleagues and has been taking odd days of sick leave in a most uncharacteristic manner.

In the end her boss decides that he must have a word with her - in a helpful rather than a disciplinary frame of mind. As he thinks about her age he wonders if the problems are to do with the menopause, but is not sure how to raise that and he wonders, too, about issues at home, for there are rumours in the staff group that Beth is not living with her husband any more and that their son has gone off to be a New Age traveller.

Beth responds quite openly to a kindly enquiry about her health; yes she knows that she is not easy to get on with now, and that she has been taking days off. She feels so tired all the time and is not sleeping well. Beth runs things over in her mind,
    'Yes, perhaps I ought to see the doctor, perhaps it is the menopause and no, everything at home is just fine.'
Her son has gone travelling - to New Zealand to see a cousin before his firm sends him to college for a couple of years to finish his engineering degree. Her husband is fine, he has recently taken up sailing.

Both leave the meeting thinking that the problem will soon be resolved. Beth has seen that she must get the doctor to give her something for her symptoms and her boss feels relieved that she will soon be her old reliable self.

What do we make of all this? Have Beth and her boss really looked at all the issues here?

Beth has been working for the same organisation for fourteen years, but the organisation is not really the same. Reorganisation and restructuring have created great insecurities over the past eighteen months, and new work responsibilities and schedules have been imposed on the workforce.

Beth finds more of her time spent with the computer and less with clients and more and more decisions are being devolved to her level, without any additional support for newly exposed staff. Perhaps some of the unhappiness lies here too, and not just in the obvious menopausal stuff, or even the secret envy she feels for the freedom both her children now have to develop their intellectual lives. Without understanding that the Systemic Issues, and quite possibly Oppression Issues, might be important, can we say we really understand Beth's situation?

These illustrations were drawn up to help illustrate the way in which *societal* and *oppression* issues are at work in personal problems. They also begin to throw light on those personal problems with a significant interpersonal or social dimension. Whilst it is important not to lose sight of the truism that your feelings are your feelings and that no-one can *make* you feel them, it is just as important to recognise that a great deal of our unhappiness has a shared, social, inter-personal, or *relationship* dimension. Amongst those kinds of problems we can list *relationship difficulties*, whether this is about isolation and loneliness, tensions with people we work and live with as colleagues, friends, family, or tensions with a central relationship where there may also be sexual concerns. Issues of abuse, physical, sexual and mental come in here because distortion of the interpersonal relationship can be a key feature of the harm that results from such abuse. Problems associated with grief and bereavement are, of course, about the loss of relationship.

If we listen to Ashley, Beth and Charlie a little more, we may understand more about their internal struggles and the issues that affect their lives.

Ashley

In Ashley's case although the Oppression Issues are clearly central to an understanding of the problem he is experiencing it is also clear that there are a number of interpersonal issues operating here. He has recently been bereaved of a significant relationship with his grandmother, and subsequent to that has suffered the further loss of familiar surroundings and friends. Ashley was consulted by his parents about the move and knew that he would miss his friends but could see the logic of going to Marketon and was willing to go along with the change: but a loss is still painful even when chosen. Perhaps his loneliness and grief are being hidden behind sharp words and macho behaviours, but they are still there affecting his interactions at every level.

Beth

Beth is suffering from issues of loss too. The organisation's rumour machine may have got it wrong about her son's travels, but they are nearer the mark about her relationship with her husband. He is still living at home, but has become irritable and distant and taken to spending more and more time with a new crowd of people who share his relatively recent passion for sailing. Beth misses the companionship she felt they had, but Ben is uncompromising about his new interest and she is beginning to realise that the youngish woman who crews for him may be a rival for his attention in other ways too. Just as Beth felt that she and Ben might give some attention to their rather flagging sexual life together his interests seem to have become focused elsewhere.

Charlie

One aspect of Charlie's current difficulties is that he is on his own. His second marriage did not survive the excited and then stormy period when he first got his redundancy money, and although his easy charm made him seem popular with women he has never managed sustained relationships. Secretly Charlie wonders about his sexuality and is disturbed by powerful dreams of enormous men showering together in the pit-head bath. He remembers being battered by his Dad for being too interested in sex and playing doctors with the neighbours' five year old when he was seven or eight. He also can't quite remember something that happened with his younger uncle the year before that. Anyway what's the point in thinking about that, he's seen those programmes about abused children on the telly. There's no way he's going to spend hours talking to some over-educated skirt with her head full of fancy ideas about the things he dreams of at night.

But what of the problems that are essentially *individual*? It is at this level that we respond to the world with feelings and each of us responds to the same situation in different ways with quite different feelings. We may be happy, sad, angry or frustrated, the list of words we might use to describe our feelings is almost limitless, see *First Steps in Counselling* p.79.

Feeling scared or sad or angry might not be too big an issue when we feel we have the resources and support to deal with what frightens or upsets us, but should we lose confidence in the support available to us, or experience repeated failure to deal effectively with feelings like these (perhaps because we feel really traumatised by events), then we begin to have problems at a new level and may begin to make adjustments to the way we deal with the world.

We might, for example, try to avoid these feelings or try to turn them into something more manageable.

Feelings can also become jumbled as we try to make sense of our experience. Thus a child who is constantly criticised for being angry (i.e. made fearful of their anger) may begin to experience anger-making situations as frightening and become withdrawn rather than angry.

The substitution of one feeling for another, the distortion of our real feeling world seems to be a very common experience and these individual internal distortions may be an important source of difficulties our lives. We could now add this information to what we already know of Ashley, Beth and Charlie.

Ashley

Ashley might be denying both sadness and fear about his losses, but acting out some of his anger in his relationships with women teachers, and getting into a pattern of withdrawal because he feels sad and lonely. We are not trying to find a label for his behaviours, rather we are trying to recognise the dimensions in operation so that we can address each of them if and when Ashley is ready.

Charlie

Charlie's problem seemed superficially to be a relatively clear cut response to systematic issues, but we have seen that failed relationships in adult life, perhaps brought about by relationships distorted through abuse in childhood, have played a significant part in his overall response. Maybe his anger is located in his disrespect for women, and his offending too. His fear and sadness come out in his current withdrawn state and apparent inability to help himself.

Beth

Beth, as we have seen, may be experiencing some effects of menopausal change, but even if this is true, it is clearly interacting with two major sets of stresses that are currently affecting her life: from the Systemic level we may identify the changes at work over the last eighteen months as inducing a sense of powerlessness, whilst the changes in her marriage are producing fears of loss and change and possibly even anger which may be only partly recognised.

Again we are not trying to find a label for Beth's 'condition'. We are trying to understand how complex issues might affect her life at many levels. It is for her to identify and name the issues, then find ways of dealing with what is happening and what she is feeling at these many levels.

It has transpired with each of the people we have met that although there may be a predominant issue when human beings have personal difficulties, there are also likely to be a range of other issues at other levels, some recognised and some unrecognised, that they might wish to deal with.

One aspect of a counselling approach to helping that has been illustrated in this chapter is that we have to be prepared to look at problems in the round, to recognise that human beings operate at a number of levels, and that although often it is appropriate to deal directly with the problem at the level at which it is presented, a really helpful response will be one that stays open to the possibility that there is more going on than immediately meets the eye.

It is not our intention to propose a model or framework within which human problems can be neatly pigeonholed, but to stretch the ways we might have of thinking about human problems. The difficulty we have is to keep seeing people as people whilst we think about problems and issues. We could draw this way of looking at how problems interact and overlap with each other like this:

Personal	Societal
	Interpersonal
	Individual
Practical	Societal
	Interpersonal
	Individual

The question remains: *How can we remember that we are dealing with people, not issues in boxes?*

The vignettes, then, also help demonstrate a further important attitude which we think is essential when approaching a human problem using counselling skills. Namely, to remember that the person we are trying to help is uncharted territory. We really know nothing about them at all and we must avoid applying our pre-conceived ideas to the situation. It would be helpful to approach each helping situation with an open mind and fresh eyes so that we don't automatically judge and categorise other people and their experience.

This is a tricky balancing act between *not* making the assumption that Beth's symptoms are menopausal because that's what happens to women of her age, whilst still being sensitive to the possible issues of age and gender. Also we would not want to *assume* that Ashley's life at school is completely defined by his blackness, but we want to be sensitive enough to not forget that as well as being Ashley, the young man we are talking to *is* black and so likely to be the victim of oppression.

Activity
You will have your own thoughts about how it is that people respond differently in essentially the same situation. What examples can you draw from your own experience of
• the ways in which babies show how different they are, and
• how we learn how parents, school friends, teachers and others 'teach' us to 'manage' our feelings.

Chapter 2 Summary

We have tried to extend the ways we might ordinarily have of thinking about human problems, here are the major points of this chapter:

1. It is not difficult to identify a very large number and range of situations where individuals feel in need of help. One fairly common-sense division of such a list is into personal and practical categories, although these will often overlap.

2. Human beings are co-operative creatures living in relationships within complex social systems.

3. Personal problems may thus be expected to be related to each of these three dimensions.

4. At the societal level we may identify personal problems that are a result of interactions with Systemic Issues or with Oppression. A predominant issue here will be power.

5. At the interpersonal level we might identify personal problems that are to do with isolation and loss or with handling the stresses of social and sexual interactions with others. The key issue here is *the relationship*.

6. At the individual level we suggest that personal problems might be to do with basic human feelings, including anger, fear and sadness, and how we have learned to deal with them.

7. A counselling skills approach to helping will be open to ways of looking at personal problems that recognise that they are multi-dimensional, and that neither the most obvious nor the most individualised response will necessarily be the most helpful.

8. Helpers using counselling skills (and professional counsellors too) have a dilemma. How do we acknowledge that people are affected by and products of their environments, their race, gender, sexual orientation etc., whilst still remembering that people are all unique individuals with their own personal responses to their world. As helpers, we need to be aware that pigeonholing the people we are helping is neither respectful nor helpful, yet at the same time be prepared to make room for the influence of oppression, society and relationships on their lives.

What is Helping?

3

In this chapter we will start thinking about helpful activities by asking you to remember an example of a helpful experience, and looking at other examples in order to develop a framework for looking at helpful activities. We are interested in what you have found helpful in the past and this will lead up to us trying to identify what makes a particular incident helpful or unhelpful.

> *Activity*
> * *Spend a few minutes recalling a fairly recent example of your own experience of being helped. It does not matter whether this was a response to a serious crisis or a minor need, whether the help was requested or offered or even if the need was predominantly practical or personal.*
> * *Once you have settled on a particular example make some notes both about what happened and about what you were feeling:*
>   * *What led up to the helping event?*
>   * *How did the need for help become apparent?*
>   * *What did your helper actually do?*
>   * *How did you respond?*
>   * *What happened afterwards?*
>   * *How do you feel about this now?*

In order to identify the helpful elements of a situation (rather like dissecting a body and naming the parts) we will begin by looking at the *structure*, *focus* and *content* of the incident concerned.

* By *structure* we mean what sort of helping relationship it is in terms of its
  * *Formality - is the relationship formal or informal? Is there any sort of agreement or contract?*
  * *Authority - is there an identifiable helper and person being helped? Do they have titles? Is there a difference in power in the roles of helper and person helped, or are they on the same level of authority?*
* By *focus* we mean where is the helping activity directed? Is it aimed:
  * *At the external world and trying to change it so that the problem disappears, or at the person themselves, trying to help them change inside.*
  * *At the whole person or just 'the problem'?*
* By *content* we mean what actually happens in the relationship that makes it helping.
  * *What helping behaviours are taking place here?*

In order to help us to look at each of these separately, we will continue with our story about Beth whom we have already met in the previous chapter.

Beth

It is Friday evening. Beth has come home from work feeling really drained and anxious. It's been a bad week at work, she has had difficulties with the new information system on the computer, and today, to cap it all, she was angry with a client on the 'phone and it seems likely that they will make a complaint about her. She feels that her professionalism has been undermined by the new management structure that has been brought in, and is beginning to wonder whether she wants to keep working under these circumstances.

When she gets home there is a note from Ben. They had had some discussion about whether he would leave on Friday evening or early Saturday for the Regatta that he was due to take part in over the weekend; he'd decided when he got back from work a bit early to cash in on that time advantage and set off straight away.

Suddenly Beth feels overwhelmed by everything that seems to be going wrong, she feels too tired to cook, too agitated to read or even to watch the television, too needy to ring a friend - and when she knocks over the cup of tea she has just made it's the last straw and she throws herself onto the settee and sobs.

Five minutes later the 'phone rings. It's her friendly younger neighbour from over the road, who has noticed that she left the car on the drive with the door open; is she all right? Beth cannot fully disguise the tears in her voice and although she says she's fine Yvonne is not convinced and, rather shyly at first, wonders if there is anything she can do. This simple kindness starts Beth crying again but as she puts the 'phone down she hears Yvonne saying she does not want to intrude but she's coming over.

Minutes later Yvonne is there, but now Beth is embarrassed. She is not sure whether she is glad to have a friendly face or would rather no-one had seen her like this. How will she explain this to Yvonne? Will all the neighbours get to know? She starts to struggle to her feet, saying something about 'closing the car door and making a fresh cup of tea and really it's very kind of Yvonne, but it's nothing really'. She is surprised to find herself quite firmly eased back onto the settee and to hear Yvonne say that she locked up the car as she came in and that she will make them both a cup of tea just as soon as she has done something about the potential stain on the carpet.

Rather surprised that her neighbour should be so active, but warmed by her kindness, Beth sits and just lets her mop up and make tea. When Yvonne sits beside her part of Beth longs to be able to ask for a hug and to tell someone everything; about work, her family, her fears about Ben, and her sense that maybe it's all too late for her now: and part of her knows that that's impossible. Yvonne puts a hand very lightly on her arm and says something vaguely reassuring. They sit drinking tea for a moment and Beth tries to say some sort of thanks. Yvonne brushes this away quite lightly and says that she does not think the tea will stain, she had popped home and brought over some new biological Nostain which she was sure wouldn't harm the carpet, and would stop the stain setting in: they even claimed that it worked with red wine if you got it on while the pile was still wet. They probably both know that spilt tea was not what Beth was really upset about but the moment for more sharing seems to pass. As Beth appears more calm Yvonne makes it clear that she must go soon to pick up her boys from badminton, will Beth be O.K. now? What can you say? As she leaves Yvonne again hushes Beth's thanks, and says 'It's O.K. We all get days like that. It's our secret, right?'

After Yvonne has gone Beth feels really grateful that she had responded so quickly to her obvious distress, but feels a bit ambivalent about seeming to share the pretence that it was a stained carpet that was upsetting her. Later she feels quite glad of this pretence because Yvonne clearly did not have much time and she is just a neighbour rather than a close friend.

Perhaps you can compare your own 'helping event' and this one now, asking yourself again about the *structure*, *focus* and *content* of the helpful events.

Structure

In the example given above, and I hope in your own example, it is possible to discern two interlinked aspects of the structure in which helping took place. Namely, and these are our names for these aspects,
- authority or power, and one way of making this explicit:
- formality or contract.

Authority or power: On the surface of it Beth's relationship with Yvonne is totally informal and there is no power dimension operating at all. This is just an example of a good neighbour operating with warmth and tact. But if you think about this further and look again at the details of the example you will see that both women were aware of issues of power and authority, e.g. Yvonne
- was to some extent intruding on Beth's privacy even with the initial phone call,
- and was certainly 'intrusive' in deciding to come over uninvited and to take over the host role whilst Beth feels vulnerable and a bit ashamed to be seen in such a state.

In every helping situation there will be questions of who holds power and authority, and having an awareness of, and dealing with, the central issues of power is an important, but often under-emphasised, aspect of helping activities. The way the power is handled may make all the difference between an act being experienced as helpful and having positive consequences and it being experienced as well intentioned but meddlesome or even harmful.

Formality or contract: One way in which power is shared and equalised in helping is through the establishment of agreements (often called contracts) about what is being offered and what each participant in a helping situation may expect of the other. There was clearly no formal contract in the situation between Yvonne and Beth but we can see the beginnings of a negotiation about what was available and what was possible going on:
- Perhaps unconsciously Yvonne signals what she can and cannot manage, in terms of time and the focus of the helping.
- Beth is unsure of what she wants and of what other boundaries are in place.
- The issue of confidentiality arises for Beth and intuitively Yvonne responds to this in her parting comment.

Needing help is not a weakness, but it seems inevitable that we feel somewhat vulnerable in situations where we ask for, or accept, assistance from others. It is this vulnerability which gives or adds to the power that the helper has, and gives rise to the need for some kind of agreement however formal or informal about the boundaries and obligations that each individual is taking on when engaging in some helpful activity. Many aspects of such a contract will be taken for granted by both parties, and so long as they share a common culture about helping, time and energy will be saved.

In a pluralistic and multi-cultural society, however, we have to be very careful not to make too many assumptions about the values and norms of our neighbours, and if there is any room for doubt about common understandings to explicitly explore what is offered and received rather than to assume that *our* particular understanding is universal. If this is not clear to you, you might consider how Beth and Yvonne's scenario above would have been different if Beth was Bob, or Yvonne was Yitzak.

Focus

Let us turn now to the question of the focus of this helping event. If Beth's story has captured you at all, you will be aware of the continuing ambivalence so far of both women about the 'real' focus of what is being offered. As we suggested in Chapter 2 there are often both practical and personal dimensions to people's problems.

In Beth's story we see Yvonne initially responding to uncharacteristic carelessness about the car door, and later focusing on the potential carpet stain. These are practical issues, but Yvonne is no fool. She could very well guess that an unlocked door and a potentially stained carpet are not the full extent of Beth's problem. Indeed, her initial approach to Beth explicitly identifies the open car door as evidence that Beth might not be all right, but because she is short of time, and feels the weight of English suburban values about not intruding etc., she chooses only to intervene at the practical activity level. Nevertheless, it will be clear to both women and is implied in Yvonne's tone, fleeting touch, and parting comment, that the point of the activity is to offer support at a more personal level as well.

So, on the one hand, helping at the practical activity level is an attempt to solve the problem by changing the external world, yet in this example it can also be seen as a socially acceptable way of making the first step to helping someone at a deeper level. Beth is aware throughout of those dimensions of the helping

that are centred on her, rather than the car door or the tea-stain, and might be longing for the possibility of a deeper contact when she could be comforted more and explore how she feels.

Content

Now we are trying to separate and identify the active ingredients in the relationship that make it helpful. In order to look into this dimension a little more deeply, we return briefly to Ashley and his life. On the opposite page we continue with Ashley's story which we would like you to read now before continuing with the main text.

This episode from Ashley's story contains a number of elements that are common in helping relationships, and some of them will become clearer in future parts of the book. Ashley's story does not provide us with a complete picture of all possible helping activities. Like real life, it shows us just a fragment of what is possible. For the moment it is worth noting that, in terms of content, it included two kinds of helping:

• *Clarification*: it helped everyone to think more clearly about the issues in two particular ways: Mr Anderson and Ashley were helping Wendy West, as a representative of the school, to understand certain dimensions of the oppressive difficulties that Ashley was experiencing. Mrs West was helping them to understand different approaches she could see to the resolution of different areas or dimensions of the problem. There was a process of clarification of ideas and perceptions going on between all the parties to the meeting.

Ashley

Ashley and his parents have gone to see the Year Head at Marketon Comprehensive. As they discuss the difficulties that he is experiencing it becomes increasingly clear to Mrs West who learns quickly, and is an experienced and sensitive year head, that there are three levels at which Ashley's difficulties will need to be addressed. There are some problems that require an immediate intervention at a practical level; e.g. it has to be made clear to the sports teacher that his nickname for Ashley and his assumption that if only he would not be so lazy, he would be ace in the school basket ball team are oppressive and unacceptable and that Ashley, like his peers, must be given the freedom of choice to engage in a specialised physical activity, or not, as he feels appropriate.

There are other issues that will respond to a problem-focused approach, e.g. the school's lack of awareness about racism and some aspects of the way Ashley handles his own anger that have led to the aggressive outbursts against some teachers. Mrs West is, however, aware that working at the levels of practical activity and problem-solving alone will not be enough, there also needs to be a focus on Ashley himself, a person-centred perspective that will give

Ashley the opportunity to identify and express feelings and work on finding his own way.

Initially Ashley and his parents had some difficulty in understanding quite why Ashley is so angry so often. It only slowly came clear to the Andersons that the oppression issues really had not been dealt with at all at this school and that Ashley is picking up a lot of the 'fallout' from that. Even so, that does not seem to be a sufficient explanation for Ashley himself; "Cos I was feeling really mad before I got here". Later, the Andersons agree that one of the really helpful bits of this session was Mrs West's response to this statement. She recognised that there could be a grief reaction going here, both about his gran and a kind of home-sickness for his London mates and familiar places. She'd told them about the time last year when she'd had to have her old dog put to sleep. She knew it was the right thing to do, had confidence in the vet, had chosen to let the old girl go rather than keep struggling: and yet she had been so angry for a couple of days. Only later had she realised that this was a normal part of grief and loss: that there is a characteristic pattern of adjustment to loss and change that commonly features anger and guilt as well as other feelings.

• *Information giving*: Towards the end when Wendy West talked about the death of her dog, she was also giving Ashley additional information about the processes of grieving and the fact that some aspects of his behaviour that he found puzzling or scary are shared by others.

Whilst there will be many occasions when clarification and information are not really appropriate, or where they really act as a kind of filler or medium for more useful features of the helping that are going on (like Yvonne's 'information' about Nostain in the earlier scenario), we cannot ignore the importance of these activities in helping people. Helping activities such as information giving and clarification are called *cognitive* activities. Cognition is a term used by psychologists to denote the domain of thought or mental processes, as opposed to feelings or emotional processes which are called *affect* (or *affective*). It is important that we acknowledge the appropriateness of both cognitive and affective activities in helping us to begin to resolve our difficulties since we are, after all, thinking as well as feeling beings.

Helping activities involving feelings include the purgative or *cathartic* effect of expressing our feelings and linking feelings to events so that we might understand them better. We will see that helping relationships in which counselling skills are used can involve a wide range of helping activities, but many will not be carried through to any great depth.

Chapter 3 Summary

1. We can analyse any helpful incident in terms of its structure, focus and content.

2. Structural issues in helping are concerned with authority and formality and help us look at the working agreement or contract which in turn helps to manage issues of power and vulnerability by attending to the issues of boundaries and expectations in the encounter.

3. The focus in a helping encounter may be:
   • on an activity which seeks to ameliorate conditions external to the person concerned, which appear to be causing distress,
   • and/or on resolving more internal, problems concerning the individual in question,
   • and/or on attending to the whole person rather than only to a particular 'problem'.

4. The content of helpful encounters can be either:
   • cognitive, or involving thought processes, including clarification, information giving etc., or
   • affective, or involving feelings, including expression of feelings etc.

Defining the Counselling Approach

4

Devina's Day

10.22 First client nearly completed. Still listening carefully: his voice and his manner are so angry, but when I reflect that back to him he just repeats his own logical words; but now seems angry with me. It's really very hard for him, if only he could see that I really admire his tenacity and that I really want to help. As we approach the end of the hour I say a little of that, summarise a bit, check that our appointment next week is also in his diary. Remind him gently that he hasn't tackled some of the things he earlier identified as central to sorting out his situation.

10.40 Have finished notes, just time for some tea before the next client. Glad to see that Dr. V is talking to Usha. It must be so hard for her coming back to work while still grieving. I don't interrupt, but I squeeze her arm as I go by. Listen to one of the G.P. trainees talking about how little input they've had on interacting with patients. I said that she seems very concerned about what she should say. I'm not sure she got the message: perhaps I should give her a bit more space - seems very anxious.

11.00 Viv (client) on time as always. Thank heavens the practice has agreed to allow us the opportunity of working for months rather than weeks. Her distress is still great but I'm not sure what it's all about. She talks about her childhood a little, but when I try to pick up on it she retreats and talks about her current relationship. There is the real dilemma here about present and past pain. Need to take this to supervision (again) I think.

12.15 Finished for this week at the practice. Saw Tony at supermarket. He clearly wanted to talk so I offered him a lift back to college. And did he talk! His relationship is not working out and he's worried that if they split up he won't have the emotional or financial resources to keep going. He seemed to want to tell me more, but I felt it better to ask him not to. I hope I did it gently enough. We did not have time to deal with it properly and I was becoming clear that he needs to explore this all more fully, and that it would not be right to do this with me. I wonder if he could use the college counsellor for this. Must ask Vic.

7.15 The class went well. Some of them were pretty cross with me when I would not tell them what the ground rules about the small groups should be, and although some got the point when I calmly reflected back this anger (even though I did not feel that calm), one or two got even crosser - until someone else in the group pointed out what was going on! Not sure how much I should let Terry know that I find her aggression, when she doesn't get her own way, intimidating - suppose I'm not sure whether this is my stuff or hers.

7.30 Kids starving by the time I got home. Sometimes amazes me that they don't think to go to the corner shop when we've run out of bread - just starve and grumble! About to have a go at the twins when I realise that Sol is really upset about something. Not the BNP thing again please. I let him know that I can see he needs some space/seems upset and he smiles at that: 'Later p'raps Mum. You've been doing it all day. Kettles on.' Sweet - I can do with a break, I'll find the right moment later if I can get him away from the computer.

In order to help us illustrate some of the features of a counselling approach, we've introduced you to Devina. Like many of us who earn a living around counselling she is a busy person with a number of different work and family roles. The thoughts that we have listened in on could be a part of 'A day in the life of...'

Devina is a professional counsellor. Her thoughts give us insight into a range of activities when she approaches the person or problem from a counselling perspective and she is clearly using counselling skills, which you will be increasingly able to identify and even give labels to as you work through this section and Section III on skills. The question that some people would ask though, is when should we consider her activities to be counselling and when should they be called something else?

The British Association for Counselling makes a distinction between the two, which can be useful, in terms of:

(i) Counselling skills: A certain kind of helping activity in which one person (the helper or counsellor) respects the values, resources and capacity for self-determination of the other(s) and seeks to provide opportunity for them (the client[s]) to work towards living in more satisfying and resourceful ways, and

(ii) Counselling: A certain kind of relationship, in which explicit agreement, and clear role demarcation are the key features.

Thus for BAC, counselling takes place only when both sides agree that it is taking place and the counsellor has no other role in the client's life. If the helper does just the same things but as part of another role they are not counselling but using counselling skills. The BAC 'definitions' focus on the *contractual arrangements* and **role relationships** in helping in order to define each situation. It's easy to apply this to Devina's diary:

• Between 9.30 and 10.30 and from 11.00 to 12.00: she was seeing clients in her role as the practice counsellor: she was *counselling*.

• At all other times she was in another role. As colleague, tutor, teacher or parent - she was undoubtedly using *counselling skills* and knowledge, but not counselling.

The trouble is that after a while this distinction can lead to a rather convoluted vocabulary and something of a sense of unreality in trying to describe helping encounters. How would Tony describe Devina's help? Can we be so sure that her morning clients think of her only as the counsellor? Many of them know that before she took her counselling diploma she once was a Practice Nurse and later a Health Visitor, why does it matter if they are not absolutely clear about whether their relationship now is counsellor/client or nurse/patient? I doubt if Sol thinks of his mother taking time to listen to him as being counselling (except when it annoys him!), but what about the G.P. trainee in the practice; won't she think that her conversation was with Devina in her role as practice counsellor, even if the young doctor would not see herself as client for those few minutes?

For these reasons we are going to use a different approach in this text. Rather than focusing on the *contractual arrangements* and *role relationships* in the way that BAC does we intend to focus on the *intentions* and *activities* of those offering help. We accept that there is a common range of skills (perhaps with some used to different degrees and with different levels of intensity), but we stress *that no activity is legitimately described as counselling unless the skills are offered within a particular set of roles, values and ethical boundaries.*

Now we need to identify and explore a framework that has become central in the understanding of helping, counselling skills and counselling: *the Core Conditions*. When the American Psychologist Carl Rogers was working on the issue of what it is to be helpful in interpersonal situations, he suggested (on the basis initially of his own experience, later backed up by research) that five elements were necessary for a relationship between two people to be helpful:

1. One person who is for the time being the client has to have some awareness or some discomfort or incongruence, leading to discomfort and distress, which gives rise to a need for change.
2. The other person, in order to be helpful has, for the time being, to be congruent,
3. respectful and
4. empathic in the relationship.
5. These attitudes or values have to communicated to the client.

In the next chapter we will explore each of the three central conditions and how they may be put into action; for the moment we will define them briefly to help us lay out the framework for helping activities.

Congruence is also called genuineness in some texts. We are talking here of two related aspects of the helper's adjustment and attitude within the relationship. In the helper there is harmony between how she experiences herself and how she wants to be in the relationship with how she feels it would be helpful to behave and how she actually does behave. Thus the helper is not playing a role but being herself and that self is a reasonably integrated expression of the needs and wants of a unique individual.

Respect, also has a lot of other names including *Unconditional Positive Regard* or (UPR), acceptance, non-judgemental and non-possessive warmth and prizing. The central value here is the recognition of the fundamental worth of every human being, not because of what they have achieved, or even of their potential, but simply because they are another living human entity with needs, drives, hopes and fears. Respect for another does not mean that we may not abhor their actions, but that we try to see their human value as separate from that, and deal with them with warmth and acceptance. This is a hard discipline at times.

Empathy is both an attitude and an activity for the helper. To be empathic is to make the effort to grasp the world as the other does. To understand and feel it in the same way, so that you stand alongside them, as if to see the world through their eyes, to process it through their backlog of experience, to feel it with their heart and all their associations. At one level this is obviously impossible, but the willingness to try, to be on the same wavelength, to set aside ones own responses enough to have some feeling of that of another seems to be a vital part of helping.

You may be able to pick out examples of the presence of these core conditions by going back through Devina's diary, and the illustration from Charlie's life should also help to clarify this:

Charlie

You may remember that Zack has come through his redundancy and the resulting stresses in his relationship rather more 'positively' than his former friend Charlie who is now divorced again, broke and depressed. One Saturday as Zack is crossing the recreation ground to meet his daughter he sees Charlie sitting on a bench staring at the canal, and having a bit of time to spare goes over to him. Zack sees himself as just an ordinary working bloke with no special helping skills, but he hates to see his old friend in such a state, and is prepared to put himself out a bit if he believes it would do any good. He has no idea what he will do or say but maybe there's something, so he sits down.

'Alright Charlie?'

'What's it look like?'

'Sorry, I'm stupid. You look pretty down at the moment. It looks really bad.'

'It is. No wife, no money no home soon, and even less pride. Don't suppose you want to lend me a few quid do you, just 'til I'm right again y'know, for old times sake.'

'Give it a miss Chas, I'm beginning to wish I hadn't bothered you. I didn't come over to offer you a handout. What the hell's going on for you?'

'Nah, you don't really want to know, I'm just an embarrassment Zack, or are you going to feel sorry for me, which is no bloody use to anyone. I'm not worth your time.'

'Shit, you sound pissed off, like you really don't like yourself any more, given up on yourself or something.'

'What would you feel like? I've lost the bloody lot. You must think I'm a right dick-head, I got everything wrong. Blew the money, lost me missus and now I'm turning into a full time piss artist.'

'Come on Charlie, I don't see it like that. Lots of the blokes found the money had disappeared. A few drinks, a nice holiday, perhaps a flash car and then what you got left doesn't seem quite enough to really do very much with and before you know it you haven't even got that much, and so on. It's a pain, it's scary how easy it goes and the trouble it makes in the family too. How did it happen with you ?'

In this short interchange we can see the rudiments of the core conditions in action. Even before he sits down Zack knows where he is coming from, he is fairly at ease with himself. His motives are reasonably straightforward, and although he doesn't know what he will do or say he's open to doing something. He is not playing any kind of role, and when he feels uncomfortable being tapped up for a loan he does not just guiltily cough up and run, but says something of what he feels. He comes into the situation congruent and tries to remain so. It can't be easy, as Charlie senses, for Zack to maintain an open non-judgemental respectful stance. Its fairly clear that Charlie has made something of a mess of all this.

Is there the hint of a judgement in Zack's question about giving up on yourself ? Yet he actually finds a way of making sense of the situation that does not judge his old workmate (*'It's happened to lots of people,'* and *'Its an easy thing to do.'*) and he communicates that warmly.

Lastly, Zack tries to be empathic, although he probably does not know the word for it. He gets off on the wrong foot (perhaps not sensing or daring to respond immediately to Charlie's despondency as an opening gambit), but he is gradually, intuitively, feeling his way in to what Charlie feels. At this stage it's bound to be a broad sweep, but so far he has avoided assuming that he knows what it was like for Charlie and is trying to find out how it was for him.

A framework for counselling and helping activities

Although Zack is clearly not a counsellor and there is no contract etc., we may say that what is happening here has some elements of a counselling approach, albeit intuitively. Zack is not trying to be a counsellor, his aims seem to have been derived from past friendship and fellow feeling. His aims may be said to be offering some kind of personal support.

In the previous chapters we introduced the idea of looking at all helping activities in terms of the practical and the personal elements. We also introduced the possibility of splitting up helping in which counselling skills might be used into different levels. Here we take this a little further to create a framework within which we can locate the helping activity and see how counselling skills might fit.

Personal Support

This is the first layer of counselling activities that we wish to distinguish. Individuals faced with personal problems, or indeed practical problems may be helped by being offered the core conditions, with no aim on the part of the helper other than to indicate concern and support for their position. It is perfectly possible for this kind of help to also go alongside practical interventions such as we saw in the earlier section when Yvonne came to Beth's aid. In that Scene Yvonne actively avoided any exploration of the emotional difficulties that Beth was experiencing, but her assistance verged on *personal support* as she could be seen to be offering a respectful approach apparently based on a reasonable self-knowledge and congruence.

Developmental Support

Going beyond personal support, moves us towards the second layer in our framework. As we have already seen being offered information is commonly seen as helpful, as is the encouragement of skills: if this is done within the context of the core conditions we can see that the counselling approach can be used for the *development* of skills and knowledge.

Problem Solving

Development of a suitable skill and knowledge base, along with continuing personal support will provide a platform for helpful encounters which seek to provide solutions to personal problems. Counselling with a problem focus, or *Problem Solving Counselling*, is seen by many as what *counselling skills* are best employed for, and the real task of the helper is seen as enabling individuals, through the process of supported analysis of problem issues, to come to a more satisfactory way of leading their lives of their own choice and creation. This layer of helping happens in many professional and voluntary roles and settings.

Therapeutic Counselling

Others see a fourth (and final) layer which encompasses the tasks of the previous three layers and goes on to address the deeper needs of the individual. It not only provides support, information or skills to enable the resolution of identifiable problems, but goes further in enabling the individual to grow through deeper hurts towards a broader maturity, creativity and self-actualisation than can be encompassed in the idea of solving a problem. This is therapeutic counselling, or counselling for personal growth and can include spiritual dimensions of ourselves as well as psychological dimensions.

Talking about Therapeutic Counselling brings us back to the BAC with which this sub-section started, for in the *Code of Ethics and Practice for Counsellors* it is made clear that BAC takes the view that no consistent distinction can be made between Counselling and Psychotherapy. We endorse this view.

Represented in a diagram, this approach may be summarised as a series of overlapping waves or layers in which the core conditions are aimed at four outcomes, each of which is valuable in its own right, and where the execution of the next wave may include elements of the activities from the wave below.

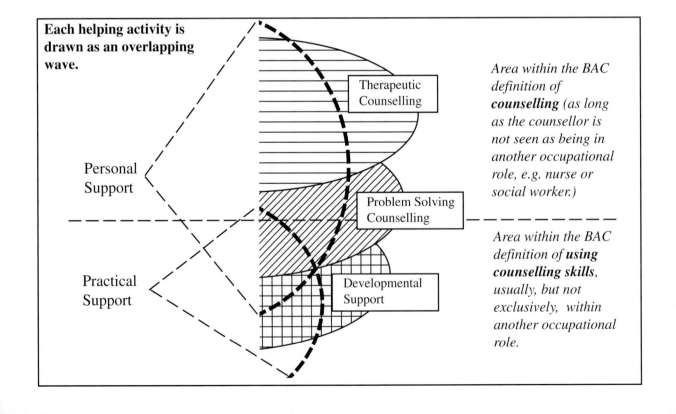

Each helping activity is drawn as an overlapping wave.

Therapeutic Counselling

Personal Support

Problem Solving Counselling

Practical Support

Developmental Support

*Area within the BAC definition of **counselling** (as long as the counsellor is not seen as being in another occupational role, e.g. nurse or social worker.)*

*Area within the BAC definition of **using counselling skills**, usually, but not exclusively, within another occupational role.*

Activity

• *Imagine the following scenario:*

   • *Your employer knows that you are on a counselling skills course and takes you to one side one day. Since you 'Know all about counselling,' would you have a word with Jim a driver who has a bit of a drink problem and sort him out? You have never met Jim before.*

      • *How do you explain to your employer exactly what using counselling skills means?*

      • *If you did agree to meet Jim, how would you explain the sort of helping you could offer him?*

Chapter 4 Summary

1. BAC makes the distinction between Counselling and the use of Counselling skills.

2. We have suggested that the central defining characteristic of counselling activities as related to the presence of the core conditions originally derived from Rogers' work.

3. These core conditions of congruence, respect and empathy are briefly defined and illustrated.

4. Four layers in an outcome model of counselling activities are identified:
   - Practical Support
   - Personal Support and assistance,
   - Developmental Support - or the development of skills and knowledge,
   - Problem Solving, and
   - Therapeutic Counselling, therapy or psychotherapy

The core conditions and their associated counselling skills facilitate each of these outcomes in different ways, and the relationship between these layers is illustrated in a model which depicts each layer as an overlapping wave of helping activity.

5. The BAC definitions of counselling and using counselling skills are also shown in relation to the model.

The Core Conditions

5

Empathy

We have already made a first attempt to define Empathy and to illustrate its use in a helpful encounter. Although we shall explore the meaning and purpose of communication of empathy here, we shall return to the practical questions of using accurate empathic responses in a helpful encounter in Chapter 9.

In Chapter 4 we wrote that empathy is both an activity and an attitude in the person of a helper. To be empathic is to make the effort to see the world of another person as if through their eyes, to sense their experience, to feel it as though you might feel it with all their associations.

It is important to note here that we do not say 'See *the* world through their eyes', but 'See *their* world through their eyes'. This acknowledges the fundamental philosophical notion that there is no testable objective reality, simply many different viewpoints. Empathy is our effort to experience someone else's reality no matter how different from ours, as if it were our own.

At one level this is obviously impossible, but the willingness to try, to be on the same wavelength, to set aside ones own response enough to have some feeling of that of another seems to be a vital part of helping.

Whilst the statement above tries to cover a number of aspects of empathic understanding, since it was Carl Rogers who developed and popularised the term perhaps we should go back to his own words for a fundamental definition:

> *'To sense the client's private world as if it were your own, but without ever losing the 'as if' quality- this is empathy and this seems essential to therapy.'*
> [Rogers, C.R. 'The Necessary and Sufficient Conditions of Therapeutic Personality Change.' *Journal of Consulting Psychology*, 1957, Vol.21, No.2, pp 95-103.]

The basic idea, developed and popularised by Rogers, does not change much over time. Why should it? What we are dealing with here seems to be a general principle of helpful social behaviour, which does not seem to be highly specific to culture whether defined by time or place. Rogers was neither inventing nor discovering the phenomenon, which seems to be a part, not just of therapy but of almost any helpful personal interaction. He was trying to explain it more clearly, particularly because he felt it important in the work of problem solving and therapeutic counselling, at a time when helping was seen by many as the provision of *expert* centred diagnosis and guidance.

Rogers was keen to demystify the helping process and wrest it from the grasp of 'experts'. Even as early as 1940 Rogers was placing emphasis on enabling anyone in need of help to understand their own feelings:

'As material is given by the client it is the therapists function to help him recognise the emotions which he feels.'
[Rogers, C.R. The Process of Therapy. Journal of Consulting Psychology, 1940, 4, pp 161-164, as quoted in Rogers, C.R. Client Centred Therapy, 1951, Boston: Houghton Mifflin.]

By 1946 he was expressing his finding that helping is the more effective when:

'the more completely the counselor concentrates upon trying to understand the client as the client sees himself. If we can provide understanding of the way the client seems to himself at this moment, he can do the rest. The therapist must concentrate on one purpose only; that of providing understanding and acceptance of the attitudes consciously held at this moment by the client as he explores step by step into the dangerous area that he has been denying to consciousness.'
[Rogers, C. R. Significant aspects of client-centred therapy, American Psychologist, 1946, 1, pp 415-422. As quoted in Rogers, C.R. 1951]

Even after almost fifty years of potential refinement, as therapists and researchers have worked with this concept, we can report that its definition has not greatly changed. The British authors of one of the most well respected texts on Person-Centred counselling of recent times write:

'Empathy is a continuing process whereby the counsellor lays aside her own way of experiencing and perceiving reality, preferring to sense and respond to the experiences and perceptions of her client. It is not a technique of responding to the client, but a way-of-being-in-relation to the client'
[Mearns, D., and Thorne, B., Person-Centred Counselling in Action. 1988 Sage: London.]

Sometimes, the position of looking at the other person's world from their point of view is called the *'internal frame of reference'*, and any other point of view is called the *'external frame of reference'*. If we are to be empathic we must try to be in this internal frame of reference and we will be looking at the skills associated with the internal frame of reference in Chapter 9. We are, however, more used to looking at the world as though there was an objective reality, something 'out there' that we can agree on. Although this may be useful in the communication which features in our day-to-day lives, it is not really a helping activity, since it is an example of the external frame of reference in that it is external to the person we are trying to help.

Since we are dealing with a relatively stable idea it seems reasonable to invite you to explore it further by asking you to undertake an exercise that Rogers put to his readers in 1951. (Rogers, C.R. 1951 ibid). The activity on the following page takes you through this exercise, and the sections quoted directly from Rogers *appear in this type-face.*

Activity
1. Imagine yourself about to meet a man in his early thirties, we could call him Frank, who you have been asked to talk to because he is clearly upset, and people know of your interest in counselling and such matters. Read the following material as if Frank launched into it after only the briefest of introductions, have paper and pen ready before you read, but don't go to the second instruction until you have read what Frank has to say:

'I don't feel very normal but I want to feel that way... I thought I'd have something to talk about - then it all goes round in circles. I was trying to think what I was going to say. Then coming here it doesn't work out. I tell you it seemed that it would be much easier before I came I tell you I just cant make a decision; I don't know what I want. I've tried to reason this thing out logically - tried to figure out which things are important to me. I thought that maybe there are two things a man might do; he might get married and raise a family. But if he was just a bachelor, just making a living - that isn't very good.

I find myself and my thoughts getting back to the days when I was a kid and I cry very easily. The dam would break through. I've been in the Army four and a half years. I had no problems then, no hopes no wishes. My only

thought was to get out, my problems, now that I am out, are as ever. I tell you, they go back to a long time before I was in the army. ... I love children.

When I was (overseas) -I tell you when I was young I swore I'd never forget my unhappy childhood - so when I saw these children... I treated them very nicely. I used to give them ice-cream cones and movies. It was just a period - I'd reverted back - and that awakened some emotions in me I thought I had long buried.
(A pause. He seems very close to tears.)

2. Write down what you are thinking and feeling about Frank and about the situation we have (in imagination) placed you in. You can read the text again as you make notes if it helps, but try to catch some of your spontaneous responses. When you have caught at least half a dozen of your thoughts/ feelings move to the third step.

3. Separate into different columns, if you can, (a) those thoughts and feelings which represent your objective frame of reference, which allows you to see Frank and this situation from the outside, and (b) and those thoughts and feelings which were more nearly empathic. Did you get any sense of what it might be like to be Frank ?

Carl Rogers suggested that you might have had some of the following thoughts and feelings in the objective or *external* frame of reference:

- *'I wonder if I should help him get started talking?'*
- *'Is this inability to get under way a type of dependence?'*
- *'Why this indecisiveness? What could be its cause?'*
- *'What is meant by this focus on marriage and the family?'*
- *'He seems to be a bachelor. I hadn't known that.'*
- *'The crying, the "dam", sound as though there must be a great deal of repression (lots of feelings bottled up).'*
- *'I feel sorry for anybody four and a half years in the army.'*
- *'Some time he will probably need to dig into those early unhappy experiences.'*
- *'What is this interest in children? Identification? Something vaguely sexual/ abusive?'*

[Adapted from Rogers (1951) p 33.]

Carl Rogers is at pains to point out that these thoughts and feelings are basically *sympathetic*, there is nothing wrong with them. In one sense they are attempts to understand the client. The locus of perceiving is still, however, outside of the client, still in the *external frame of reference*. They may be sympathetic but they are not *empathic*.

By way of comparison the thoughts which might go through your mind if you were quite successful in getting hold of the client's *internal frame of reference* would tend, Rogers suggests, to be of the following order:

- *'You are wanting to struggle towards normality aren't you?'*
- *'It's really hard for you to get started.'*
- *'Decision-making just seems impossible to you (at the moment).'*
- *'You want marriage, but it doesn't seem to you to be much of a possibility.'*
- *'You feel yourself brimming over with childish feelings.'*
- *'To you the army represented stagnation (standing still).'*
- *'Being very nice to children has somehow had meaning for you.'*
- *'But it was - and is - a disturbing experience for you.'*

[Rogers (1951) p 34.]

These thoughts and feelings are not presented in the way they might actually be said in a helping encounter, and it's quite likely that your notes are not written as if you were addressing Frank. If responses were put as baldly and definitely as this in an encounter that was intended to be helpful they might well appear expert and diagnostic, and thus not be very helpful; but as internal *cognitive (thinking)* and *affective (feeling)* responses they represent a real attempt at adopting the client's frame of reference', the *internal frame of reference*.

We would also like you to put this in the context of Ashley, Beth and Charlie. You may need to check back on each of their stories so far so that they come to life for you a bit before you complete this next activity.

If you think you did manage to get in tune with Ashley or Beth or Charlie how did you do it? What did you actually do? If you are white you don't have a black person's experience of racial oppression, but if you felt that this was one of the things that Ashley might have been writing about what did you do to try to get alongside him? If you are a young male you probably don't have Beth's experiences of being a mother with a grown up family, a job and a marriage that is disintegrating around you. So what guidelines did you use to help you with a list of adjectives to describe her feeling world? Charlie may be seeing his world as disintegrating too, but unless you have been in his situation how can you know what he might put on his list or do next?

To find any kind of response to the above questions you will have to have undertaken some first steps in conscious empathy. Even after such a short exercise, you may have noticed that empathising contains a number of elements:

• It involves an act of imagination. We may need the springboard of some experience that seems to us to have something in common with the subject of our attention. But we need to go beyond remembering how we felt, or pondering how we might feel, to make a link with an experience that is not our own.

• Empathising requires us to perceive clearly and think quite hard, although not always consciously, to identify the parts of the subject's world that are important to them, rather than what is, or might be, important to us.

• In addition to the thoughts, there is also a feeling content. This is not a question of identification, of taking over another person's feelings, nor is it about what I would feel if I were you - you are only yourself and no-one else: but you can, if you are willing, allow yourself to resonate with their feelings if they are expressed, or (in a live situation) as you sense them.

• Empathy is not just listening to the other person or sensing what is going in their world. In order to be present in a relationship, empathy has to be *received* by the person being helped. This means that empathy is *active* and must be actively communicated by the listener or helper. So there are two phases in empathy:
  • *Discrimination,* or listening to and sensing the world of the other, and
  • *Communication,* or reflection and feedback to the other that their world has been accurately perceived.

Only when both discrimination and communication have taken place can empathy be *experienced* or received by the other person. Since the core conditions must be experienced or received by the person being helped before we can say they are truly present, then communication or reflection and feedback is the essential skill element of empathy.

Respect

The concept of **Respect** has been given many different labels and is made up of a number of interwoven strands. In this section I want to explore some of these labels in order to discover what each tells us about this core condition and its strands, and once again I will provide an activity and examples for you to work through to clarify the central ideas for yourself, by seeking to put them into a form that is more grounded in *your* experience.

In Chapter 4 you were offered the following:
'Respect, also has a lot of other names including Unconditional Positive Regard (UPR), acceptance, non-judgemental, and non-possessive warmth, and prizing. The central value here is the recognition of the fundamental worth of every human being, not because of what they have achieved or even of their potential but simply because they are another living human entity with needs, drives, hopes and fears. Respect for another does not mean that we may not abhor their actions, but that we try to see their human value as separate from that, and deal with them with warmth and acceptance. This is a hard discipline at times.'

Mearns and Thorne (ibid) are not at all keen on using the word 'respect' to identify this core condition because they feel that it carries with it overtones of duty and that it may have an indication for many people of a certain aloofness and lack of warmth I am happy to acknowledge that this label may have some undesirable shortcomings and overtones, but I have always found its directness and brevity helpful.

Rogers (1957) himself preferred the terms warmth, acceptance and unconditional positive regard, and he made extensive use of the term *prizing* in later years. I have a sense that those teaching and writing in this area are some way from agreement about a *title* for this construct, but are much nearer consensus on its *content*. The essential characteristics seem to be:

• The recognition by the helper of a common humanity shared by the two (or more) parties to the interaction, and the acknowledgement that whatever the other has done (or even is doing) they do not forfeit that humanity. *'There but for fortune go you or I,'* might be one way to summarise this feature.

• An openness to seeing this common humanity, made up of strengths and weaknesses, as tolerable or manageable in oneself and in others. An understanding that our wholeness as people is made up of light and shade, that we are creatures of feeling as well as reason, of uncertainty and choice, so it cannot be otherwise.

• A positive feeling about oneself and one's integrity (self-respect) which allows one to move towards acceptance of the wholeness and integrity of others, and to approach every human being with warmth and hope predominant (rather than fear and disgust, with the desire to control if not destroy, that are consequent on such feelings.).

The challenge of respect
I will use the following illustration from Georgie's story to explain the point further.

Georgie

Georgie does not seem to be very bright and he has few social skills. He attended a special school from when he started to fall behind at about seven until he left school three years ago. He is a big shambling man who does not work, and lives in rather poorly run 'sheltered' accommodation where he is expected to be out during the day. He goes to the local recreation ground most days. He is usually on his own. Sometimes he sits by the swings, and talks to the children playing there. One day it emerges that he has been inviting children to go for walks with him, and eventually one of the children, Ruth, who has been talking to him regularly, tells her mum of the games they sometimes play. Ruth seems to be saying that she has been sexually abused. Her mum is angry and frightened by Ruth's story.

Activity
• *Can you quickly catch your feeling about this?*
• *What words come to your mind to describe Georgie?*
• *What do you think the local paper will print?*
• *What will the tabloids say if they get hold of this?*
• *What have you assumed about Georgie's guilt or innocence*

Amongst the words that might be around are:
    simple
    pervert
    abnormal
    animal
    sick
    sad case
    danger
    molester....
and this shows what a hard discipline respect is.

None of these words help us to see a person. Even the kindest and most 'understanding' label of this type is still one that distances and emphasises the difference between Georgie and the rest of us, rather than trying to focus on our common humanity; on the person (who is assumed to have done something dreadful).

Acceptance is sometimes very difficult and given that we don't know what really happened in the park in the illustration above, we are prey to our own imagination and prejudice. I am not suggesting that sexual games with children are at all acceptable, that anyone else can be expected to carry the can for such actions, or that the prime focus for our care and understanding should be other than the children whose lives may have been damaged by the actions. I have used a powerful example to help you to notice just how difficult it is to carry out the elements of respect; to notice how quickly we tend to retreat to labelling and dehumanising people on the basis of their assumed, or real, actions.

This tendency to distance ourselves from people on the basis of their behaviour, or our assumptions about their behaviour, is also evident when their actions are much less profound, and have no obvious victims but themselves. What about Charlie for instance? Many people would find him difficult to help because they would not be able to put out of their minds their judgement that he is a waster or work-shy, that he is a fool for not making the most of the opportunity that his redundancy money offered, that he's just a drunk etc.

And that distance makes it less likely that we will be able to help. The identification of the importance of respect is not an abstract moral consideration. If we explore the alternative title of unconditional positive regard we may see this more readily as an intensely practical issue.

Judgement and self-development
When human beings are very young they seem to register and express their feelings easily; and straightforwardly direct their limited powers to getting their needs met. This directness is not always convenient and manageable for those who have care of infants, and from very early on the carers of small children are seeking to shape infant responses to make them physically and emotionally more manageable.

In the next vignette we present the story of Helen, from a very early age to her teens. We have deliberately made many assumptions about why Helen and her parents Ian and Jill do things in order to illustrate some points about how being judged might affect us as developing persons.

Helen

When four month old Helen starts cooing and then yelling at half past three in the morning because she seems to have had enough sleep for the moment and is bored because she can't see much in the dark, Ian and Jill don't immediately rush to provide her with stimulation, to be with her for an hour or so of bright chatter and play. It's not possible for them to do so, they need their sleep because they have to fit in with the ordered demands of the 'civilised' world, so they either try to ignore Helen or they seek to pacify her. They try to shape her behaviour away from her needs and feelings as she experiences them, towards what they can manage.

This is reality and necessity but it is also part of a process whereby we begin to be distanced from what Rogers calls our 'organismic self' by the 'conditions of worth' that are applied to us as we grow...

Ian grew up with an angry mother, and Jill has had years of conditioning that suggest that women don't get angry, so two or three years later when Helen experiences the frustration of not being able to reach a toy that has absent mindedly been set on a table out of her grasp, they both (for different reasons, and not from a consciously thought out policy) react with shock and horror to her angry outburst.

With such reactions, totally without malicious intent, Helen learns to distance herself again from her real feelings to set aside her organismic self in favour of what is in some sense a false self. The fear of anger is so strong in her family that by the time she is a teenager she has completely lost touch with her capacity to experience or express such feelings, and presents to the world a sweet natured acceptance. But the anger is still there, the results of minor frustrations and conflicts that are inevitable in growing up, and the false self that has been created to mask it in line with her parental (and societal) expectations is now beginning to distort her experience of the world. The energy begins to be experienced as anxiety and as exams approach, Helen becomes increasingly disabled.

It won't help for someone to tell Helen that there is nothing to be anxious of, or to insist that she pull herself together. It won't even help if someone explains to her how she has built a false self that is turning anger into fear and that all she has to do is to let out some of the anger and she will feel less anxious and more able to cope. It's probably true, but to get near to doing that Helen has to experience a different pattern of acceptance, where there are no conditions to which she has to fit to make herself acceptable or worthwhile. She has to experience, being valued as she really is, being offered Unconditional Positive Regard, especially in relation to those aspects of her behaviour and feelings that she has learned were unacceptable, so that she can really experience her organismic self again, and then choose more freely how she wishes to express her real feelings.

With this example we may see the practicality of the so-called nonjudgemental position. It appears that if we want people to be able to change we have to give them the opportunity to get more in touch with their real self, so that they can give up distorted patterns of feeling and motivation and act more in line with their essential capacity to be social and co-operative. The only way to give them this opportunity, it seems, is to accept them unconditionally, to offer them warm respect as a fellow struggling human being, no matter how inconvenient it may be for those around them.

Congruence

In this chapter we are going to look at the third of the Core Conditions for a helpful relationship. Once again I will review the definition that has already been given, and explore the concept a little: we shall see that, like Respect, it may be called one or two different things and is also demanding for the potential helper. As before we shall try to explore this through examples, returning to the scenario with Georgie among other things.

In Chapter 4 we said that congruence is also called genuineness in some texts. We are talking here of two related aspects of the helper's adjustment and attitude within the relationship. In the helper
   • there is harmony between how she experiences herself and how she wants to be in the relationship, and
   • with how she feels it would be helpful to behave and how she actually does behave.
Thus the helper is not playing a role but being herself and that self is a reasonably integrated expression of the needs and wants of a unique individual.

Robert Carkhuff in an early important work on helping activities in human relations (Carkhuff 1969) explored some aspects of both of these dimensions in his concept of 'Facilitative Genuineness'. We can adapt one of Carkhuff's illustrations of this for our own purposes here.

Beth

A few days after the incident we explored earlier she is again called in to see her boss, who has been alerted to the fact that she is feeling dreadful because she believes that all her work is now of poor quality. Keith has always got on well enough with Beth, values her work and wants to encourage her. He invites her to review her work of the last couple of weeks and focuses on what has been going well This is gratifying for Beth (who thought she was in for a rocket or further slightly embarrassed enquiries about her menopausal state'.) but it also makes her a little suspicious- 'Is this for real Keith, or are you just trying to buck me up a bit?'

What does Keith say now? Some people would be inclined to hide behind a formal mask, their role or generalisation:

'I feel sure that its always useful for a manager to undertake an affirmative review with staff from time to time.'

Others, perhaps having learned a bit about helping, would know that reflection can be helpful (and in this context would also avoid too close a scrutiny of motives) :

'I wonder why you feel doubtful about this positive feedback Beth?'

But Keith could also come clean:

'You don't miss a trick do you Beth? I really do appreciate you and the work that you do, and I've been careful to say what I meant in reviewing the positives this morning. But as

I said to you last time we met I'm also really worried about some aspects of your performance and since you seemed so depressed in the last couple of days I was trying to find a way to give you something positive to work on. Now I'm getting anxious that I've made things worse, so I'm wondering how we can move from here.'

Let's assume that Keith doesn't want to hide behind formality, generalisation, or his role and is unwilling to deflect the question because he has a simple belief that honesty is more important than that. So he makes the third reply. Is it helpful ?

The evidence suggests that it is. Whether she says so directly or not it seems likely that Beth will respond something like this.

'I was really anxious that you were going to try to flannel me, and that would be so patronising. At least I can see that your intentions were good, and its actually as helpful to know that there was a personal element in this as anything else. I don't want you to be uncomfortable about it, but I'm glad you feel a bit embarrassed, because it feels real.'

Keith's response can be seen as moving towards the higher levels of facilitative genuineness as Carkhuff suggests, that this occurs when

'The helper appears freely and deeply himself in a non-exploitative relationship with the person being helped.'

Carkhuff also offers an example where

> 'The helper is completely spontaneous in his interaction and open to experiences of all types, both pleasant and hurtful; and... the helpers comments are employed constructively to open a further level of enquiry for both the helper and the person being helped.'

Carkhuff (1969a) pp 182-183

Perhaps you can see in this example and the definition, aspects of the two main dimensions that appeared in the initial statement about congruence:

- on the one hand spontaneity and openness to experience which links in with the helper being herself, and
- on the other hand the helper responding constructively which links with the idea of wanting to behave in ways that would be helpful.

Together ,these dimensions of congruence also give such genuine utterances a *respectful* tone. Almost as if the helper is saying *'I respect you and value you enough to be open and real in a constructive way'*. This illustrates how, at certain times, the core conditions are difficult to separate into discrete behaviours and skills.

Another way into this is to explore the concept of *'authenticity'*. John Rowan (Rowan 1983) recognises that the exploration of this concept might lead into deep philosophical waters but he presents some useful ideas when he argues that there are three levels at which any of us are operating most of the time:

I	Positive but phony
II	Negative self-image
III	The self: who you really are

He makes it clear that, in his view, helping someone is not about bolstering up their phony image or feeding their negative self-image, but about helping them to know, value and express their real self. It seems obvious that a helper is not likely to be able to do this unless they are operating from who they really are: unless they are being authentic.

We may then see that the role of not having a role - but being real - has two elements:

- As **receivers** of communication we aim to be genuine and to stay in touch with who we really are, to feel the feelings, notice the range of thoughts and images that are stimulated, and be aware of shifting responses and motivations.

- As **senders** of communication we aim to be congruent, seeking to ensure that at every level we are not concealing our intentions, whilst refraining from judging, attacking or denigrating. Rather, we are seeking to promote enquiry, exploration and motivation to try different thoughts feelings and actions in the other that are in line with their own real self.

And there may seem to be a paradox in this latter part because sometimes the response that seems to come from our true self, (what seems like an authentic response) is not gentle and reflective and expansive, but appalled, confrontative, angry; even violent and attacking at times. So do we just express that on the grounds that to fail to do so would be to be inauthentic, incongruent etc? The answer seems to lie in remembering who we are there for, and that so long as we know what we really feel, and offer it to others when they can use it and in a way that is as accessible as possible then we remain congruent and helpful. Authenticity is about not forcing our world on others.

To illustrate some of these ideas, let's go back to hear a bit more about Georgie.

Georgie

Len is a police constable who is on cell duty just after Georgie is brought in. He's a young officer with a family, including a little girl about Ruth's age. Len does not identify with the macho culture that many think typifies police work. He thinks of himself as tough but quite gentle and his real interest in children's welfare means that he has been training to do Child Welfare Liaison, so he has learned a bit about helping.

Georgie was really upset when they brought him in, alternately crying and shouting that he's sorry and he hasn't hurt anyone, and being sullen and angry, sitting in the cell banging his head and denying that he did anything. Len is concerned that Georgie might hurt himself, and so decides to visit the cells on a regular and frequent basis. He looks in on Georgie making somewhat vague, 'calming' comments, but after a couple of hours Len notices that Georgie has changed, he is sitting on the bed shaking and weeping silently.

Len decides to make him a cup of tea and talk a bit. Seeing this big shambling youth just silently sobbing engages him somehow. He has no investigative role, he just has to keep the suspect safe and secure. Len hopes that a few minutes general chat may help

Georgie to calm down, he tries the football and the weather, but Georgie is not up to that. Len wonders if there is anyone Georgie needs to tell and that triggers another tearful outburst and Georgie breaks again into half-fantasies about how everyone is going to hate him and that he will be beaten up and no-one will believe he didn't do anything to them. Len stays calm on the outside, he's a good officer, but inside he feels something go as he hears Georgie beginning to justify and explain his games with the girls. Len thinks of his own little girl and is suddenly overcome with the idea that if Georgie *did* do it he would 'knee him in the balls so that he'll not be able to do it again.' But part of him can still see the frightened youth who touched a more gentle chord a few minutes before.

Both his professionalism and the bit of knowledge he has about helping line up to enable him to make a gentle empathic comment: 'And now you are really scared about what's going to happen to you.' As Georgie responds to this Len finds his compassionate self more and more engaged. He listens empathically and with respect for Georgie's hurt humanity. After a bit Georgie seems calmer, and Len gets him to drink his tea and then leaves.

I think I would initially be inclined to answer the question as follows:

• Len has certainly acted properly in his role as a police officer and he has been quite kind.

• He has offered some empathy and respect, but the example suggests on first reading that Len has not been authentic, because he kept a tight rein on his angry and vengeful gut level responses (which many of us might share about suspected or assumed abuse).

• On reflection, I tend to the view that Len was helpful here, and that in many ways he was being authentic with Georgie:

    • Throughout the interaction Len was being genuine, he was recognising in himself a range of feelings about this man, and suppressing neither his compassion or his anger.

    • He was also being congruent in that he was acting (in bringing the cup of tea and making some effort to help Georgie to feel less afraid) on a real felt impulse, albeit one that was a 'minority' feeling for him.

    • He did not allow his hostile feelings to have expression because they were *his*

feelings, and were clearly judgemental and not obviously constructive.

Had the conversation continued however, the situation may have changed. Just as Len is leaving Georgie looks up to say thank-you for the tea and goes on:

'I'm glad someone listened. I'm glad you aren't angry with me and won't hurt me'.

If you were Len, and determined to be helpful, how would you now respond to Georgie? Take a few minutes to think about possible responses (as Len) before reading on.

Difficult isn't it? The obvious temptation is to leave Georgie feeling mildly less bad than he did. He has calmed down, so Len might say:

'Mmm, that's right, you just don't get het up. I'll bring you another cuppa in a bit.'

But this is flannel, it damages the possibility of later communication because it is not really authentic and so in some ways is disrespectful. To stay authentic here Len will have to find a way of challenging the assumptions that are in Georgie's statement, for example:

'Listen Georgie is not as simple as that. You are dead right: I'm not going to hurt you, and while you are here I'll do everything I can to stop anyone else hurting you. But I am angry that you might have frightened Ruth and put yourself and her in a situation that has risks and could be misunderstood. And its hard, really really hard to listen to you talking about it, and making excuses about playing with little

girls. Sure if you want to talk I'll listen when I can make a bit of time, but I don't have to like what you say, and there's no way I'm going to get into deciding what you have and haven't done.'

Authenticity in real life

There is a problem here for Len, he is not a social worker or a counsellor. It isn't his job to try to get Georgie to extend his thinking or even change his behaviour. What should he do given that being authentic isn't a part of our usual polite social repertoire? Len wants to help, but as a fellow human being, not from the role of a professional helper. This *role of having no role* is a common dilemma for many of us wanting to use counselling skills. The key to being authentic lies in the relationship between the people concerned. Len's response will have an effect upon Georgie because in this moment they have made a reasonably powerful connection at a human level.

If Len's response were similar to the last response illustrated above, the effect might well be a little less calming in the short term, but probably more helpful in the medium to long term. It might also be the case that Georgie may need to hear this message a couple of times before it all goes in, but even from this brief encounter, he will be experiencing more of the authentic response he has already had from Len and will know that he can trust him to be straight.

Again the powerful example helps to bring out the process quite clearly, but it may seem a long way from your everyday experience. No doubt we all have experiences from time to time where we know we are not getting authentic responses and we are aware at some level of the consequences of that. For example, some readers will be very familiar with the getting ready to go out scenario where a partner or a teenager wants feedback on their appearance. If this is familiar to you, you know its a minefield. There is seldom a problem if you really like what the inquirer is wearing, the way they've done their hair or the ear stud they've chosen. It gets more difficult if you have mixed feelings; but its most difficult of all if you have got into the habit of saying you like something even when you don't. If *they* like what they've chosen, your affirmation may be assumed and the actual content of your feedback more or less swept away in their confidence. But if your inquirer has doubts, or is actively seeking reassurance then your inauthenticity will jangle and you may get into a long round of *'Yes, but do you really like it?'* and *'Is it really me?'* Inauthenticity leads to mistrust, and mistrust is no foundation for being helped.

Chapter 5 Summary

Empathy

1. A definition of **empathy** is offered, drawing both on work done early in the exploration of this concept and on modern texts.

2. There is a difference between the 'internal' frame of reference and other *apparently* helpful responses which tend to encourage us to see the other person as an object.

3. The essential elements of empathising are: (i) imagination rather than identification, (ii) perception and thought about the world of the other, and (iii) resonance of feeling.

Respect

1. Although there is considerable disagreement about the most suitable *name* for the concept that we are calling **respect** there is more consensus about its *meaning*.

2. There are three elements, (i) acceptance of the common humanity of both persons in a helping relationship, (ii) acceptance that this is made up of light and shade, and (iii) acceptance of self or a measure of self-respect on the part of the helper that helps them adopt a non-judgemental approach to the person they are helping.

3. It is sometimes very difficult to provide respect for people who may seek or need help from us. It is easy to retreat to labelling which depersonalises the person who may need help.

4. This respectful approach is necessary if we are to avoid the factors which cause disturbance, i.e. in the way that we move away from our 'core' or 'organismic self' during the process of socialisation. This follows as a result of the 'conditions of worth' applied by 'significant others'. If or when the distortion of our *self* thus brought about becomes too much at odds with our experience, we may need a significant relationship that offers unconditional positive regard if we are to let go of the *false self* and become more our *real self* in order to fulfil more of our real potential. Every time we receive non-judgemental warmth and acceptance can help us to move on.

5. There are varying names for this core condition used throughout the book depending on the context, but we slightly prefer 'respect' or non-judgemental warmth, with 'Unconditional Positive Regard' (abbreviated to UPR) and 'acceptance' coming in close behind.

continued ...

Chapter 5 Summary continued

Congruence

1 Definitions of **congruence** from earlier chapters and from the work of Carkhuff indicate two dimensions to this concept, (i) openness to experience and spontaneity and (ii) constructive honesty.

2. The idea of **authenticity**, is drawn from humanistic psychology. This emphasis on a helper being authentic, was illustrated by John Rowan's model of the location of the *real self*.

3. Authenticity can be divided up in a slightly different way to congruence. This division produces the elements of (i) *genuineness*, where an individual knows and acknowledges to themselves what they are thinking and feeling and how they are motivated to act, and (ii) *congruence* where the individual seeks to ensure that their actual responses to others reflect what is happening in their real self in a constructive way. In other words, my behaviour will constructively reflect what's happening inside me.

4. Some of the paradox of this limited openness (the role of having no role) is explored through both returning to Georgie's story, involving the highly emotive issue of accusations of sexual abuse, and looking at issues of authenticity and helpfulness in more everyday situations.

The Core Conditions Plus ?

6

In the first chapters of this section we have tried to develop and extend the ways that we can think about human problems and responses to them. We started with the distinction between practical and personal problems, and noted that in reality the boundaries between the two were variable and permeable. Focusing on 'personal problems' we saw that personal issues were not just individual issues - that many (perhaps all) problems that affect us personally will have dimensions that are to do with:

    i) society (including issues of oppression),
    ii) interpersonal relationships, as well as,
    iii) individual issues to do with our reactions
    to our history and present experience.

Then we saw that helping (or more broadly responses to human problems) could also be seen on the dimensions of personal or practical, but that a more subtle focus would distinguish three elements:
• practical activities to ameliorate the problem;
• attending to the internal response to the problem with a view to creating better resolutions (i.e. problem solving), or
• attending to the person who may be seen as 'having' the problem.

Further we suggested that helpful responses could be understood by looking at how the helping was structured: attending to issues of formalisation and the way power and authority are handled in the emerging relationship. Finally we looked at how the

content of helpful interactions could include cognitive elements such as clarification and information, and feeling elements such as expression of emotion.

This analysis of problems and helpful responses lead us towards trying to see what counselling as a specific kind of helpful response was really about. After looking at the BAC distinction between Counselling and the use of Counselling Skills in another functional role, we suggested a different approach to looking at interpersonal helping in which it takes place in four rather different ways, which are bound together by the common philosophy . These are:

    i)   Personal Support
    ii) Developmental Support
    iii) Problem Solving Counselling
    iv) Therapeutic Counselling

What these approaches could have in common would be the core conditions of empathy, respect and congruence which we have spent the last three chapters exploring in some detail.

The question for this chapter is whether these three core conditions are really all that needs to be understood and put into practice in order to be helpful, or whether there are other key features to which attention must be paid. It's a huge debate, and some would it see it as the central theoretical issue for counsellors and psychologists and others interested to understand and define this approach to helping more fully. We don't think this is the kind of course for dealing with the abstract issue, but it seems helpful to canvass a number of other considerations that might need exploration as we build an understanding of the counselling approach, and to look at a few of the other factors which have been proposed as additions to the Person-Centred Core Conditions.

Skills or qualities?

If you look back at any of the helping incidents that have appeared already: for instance the brief interactions between Beth and Yvonne or Charlie and Zack, it will be evident that there are other features of the interaction that we could investigate apart from the presence or absence of the core conditions. We could, for example, ask why Yvonne phoned before she came over on that Friday evening, what were the factors that led her to ease Beth physically back into her chair? Or led her to make the parting remark about 'our little secret'. With Zack and Charlie we could ask why Zack just casually went over and sat beside Charlie? Or about particular words he chose etc.

These seem to be sensible questions and they are not obviously answered by an analysis that looks only for the presence or absence of the core conditions. Core conditions tell us something of the kinds of things that people might say and do, but in a rather broad sweep, essentially related to the values that come into the interaction and how they are put into practice. The questions we have asked above are rather more detailed in some ways and can be understood most easily as questions about Skills - learned patterns of activity that are applied in ways that are appropriate to the aims of the worker and the context in which he or she is operating.

McLeod (1993) in a recent textbook on counselling, has pointed out that although seeking to understand counselling activities in terms of skills has a fairly long and respectable history, there are three reasons why looking at the task of the counsellor in this way is inappropriate:

'The first is that many of the essential abilities of the counsellor refer to internal, unobservable processes.

The second problem lies in the fact that it would appear that one of the differences between truly effective and less able counsellors is that the former are able to see their own actions, and those of the client in the context of the total meaning of the relationship.

Finally it can be argued that personal qualities are at least as important as skills.'

There is clearly some force to the argument that suggests that counselling is about personal qualities and attitudes and yet many writers researchers and practical trainers continue to find a skills formulation useful. McLeod's objections can be partially circumvented if we allow that the term skill, although developed within psychology to describe relatively short and discrete patterns of behaviour (such as might be entailed in production line manufacturing), had a previous meaning (viz. the skilled craft worker) which was rather less specifically behavioural and did not necessarily refer to a discrete 'piece' of behaviour. Most people still use the term in this way when referring to a tennis player or a musician as skilled. They are not only referring to their individual behaviours, but to some extent also to their more complex capacity to read the game or interpret the piece they are playing.

In seeking to add an understanding of helping skills to an understanding of the core conditions, we are not arguing here that they are more important than the personal qualities identified in the core conditions, but we have little doubt that more experienced helpers become more skilful, and it seems a useful way of describing some significant aspects of how core conditions are understood in practical terms. So, we would suggest that there are two equally important elements to the core conditions; firstly the personal qualities and attitudes which spring from the core conditions, and secondly there are the skills through which the core conditions are presented in a relationship.

The next section of the book is an acknowledgement of this second element of the core conditions, namely skills, and further it is an acknowledgement that they can be learned and usefully transferred to a variety of helping settings.

Another level at which we can analyse counselling and helping activities is also visible in the helping encounters we have been revisiting above. Yvonne noticed a potential problem (the car door left open), she initiated some activity (phoned and came over), she assessed the situation (Beth's level of upset, the spilt tea) and made some sort of plan of action, which she then carried out (doing a bit of looking after, making fresh tea and mopping up). She then brought the interaction to a close and left. If you look back at that example on page 26, you will see the steps were not quite as neat and separate as this description

might suggest but that there was some kind of progression in the activities, crudely put; from problem through helping or assistance to solution or resolution.

As with skills analysis there has been a respectable tradition for some years now of seeking to identify a model of the process of helpful interactions. Gerard Egan (1994) in particular has been active in seeking to generate a model of helping processes which would hold for *any* assisted change. Since he seems to have some success in identifying major components of such a model it seems wilful not to pay some attention to this and other models (some of which suggest no more than the value of identifying beginnings, middles and endings). We briefly attend to this in Chapter 7.

Necessary and sufficient
In 1957, Carl Rogers wrote that the core conditions were *'necessary and sufficient'* for therapeutic change. By this he meant that they work rather like essential nutrients given to a plant:

Necessary:
　　All three core conditions must be present before helpful change can take place. So although change and growth *of a sort* can take place if only one or two of the core conditions are present, for lasting, personally fulfilling resolution to a problem, all three must be present. A plant will grow without the essential ingredient of light, but it will be pale and leggy and the growth will not be maintained.

Sufficient:

> If all three core conditions are present then lasting, personally meaningful change and resolution will take place *whether we intend it or not*. The core conditions are all that is needed, they are the *only* active ingredients. You don't have to be a gardener to realise that if you accidentally give a seed the right conditions, it will grow anywhere whether you want it to or not.

Such a suggestion is as challenging today as it was in 1957. The challenge it presents is at a number of levels;

- It is another example of Rogers' assault on 'experts' and expert helping.
- It puts the responsibility for growth and change on the individual, leaving the helper the task of providing the right conditions.
- It suggests that any other techniques are merely decorative trappings serving no useful purpose to the central helping effort.

As we have mentioned above, we don't think it is appropriate to try to do justice to the ensuing debate here, but we will take time to let you consider the main issues from your own experience.

But first we want to ask whether there might be other conditions that seem central to making an encounter helpful. For the greater part of his working life Rogers himself continued to explore and analyse his core conditions, and at various times he seemed to have felt that each of them was in some sense primary, but it was only very late in his work (Rogers 1986) that he introduced what seemed to some to be a fourth condition, which he believed became possible in well established and intimate helping relationships where it provided an almost spiritual or transpersonal medium for change. He called the condition *'presence'* but wrote relatively little about it and does not seem to have regarded it as an essential element for most kinds of change.

If Rogers kept modestly to a single, limited, addition to the list, others have not been so modest, but only three characteristics seem to us to appear, in some form, in a sufficient range of studies to warrant discussion here. These three are

- Concreteness,
- Immediacy and
- Reassurance.

The first two arise from the empirical work of Robert Carkhuff. He took up the Person-Centred theme of the core conditions but set about exploring their presence through more experimental rather than clinical work. He found (Carkhuff 1969) that therapists who were judged to be helpful consistently produced something like the three Person-Centred conditions plus these two. In order to help work towards an understanding of the terms 'concreteness' and 'immediacy', we will return to another episode in Ashley's story.

Ashley

Ashley has managed not to get himself suspended, and the school is beginning to sort itself out about its anti-oppressive practice, but problems don't evaporate overnight. Mooching down the corridor one day he more or less bumps into Wendy West, and when quite mildly reprimanded for not looking where he was going he's a bit lippy and aggressive and so he finds himself spoken to sharply and wheeled into Mrs West's office for a more private conversation. Mrs West is actually a bit upset by his uncalled for rudeness, but she decides there is nothing to be gained by a retaliatory or punitive position and opens the proceedings with a pretty mild

'What's up Ash? That was a bit out of order wasn't it?'

'Was it? Yeah, if you say so. I suppose you want an apology.'

'That's not the most important thing. Can't you tell me what's up?'

'Do I have to? What's it to you if I'm down? Look I'm sorry I was out of order. I'm just a bit stuck with things at the moment.'

'Ash, I can't make you talk to me and I don't want to pry, but it might help to talk a bit: neither of us have got very long, but I'll listen if you want to talk.'

'What's to talk Mrs West? I'm tired and down is all. I don't know what its about.'

'Tell me a bit more about how it actually feels Ash.'

'Oh I dunno It sort of feels heavy, and a bit like I want to be sick. It's a bit like a hangover after a late night, but it doesn't go off - and no I haven't been boozing mid-week. Its just a heavy feeling that comes on sometimes.'

'Can you remember the last time you felt like this?'

'Yeah It was a few week's ago. I'd been to see a movie with some of the guys from my class. We'd had a nice time, but the following morning I started to feel really down, Hey but that's all history now, you don't want me to rattle on about that.'

'Let's just explore this a bit. Was there something special about the movie, or was it the people you went with?'

'The guys were fine and the movie was fine. I don't figure it. I just woke up the following morning with this feeling.'

'And this time? Was that connected to an evening out with the others, or going to a movie?'

'Not really, I was out last night: went round to Nic's to do some homework together, came back quite late. House was very quiet. My folks go to bed quite early. Not like before we moved, when my Gran...'

'When your Gran...?'

'Stop it. I don't want to talk about it. Don't pry Mrs West, it doesn't suit you.'

'I'm sorry Ash. I notice that you were happy to explore the feeling a bit, to tell me what it felt like and when it arose, but as soon as you mentioned your Gran, everything changed, you got distracted and then irritable.'

'I don't have to talk about it with you do I? Back off will you What are you keeping me here for anyway? I said I was sorry for being rude in the corridor. What more d'you want?'

'I'm really not interested in the apology, its you being upset and down that really matter's here, and I notice that if I try to get you to tell me a bit about your Gran you get really quite aggressive with me again. Can you see that?'

'Don't push it Mrs West, please, I'll not get anywhere by talking about it. I'll go now if that's alright I'm sorry if I was rude. I know you are only trying to be helpful, but I don't need it, right?'

'Ashley please listen for just a moment longer. I really don't want to force you to talk to me. I couldn't anyway. You are free to go, but I can't help noticing that this conversation seemed to become more difficult for you, that I became more difficult to be around, when you thought about your Gran. I can see you really miss her, and sometime you might want to talk about that.'

We have already seen that Wendy West isn't a counsellor, and this conversation has elements of reprimand and authority in it. It starts off in a somewhat inquisitorial style, but she is someone who sets some store by the counselling approach and it is evident that she is attending to Ashley and not just to the school norms about not being rude to staff. In this instance, as well as beginning to provide some semblance of the core conditions, we can see Wendy trying to move away from the vague and general (*'I'm down, I'm just a bit stuck with things at the moment'*) to something more specific about the feelings and the circumstances. I'm not sure that the only way to do this is by repeated questions, indeed as we shall see later in Chapter 10, it is often more helpful to avoid this inquisitorial style, but in this instance the questions are good examples of seeking specificity or *concreteness*.

We cannot really deal with an issue whilst it remains vague. We can neither think about it with any clarity, nor feel the feelings with any sharpness, so the route to understanding is lost in the fog. Vagueness, generalising etc. can be seen as a kind of defence, an avoidance of painful issues, and to resolve these issues we have to find ways to contact them, we have to become more concrete in our appreciation of the problem. Carkhuff's research showed that therapist effectiveness was correlated with their perceived willingness to work with the specifics of a problem, to see its concrete manifestations, and to enable their clients to do so too. As the example above also suggests this principle might also apply to workers who see themselves offering help which is not precisely therapy, but personal support etc.

In the example Wendy West's attempts at concreteness are seen to be getting somewhere when Ashley starts to get angry again and seeks to withdraw. She has helped him to bump up against what may be at the heart of his 'bad mood', and he is reacting against that. Perhaps the responses that Wendy makes here surprise you a little. She neither backs off or interprets his behaviour (or retreats behind the authority of her teacher role) but quite gently persists in pointing out to him, what she observes and what seems to be happening between them at the moment, as it happens.

Such behaviour is counter-cultural for many in Britain, it is in some ways perceived as rather rude to comment on what is happening as it happens (just think how embarrassed we can be when a young person on a bus hasn't learned that particular social norm and keeps offering its carer a running commentary on what they are doing, what others around are doing etc. (*'Why does that man keep looking at us Daddy? No I won't shush. Why have you gone all pink Daddy? Haven't you brought your hanky? Mummy says I'm not to do that, that it's rude to pick you nose, so why are you doing it Daddy?'* etc.). Nevertheless such *immediacy* is also associated with helper effectiveness in Carkhuff's work. It seems to work because it provides a kind of challenge to move on to insight without being confrontational, and because it emphasis the openness and acceptance of the relationship.

Finally a few words about *reassurance*. In many ways it seems unlikely that this could find a place amongst what may sometimes appear to be the rather austere characteristics of respect, congruence, immediacy and concreteness. But in empirical studies of what people find helpful from their helpers it does indeed emerge, to remind us perhaps of the need for helping to be a really human activity characterised by consistency and warmth.

It is not precisely clear what it is that clients find reassuring in their interactions with helpers, but it does seem likely to be related both to their perceived openness and warmth and their capacity not to be rattled by the problems and issues that the client brings. Our understanding of reassurance from the studies that have suggested that it may be a key factor in helping processes, makes it clear that the focus here is not on any kind of 'There there' response, or minimisation of the problem, or over-confident assurance that this can all be sorted, but rather on the worker's capacity to work with what the client brings. It is their capacity not to be flapped or panicked and to hold the problems and issues with the client with warmth and perhaps even some lightness.

Maybe that's a lot to read into a single concept like reassurance, but like the original core conditions (and others that have been proposed) each word we use covers a constellation of ideas, which are themselves only aspects of the helpful relationship as a whole.

We might also gather from this that reassurance is not necessarily something that the helper does, rather it is something that the help-seeker picks up or receives. So, the helper need not strive to dispense reassurance, but act in a way or have the general quality of being reassuring for the person they are trying to help. For some help-seekers, it may be enough to say that we will be there for them and not judge them.

Activity
• *What does your experience of helping and being a helper tell you about the core conditions?*
• *Do you think helping activity is best thought of as skills-based or are personal qualities more important?*
• *Are they necessary and sufficient or do you think other conditions need to be fulfilled before helpful change can take place?*

You might find it useful to debate these questions with others on your course.

Chapter 6 Summary

1. What, if anything, needs to be added to Rogers original three core conditions to understand helpful activities and the counselling approach more fully?

2. The core conditions can be looked at in terms of two elements; skills and qualities or attitudes.

3. Rogers suggested that the core conditions are *necessary and sufficient* for helpful change to take place. Others have suggested that more core conditions are needed under some or all circumstances, these include, concreteness, immediacy and reassurance. No firm conclusion about the need to revise/add to the basic three is given.

Section II
Theoretical Interlude

Psychodynamic Approaches: Freudian Psychoanalysis
Page 70

Cognitive Behavioural Approaches: Rational Emotive Behaviour Therapy
Page 75

Humanistic Approaches: Person-Centred Therapy
Page 80

Integrative Approaches
Page 86

Some final thoughts on theory
Page 89

Theoretical Interlude

7

Our intention in Section I was to suggest ways of extending our thinking about human problems and how we might put together ways of helping other people. In the latter part of that section we started to explore at least one particular theory by looking at the core conditions from the Person-Centred approach pioneered by Carl Rogers.

If you have already studied counselling and helping through an introductory course or independent reading, you will probably be aware that there are a number of different approaches to understanding how people develop, what makes people tick, how they react when faced with problems and challenges, and how they change. Although we feel that Person-Centred concepts have been shown to be central to all helping interactions, we do not wish to ignore these other ideas.

In the earlier book in this series, *First Steps in Counselling Ch 2, pp 13-38,* I explored where counselling ideas come from. It would be good start if you could (re)read that section as a prelude to the material we want to explore here.

To summarise the main proposition of that section in a few words, I argue that ideas current in counselling and helping, not only in the 'profession' but also in the common public domain, are derived from three intellectual traditions in psychology - the psychoanalytic, behavioural and humanistic traditions. In this *Theoretical Interlude* we aim to

explore this material a bit further by asking how these three approaches view:
- the development and structure of human personality;
- how we organise and explain our experiences, our *mental life*;
- explanations for common human problems;
- the best ways of helping people in psychological distress.

In order to further balance the picture we will also look at some issues raised by supporters of integrative or eclectic approaches.

We have called this our *Theoretical Interlude* for a couple of reasons; firstly we wanted to underscore the idea that this book is intended to support readers developing their counselling skills and weaving theory in and out of the skills, whilst desirable and achievable on a course, meant that the skills became buried under a mountain of theory. Secondly, we wanted to acknowledge that some students on counselling skills courses intend to develop skills to take back to their existing work settings in, e.g. nursing, social work or teaching, whilst others intend to go on to professional counsellor training. The first group will be interested in *helping theory,* whilst the latter group will want some *counselling theory*. It is difficult to pitch the theory in-between, so we have gone more for the *counselling theory* end of things to give both groups access to the next step in theory. The *Interlude* can be separated from or integrated with skills as you wish.

Psychodynamic approaches: Freudian Psychoanalysis.

Psychodynamic approaches to common human problems did not appear suddenly, they have been developing over the past 100 years, since the first tentative beginnings in the work of Sigmund Freud in the late 1890s. Freud based his ideas on case studies and his own self-analysis. Both of these methods are open to us all to gain insight into common human problems, which is why we encourage evaluation of new ideas through our own experience.

Psychodynamic approaches all owe their existence to the work of Freud. Different approaches have developed different themes or emphases over the years and some now make claims to be completely separate approaches. This section introduces some of the ideas around which a number of psychodynamic approaches are gathered.

The key to a psychodynamic understanding of common human problems lies in the nature of human personality and how, as it develops, it incorporates potentially pathological flaws. To begin, we will briefly recap the material covered in *First Steps in Counselling*.

Human personality

Freud was one of the first thinkers to give the mind or psyche a structure which acknowledged the influences of both constitution, heredity or genetic structure on the one hand and nurture, culture or the environment on the other. He proposed three structures or *objects* within the human personality and that a balance must be kept between the influences of all three. This balance is called *dynamic equilibrium* and helps us understand the term 'psychodynamic', which alludes to vibrant balance, living movement and involvement of the psyche or mind in all aspects of life.

At birth the infant comes ready-equipped with a set of instincts and energies that

> '...contain everything that is inherited, that is present at birth, that is laid down in the constitution - above all, therefore, the instincts.'
> Freud, 1940

Freud called this the *id*, the core of our being that seeks satisfaction of its basic (largely sexual according to Freud, but adapted by others to emphasise more social needs) impulses regardless of the consequences - easily recognisable in a newborn baby! The id follows the *pleasure principle* in seeking immediate gratification of these primary processes. The primary needs of the id are problematic because in most societies they are largely taboo impulses, of which we will hear more, later.

The *super-ego* develops as an internalised version of the parents as, according to Freud, the child identifies with the same-sexed parent at around the age of five. The child takes in a series of *'You can't do this'* messages from the parents which become internalised as *'I can't do this'*. The id is thus constrained.

The final part of the personality, *the ego*, develops to manage this tension between id and super-ego by calculating the consequences of any behaviour and aiming to satisfy the id and appease the super-ego. The ego follows the *reality principle*.

Well-balanced adults are governed by the ego. If *dynamic equilibrium* is not struck between the *objects* then pathology results, with guilt and anxiety characterising the neurotic person dominated by the super-ego, and a failure to distinguish between right and wrong and lack of remorse characterising the amoral psychopath dominated by the id.

Conscious and unconscious mental life

Freud will probably be best remembered for his development of the ideas of mental life. He proposed that there were three domains of mental life; the *conscious* domain, the *pre-conscious* domain and the *unconscious* domain. We might picture these domains stacked on top of each other with the unconscious at the bottom; inaccessible, hidden and unknown. The pre-conscious is in the middle acting as a half-way house and the conscious on top; known, available and present as the mediator of everyday living, see p 20 *First Steps in Counselling*.

The unconscious is the domain of the taboo id impulses which are the source of the very life of the organism, being concerned with survival, sex, comfort, and bodily functions. These impulses must be kept hidden from our awareness, confined to the unconscious domain, denied admission to the conscious in their raw, rather offensive form. It is by keeping these impulses 'in their proper place' that a healthy dynamic equilibrium is maintained by the ego. However, there is a problem. As well as being taboo, the id energy is also life-giving and life-sustaining; it is the source of our creative energy and we need these impulses to live a fulfilling life.

The ego defends the conscious mind against raw id impulses by creating a barrier thorough which they can only gain admission by various circuitous routes, becoming acceptable in the process. This re-routing creates what are called *ego defences* or *defence mechanisms*. Since id energy must gain expression somehow (the id *demands* it!) we are all using defence mechanisms all of the time.

Ego defences can be successful; allowing expression of the forbidden impulse in a way that gives the id satisfaction, or unsuccessful; simply preventing expression and causing the impulse to re-present itself over and over again, each time demanding satisfaction. Unsuccessful ego-defence leaves undischarged energy in the system which must go somewhere and so is eventually expressed as anxiety.

Successful ego-defence is called:
sublimation and is achieved by deflecting the impulse into an acceptable activity, so:
- the desire to handle faeces becomes an interest in pottery,
- the impulse to be aggressive is satisfied by playing competitive sport.

Unsuccessful ego defences are manifold, we will look at a few:
- *Repression* is the process of keeping taboo impulses and any related ideas out of consciousness - so that we are completely unaware of them. For example, my repression of attraction to other men means that I have no hint of its existence. I cannot be made conscious of it by suggestion or logical argument. Repression is a natural involuntary process according to Freud, not a learning process, so I would not repress my homosexuality because my parents told me it

was bad; repression is an unconscious automatic process.

• *Reaction-formation* is the formation of feelings in the conscious that are the opposite of the unconscious id impulses. Examples are love becoming hate, whilst over moralising and disgust are reactions against sexuality. Once again, the defence process is unconscious and cannot be appealed to by reason.

• *Projection* is the attribution of our own taboo impulses to others. So 'I hate him' becomes 'he hates me'. Combined with reaction-formation a chain of events is revealed; 'I love him' becomes 'I hate him' (via reaction-formation) which in turn becomes 'He hates me' (via projection). Since the original taboo impulses are unconscious and therefore not known to us, the process of projection is also unconscious. A common form of projection is when self hatred (which is unacceptable) is projected onto the other person as *'You don't like me,'* or, *'You hate me!'*

• *Turning against self* might seem to be an idea in conflict with projection, yet it is still another way of denying an unacceptable impulse. This time if I have aggressive feelings towards someone I love (an unacceptable impulse) I can turn them back upon myself. This leads to self-doubt, self-loathing and in extreme cases, self-harm and suicide.

A way of looking at common human problems?
It is a fairly common first reaction to psychodynamic ideas that they have no relevance to common human problems. Yet as we have seen, psychodynamic theory concerns itself with explaining the origin of such everyday experiences as anxiety, guilt, aggression, self-doubt and unsatisfactory relationships. The question remains, however, as to whether these feelings and issues are the result of human problems or the cause of them. There are many more layers of psychodynamic theory which seek to explain more and more about human mental life. The approach attempts to do justice to the complexity of human experience whilst providing a core of explanations that have an elegant simplicity.

Some critics argue, however that the emphasis on sexual, violent energy in the core of human personality (the id) is not in accord with their experience. This is, of course, not news to psychodynamic practitioners and theorists, since the energies of the id are confined to the unconscious and we should not expect our experience to do the impossible, i.e. bring the unacceptable unconscious impulses to our conscious attention for the purposes of theoretical discourse!

Activity
•*Take some time to debate these points with a friend, fellow student or yourself.*
   • *What does your experience of yourself and others tell you?*
   • *Do you notice some of these processes going on in other people's lives?*
   • *Do you think they might be going on in yours?*
   • *Do you think you could bring these into awareness and accept them, or do you believe that they really originate in unacceptable impulses forever beyond your own conscious awareness?*

A view of the helper and helping process

Each set of distinct ideas about human distress bring a different 'flavour' to the helping process. It could be argued that the whole question of *'What is helping?'* was opened by Freud and has been vigorously conducted by psychodynamic practitioners the world over, ever since.

This section looks at how psychodynamic approaches have contributed to our understanding of the way in which helping relationships are constructed. We have already looked at some aspects of theory and now we will briefly consider some of the general philosophy of helping that has been informed by psychodynamic theory.

The helper is:
- a knowledgeable expert,
- fully conversant with the psychodynamic theoretical framework.

The relationship is:
- structured upon the theoretical framework of the helper,
- focused equally around the experience of the person being helped and knowledge of the helper,
- is hierarchical with the helper as expert.

The main active skills are:
- information collection from the person being helped and subsequent assessment/diagnosis,
- interpretation of thoughts, feelings and behaviour of the person being helped according to the theoretical framework.

The helping process is:
- led, directed and driven by the helper according to their expert opinion,
- is out of the hands and beyond the reach or understanding of the person being helped,
- trying to reveal the previously unconscious motives that drive an individual's thoughts, feelings and behaviour,
- aiming to restore executive control of our lives to the conscious part of our personality.

The model assumes:
- that people cannot help themselves, but need their experiences interpreted by others,
- core self is destructive and antisocial, so people must be protected during helping,
- helping can be dangerous,
- helping can only be done by experts.

For the majority of psychodynamic practitioners, helping is a skilled professional activity with few skills which transfer easily to less formal helping settings. The level of knowledge and personal preparation required to make helpful interpretations will ordinarily rule out the use of psychodynamic methods as a sub-set of counselling skills.

There are psychodynamic practitioners who have actively challenged the role of the expert in psychodynamic helping, see for example the work of John Southgate and Rosemary Randall (1978) and the recent popularisation of psychodynamic counselling (as opposed to psychoanalytic psychotherapy) by the publication of books emphasising skills rather than knowledge, e.g. Jacobs (1988).

Psychodynamic ideas have been in continuous development for 100 years. Of the many offshoots, some have attempted to make the ideas accessible to everyone and to enable everyone to be their own expert. One such approach that has enjoyed considerable popularity is Transactional Analysis developed by Eric Berne. The radical contribution made by Berne was the demystification of the core psychodynamic ideas by the use of accessible everyday terms like 'parent', 'adult',' child' and 'games'.

The helping process, according to most psychodynamic approaches, could be represented as follows:

> *Activity*
> - *Take a few moments to consider these propositions regarding the nature of the helping process.*
> *It might help to think of times you have needed help yourself or times you have helped someone.*
> - *Can you apply these ideas to those situations?*

> Inborn instincts are the foundations upon which childhood experiences build our personality.

> Our true motives are unconscious and hidden from us because the instincts and urges are unacceptable and taboo.

> Our unconscious only lets itself be known to us indirectly through symbolic events like dreams or defence mechanisms. We cannot see this without expert interpretation of our thoughts, feelings and behaviour.

> Using their expert knowledge and skill, the helper interprets our experiences and behaviour (e.g. dreams) to unveil our unconscious motives, giving us an opportunity to be free of these unconscious controls.

Cognitive Behavioural approaches: Rational Emotive Behaviour Therapy

Cognitive Behavioural approaches concern themselves with how thinking (cognitions) affect behaviour. Few people would suggest that *feelings* had little-or-nothing to do with human problems, so much of psychology had concerned itself with the links between emotion and behaviour. *Thoughts* and *thinking*, on the other hand received little attention until the pioneering work of Albert Ellis in the late 1950s and early 1960s. He first called his approach Rational Emotive Therapy (RET), and later amended its title to Rational Emotive Behaviour Therapy (REBT), in order to emphasise the active way in which practitioners intervene at a behavioural level in their clients' lives (more of this later).

When someone has a problem in their life and seeks help, they often quite naturally focus on two elements of their experience; their feelings (because unpleasant feelings really hurt) and their behaviour (because it is inconvenient, or disturbing to themselves and others). Cognitive behavioural approaches and REBT in particular, propose that the sequence of disturbance involves thought processes in the following way:

Experience -> Thought -> Feeling -> Behaviour

Ellis is fond of quoting the first century Roman philosopher Epictetus who said *'Men are disturbed not by things but by the views which they take of them.'*

Human Personality

Although Ellis trained and began his practice as a psychoanalytic psychotherapist, it is difficult to see any influence from this source in terms of personality theory in REBT. Rather, it would appear that the scientific behavioural roots of REBT give it the underlying assumption that human personality has no specific structure in the way that Freud saw it.

Ellis does not divide the personality up into different elements with different origins and functions. The behavioural view is that human personality is almost exclusively learned, with only the minimum of an inborn framework comprising our basic survival needs. So all of our systems of thinking, feeling and behaving are learned from interactions with significant others (e.g. our parents, teachers and peers). There is no internal division into inborn impulses and parental messages or conscience. In fact, books describing REBT and other cognitive behavioural approaches rarely if ever have 'personality' as an entry in the index.

This does not mean to say that Ellis is not concerned with internal psychological *processes*, it simply means that, in common with other behavioural psychologists, Ellis does not need to propose a *structure* in order to understand these processes. In lieu of a personality structure, Ellis does propose some basic qualities of human beings or assumptions about human nature that unite all people. These basic features of human nature help us towards understanding how our mental processes work and include:

- humans are goal-directed and feel satisfied when goals are met, in other words, whilst we might have survival goals at a basic physiological level, we are most fulfilled when we set ourselves goals in life which we seek to achieve through purposeful activity.

• Humans demonstrate a social dimension in their goal seeking behaviour, i.e. it is not entirely selfish. Ellis describes this as *responsible hedonism*, or the tendency to be mindful of others when pursuing our individual goals.

• Human beings are naturally empirical, i.e. we make and test hypotheses about the world and act upon our findings.

• Human beings are introspective, meaning that we can think about thinking and analyse our own internal processes.

• Humans have two biologically based tendencies that operate in opposition, one is to think rationally and the other is to think irrationally.

[Rational, *in REBT terms, means anything which helps achieve the above mentioned personally-meaningful goals. REBT does not make an absolute definition of rationality, it is logical, pragmatic, based in reality and therefore flexible and adaptable in content.* Irrational *describes anything which obstructs, blocks or prevents us meeting our personally-meaningful goals. Again there is nothing absolutely irrational. The definitions are person-specific.*]

Irrational and rational mental life

Mental life is best understood as the struggle to think and behave rationally against the basic biological tendency to be irrational. REBT does not attempt to understand why the irrational tendency seems to win

so often, he merely notes this fact and plots strategies to replace irrational with rational thinking.

In addition to cataloguing the irrational thought processes most often used by humans, Ellis described the fundamental process within which irrational thoughts take hold as the **ABC** of RE(B)T:

A stands for **Activating event**
> This is usually some noxious or unpleasant experience, e.g. being unsuccessful in an application for a job.

B stands for **Beliefs**
> This is the person's belief system, which is usually irrational, e.g. saying to yourself *'I'm a failure and a useless person because I've not been selected for the job.'*

C stands for **Consequences**
> The consequence of the A-B chain is usually an uncomfortable emotional reaction and behaviour.

The problem is that we have a range of irrational beliefs to apply to most everyday experiences leading to a string of unpleasant emotional reactions. This discomfort leads us to seek relief in the form of therapy. Ellis identified several types of irrational belief including:

• *Musturbation*, or telling yourself the three Major Musts:
> • I *must* do well or get approval (and I'm a failure if I don't).
> • You *must* treat me kindly and be nice to me (and you're a bad person if you don't).
> • The world *must* give me everything I want quickly and easily (and it will be absolutely awful if it doesn't).

• *Awfulizing* is more than making a mountain out of a molehill, e.g. it is the taking of an event or experience which may be *upsetting* or *distressing* (such a not getting a job) and believing that it is *awful*, a *catastrophe*, or *the end of the world*.

• *Personalisation*, where we irrationally relate external events to ourselves. This could surface as blaming ourselves when things go wrong, paranoia or that things are done specially for our benefit.

• *Overgeneralisation* is the tendency to draw a general rule out of one or two unrelated instances, such as saying I'm no good at job interviews on the basis of one or two failed applications.

Ellis called this type of irrational rumination *self-talk* and from this selection of irrational thought strategies, it is easy to see how an activating event can lead to an irrational emotional reaction. We then construct behaviours based on this irrational, unpleasant, emotional reaction, e.g. in the example of failing a job interview, I might decide that I'm never going to succeed, so I stop applying for jobs. The behaviour now becomes part of a self fulfilling prophecy - I really am unemployable!

A way of looking at common human problems?
If a common first reaction to psychodynamic ideas is to dismiss them as irrelevant, then an equally common reaction to the ideas proposed by REBT is one of instant recognition. Many people can recognise their irrational thought processes as described by Ellis and we would own up to being closet musturbators and awfulizers. However, many people reject the notion that lasting change can be achieved by argument and refutation, however irrational one's position is. It seems to many that if defeating the self-defeating beliefs was so easy they might have been argued out of their troubles much earlier.

Also, the very idea of adopting an argumentative, adversarial *'helping'* style just does not sit happily with most helpers. Ellis himself questioned the value of warmth as a core condition since it led in his view to the helper *'pleasing'* the client in unhelpful ways, which could lead to irrational beliefs going unchallenged. For many helpers who see helping and non-judgemental warmth as inseparable, the expression of caring through the kind of supportive challenge advocated by REBT practitioners is unacceptable.

Activity
•*Take some time to debate the following points with a friend, fellow student or yourself.*
  • *What does your experience of yourself and others tell you?*
  • *Do you notice some of these processes such as 'musturbation' and 'awfulising' going on in other people's lives?*
  • *Do you think they might be going on in yours?*
  • *Do you think you could change your 'irrational' beliefs through argument and refutation, or do you require a helper to be warm and accepting?*

A view of the helper and helping process

There can be little doubt as to the influence of cognitive-behavioural approaches to helping on our understanding of human change processes in the past forty or so years. Any answer to the question '*What is helping*' now routinely involves a consideration of the cognitive domain or thoughts and thinking, where previously, some of us may have been tempted to think of counselling as being involved exclusively with feelings. Albert Ellis in particular was concerned with illuminating the possible connection between thoughts and feelings, and so his view of the helping process is one in which the thought processes of the person being helped are seen as primary.

In common with some other approaches, the theory of REBT leads to a clear formulation of the helping process from which springs a set of congruent helping skills. As might be expected, the skills put a high premium on thinking, logic, reasoning and the helper's ability to communicate clearly with the person being helped.

The helper is:
- a knowledgeable expert who understands the relationship between thinking and emotion,
- skilled in the application of the principles of rational-emotive therapy,

The relationship is:
- structured upon the theoretical framework of the helper,
- focused equally around the experience of the person being helped and knowledge of the helper,
- a vehicle through which the person being helped can learn a more rational way of living; this learning is not relationship-bound, it can take place through other channels,
- is hierarchical; the helper is in the role of expert.
- based on the REBT 'core conditions' of empathic understanding, argument and challenge.

The main active skills are:
- information collection from person being helped and subsequent teaching of rational ways of thinking through:
    - understanding and diagnosis of the client's irrational ABC structure,
    - explaining the experience - belief-emotion-behaviour chain to the client to improve self-understanding,
    - argument and disputation of irrational thoughts,
    - teaching the client that neither events nor other people cause feelings,
    - planning homework through which the person being helped can experience the benefits of the rationality of their new strategies for thinking and feeling.

The helping process is:
- actively led, directed and driven by the helper according to their expert opinion,
- one that uses many modes, techniques or methods of communication according to their perceived utility,
- a shared responsibility between helper and person being helped - the person being helped must show commitment through, e.g. doing homework between sessions,
- trying to unveil the irrational thought processes that govern our emotional lives, dominate decisions and invisibly make much of our everyday behaviour self-defeating,

• aiming to assign executive control of our lives to rational, self-affirming, reality-based thought processes.

The model assumes:
• that people usually cannot help themselves, although there is some room for self-generated, self-awareness development;
• experiences, beliefs and behaviour are interpreted by the helper;
• core psychological processes have a biological tendency to be irrational;
• the helping process, whilst robust, is safe, adversarial, yet affirmative and empowering, not dangerous;
• helping can be done most effectively by experts, but that people come to see their irrational beliefs and change them through a variety of experiences.

Although the majority of REBT practitioners are professionals, both they and Ellis are dedicated to the popularisation of the ideas enshrined in REBT theory. Ellis has written a number of very accessible self-help books in the view that people can become effective self-therapists when armed with the right techniques. Perhaps this approach will appeal to a wider audience if it is felt more acceptable to refute your own irrational ideas with logical reality-based arguments, rather than have a therapist do it in an apparently cold and uncaring way.

Of course, the tendency to see therapists that argue with me as 'cold and uncaring', and therefore useless and unhelpful is a good example of one of the Major Musts:

You must treat me kindly and be nice to me (and you're a bad person if you don't).

> *Activity*
> • *Take a few moments to consider these propositions regarding the nature of the helping process. It might help to think of times you have needed help yourself or times you have helped someone.*
> • *Can you apply these ideas to those situations?*

Humans are happiest when they set up, and are working towards, personally meaningful goals in their lives.

Unfortunately people have an inborn tendency to think in irrational ways

This leads to the ABC chain - an activating event is interpreted by an irrational belief system leading to an unpleasant emotional consequence. (Epictetus said 'Men are not disturbed by things, but by their view of things.')

Using their expert knowledge and skill, the helper argues with us, refuting and challenging our irrational belief system, thus breaking the ABC chain. They set us homework and behavioural tasks to reinforce the positive outcomes of rational thinking.

Humanistic approaches: Person-Centred Therapy

Humanistic approaches to common human problems are built around the idea that human beings are motivated by the need to realise as much of their potential as possible. This *actualising tendency* is the fundamental energy that drives human behaviour and it applies to all domains of human life. This energy at the core of each person is good, social, forward-looking and constructively creative. It has the potential to enable a person to find fulfilment in their life if certain physiological and physical safety needs are met. We have touched on this idea already in Chapter 2 when we looked at whether problems originated inside a person or outside a person. So, for example, can a person find true fulfilment if their needs for food and shelter are unmet?

Another distinguishing feature of humanistic approaches, and the Person-Centred approach in particular is that they are *phenomenological* approaches. Phenomenology is the belief that our knowledge is based on our own experience, on attending to phenomena as they are subjectively experienced.

A distinguished contribution to our understanding of human distress and disturbance was made by Carl Rogers and it is the Person-Centred Approach which he developed until his death in 1987 that we will focus on in this section. Indeed we hope that it is clear that the present book reflects the authors' commitment to humanistic and largely Rogerian Person-Centred ideas, skills and frameworks for helping relationships.

It may seem to some readers that all there is to the Person-Centred Approach is the so-called 'core conditions'. In fact the Person-Centred Approach is one of the most complete approaches, since Rogers laid a clear philosophical basis for his ideas, proposed a comprehensive personality theory and, in addition, outlined a detailed skills and attitudes-based framework for helping activities (known as the 'core conditions'). The latter receives more coverage in Chapter 5.

Human personality

Rogers proposed that human personality had two components; the *core self* and the *self-concept*. The core self is the seat of the *actualising tendency* described above and is present at birth. The self concept is acquired or learned and the process of its modification as a consequence of experience, continues throughout life.

Core self	Self Concept
inborn	acquired
innate	learned
consistent	modifiable
unchanging	
irreducible	

• *Core self*: This is the basic human self or *organismic* self as Seeman (1983) called it. It is the life energy of the human organism and gives each of us our unique sense of being. It is irreducible, there is no more fundamental human element to our personality. In the core self are located the essentially 'good' creative energies that make up the self actualising tendency and which have the potential for self-fulfilling, self-healing growth. It is here that the organism values experiences and makes primary, vital decisions that determine who we are and how we express our singular and distinctive selves. We might recognise the influence of our organismic self in 'peak experiences', choice of life partner, choice of job or the ways we express our sexuality.

- *Self-concept*: This is the part of human personality that is acquired through experiences, particularly experiences where other people judge us and give us approval on certain conditions. Rogers suggested that the self-concept consists of a network of linked units, each unit comprising an experience or self-observation and *the value attached to it,* i.e. whether we feel good or bad as a result of the experience.

The acquisition of these 'units' can take two pathways:

- *a 'healthy' one* in which the individual has an experience and values it according to the organismic valuing process located in their core self.
  For example, as a young boy I might experience attraction towards men and sexual arousal. If I enjoyed the feeling attraction and sexual arousal then I would attach a positive value to it in my self-concept. 'I am attracted to men and like it'.

- *an 'unhealthy' one* in which the individual has an experience but someone else evaluates the experience and the individual takes on board the other person's valuing of the experience *as if it were their own.*
  For example, if as a young boy I experience

attraction and arousal in the presence of men, my parents might disapprove and say that such attraction and arousal is unnatural, evil and bad. I would then take the experience of attraction and arousal into my self concept with my parents' values attached, but I would remember the values as though they were my own. 'I am attracted to men, it is unnatural and I am bad.'

The process of taking these 'units' in in this unhealthy way is called *introjection*, and leads to a self-concept that is not in harmony with or *congruent* with the core self. Such a self concept is vulnerable because it is built upon *introjected values* which have been acquired not through an organismic valuing process, but by a process of introjection. The incongruence between the self concept and core self will be revealed by life experiences which continue to challenge the introjected values. I will continue to be attracted to, and aroused in the presence, of men and will therefore continue to feel bad, anxious and disturbed by my feelings.

Mental life
In common with other major theorists, Rogers believed that the 'human condition' was that we cannot escape being brought up without acquiring a fundamentally flawed personality. We may be functional on the surface, but have what he called 'potential psychological tension', caused by introjected values, just waiting to be revealed.

Everyday life becomes an effort to keep experiences within the limited range that the flawed self-concept can handle without feeling too threatened by incongruence. So, I avoid the sort of contact with men that may lead to disturbing attraction and arousal. I marry and have children to create life experiences that will be comforting to my self concept rather than challenging to it.

Identifying introjected values is a tricky business since if we have taken them in *as though they were our own* we will have difficulty distinguishing them from values that we have acquired authentically from our own organismic valuing process. Also, Rogers proposed two ways of dealing with experiences that are incongruent with our introjected values, which we develop to protect our vulnerable self-concept from these disturbing incongruent experiences:

• *Denial*: experiences that are not in accord with our self concept they are simply denied; it's as if they didn't happen. This is a wide-ranging process from forgetting to disbelief. *For example, if asked if I've ever been attracted to or aroused by men, I would not be able to remember any instances. Also, if my wife told me that I had been behaving in a flirtatious way towards a man at a party, I would not believe her.*

• *Distortion*: experiences are changed or distorted so that they do fit in with the introjected elements of the self-concept. Distortion can take almost any form and is as varied as our creative abilities allow. *For example, I could distort the occasions on which I felt attracted to and aroused by men by saying to myself that the men were very effeminate and looked like women, so what would any red-blooded man feel? My so-called flirtatious behaviour at the party could* *be put down to my wife not understanding the way I am ordinarily friendly to men. So these experiences are now rendered acceptable to my self-concept.*

A way of looking at common human problems?

The self-concept is built around some fundamental pieces of value-laden information rather like key stones in an arch. Take away the key stone and the arch falls down; take away some key values and the self concept is likely to begin to disintegrate. An introjected value is vulnerable to being dislodged because it is only cemented flimsily in place - after all it is *someone else's value*! An authentic value is securely in place since it is tied into the self-structure by being the product of the *organismic valuing process*.

The key values around which my self concept is likely to be built are my heterosexuality, being employed, being able-bodied, having a loyal female life-partner and children. If some or all of these turn out to be introjected, my self concept will be intact as long as none of these is challenged. Experiences such as being increasingly attracted to men, losing my job, disablement due to an accident, divorce, or discovering I am infertile, are likely to stress my self-concept to the point of collapse.

When faced with change in this way, a healthy self-concept has a flexible organismic valuing process to help repair the damage. An unhealthy self-concept has only the cockeyed process of introjection, and the consequence is that the person concerned may feel that their life and its meaning is falling apart, with no way in sight of putting it back together again.

Unfortunately, space allows only this rather over-simplified and brutal charting of the course of human distress. Readers must continue to bear in mind some other central tenets of person-centred theory, namely:
- there is no objective reality,
- everyone's experience is different,
- the client and their unique experience is paramount,
- the client's self healing process will be at the centre of the helping relationship.

Rogers' assertion that the majority of adults (that includes us!) have a flawed self-structure, in no way minimises the pain, distress, disorientation and fear caused by the demise of a self concept packed with introjected values being pushed uncomfortably up against incongruent life experiences. Such distress is all too common in our own lives and the lives of people we know and love. A largely introjected self concept is very vulnerable to abrupt, rapid or violent change in the world around us. Redundancy, divorce, bereavement, feeling unfulfilled in your job, overnight success, illness, achieving a life's ambition or watching your last chance slip away are the stuff of ordinary lives.

A view of the helper and helping process
The work of Carl Rogers did more to re-construct our notions of what helping is than any other major thinker since Freud. The person-centred approach was a radical new way of understanding the helping process when it appeared as *Client-Centred Therapy* in the early 1950s and remains a challenge to our notions of helping in the 1990s.

Rogers was not simply the first to put the word 'relationship' into our appreciation of helping, he put it at the forefront of the helping process. At the centre of this helping process was the person being helped; another radical proposal for the time, since up to that point helping had been constructed around the helper, their knowledge, expertise, needs and professional status.

These were not mere statements of liberal political dogma, but firmly rooted in the emerging humanistic psychology of the 1950s and 60s, which put the emphasis on the person's capacity for self-understanding and self-healing. Such radical positions have fundamental effects upon the construction of the helping process. These set the Person-Centred approach apart from other approaches to helping. This is clear from the core tenets of the theory and should become even more distinct in the following section.

The helper is:
- a co-operative companion rather than expert,
- skilled in the provision of a safe environment in which the person being helped can contact and activate their own self-healing energy,

The relationship is:
- either seen as unstructured or structured upon the needs of the person being helped,
- focused around the experience of the person being helped,
- is non-hierarchical; the helper is not in the role of expert.

The main active skills are:
- providing certain 'core conditions' for effective helping, namely:
  - good psychological contact,
  - empathy,
  - congruence or authenticity,

- non-judgemental warmth, which of course means no interpretation of the other person's experience.

The helping process is:

- directed and driven by the person being helped:
  - however mysterious this may seem to the helper,
  - however long it may take (healing wisdom is located in the person being helped),
- is out of the hands and beyond the reach of the helper, they simply facilitate the emergence of the process,
- an attempt to empower the individual's capacity for self-help,
- aiming to restore executive control of our lives to the organismic core of our personality.

The model assumes:

- that only people can help themselves,
- there is no need for their experiences to be interpreted by others, indeed interpretation is philosophically invalid and practically damaging to the helping process,
- core self is intrinsically positive, social and healing so people can be encouraged to connect with their core self without fear,
- the person-centred helping process, based on the core conditions, is affirmative and empowering, not dangerous,
- helping can be done by anyone who provides the core conditions, regardless of age, status, or professional qualification.

The real ramifications of this approach can be felt in the way it gives the helping process back to ordinary people. Indeed, what could be more ordinary than the human qualities of empathy, genuineness and non-judgemental warmth? If the change process really is located in each one of us, just waiting to be activated by the core conditions within a relationship, then the challenge is a serious one to all who seek to keep helping for the 'experts'.

Activity
- *Take a few moments to consider these propositions regarding the nature of the helping process. It might help to think of times you have needed help yourself or times you have helped someone.*
- *Can you apply these ideas to those situations?*

The process of helping following a Person-Centred model can be summarised in the following diagram. It seems to be well suited to helping in a wide range of situations with its emphasis upon developing generic helping skills rather than particular expert knowledge.

Human beings have an inborn capacity to grow and achieve their full potential. It is called the actualising tendency.

The self actualising tendency can be harnessed, given the right conditions, and human beings can then solve their own problems and heal their own psychological hurts.

The 'right conditions' are the core conditions of empathy, congruence and non-judgemental warmth.

The helper provides these core conditions, enabling us to explore our own experiences, strengthen our self-concept and our tendency towards self-actualisation.

This restores control of our lives to our core organismic self, facilitating a more fulfilling life.

Integrative approaches

It may be that after looking at what the major theorists have to say, you feel that none really covers all of the ground. It may be that you like some of the ideas put forward by Freud, some of Carl Rogers' ideas and some of the proposals of Albert Ellis. Perhaps you would like to draw together and blend ideas from many sources.

This is not new notion. Putting together an approach derived from the 'best' that other approaches have to offer was popularised by Gerard Egan in the 1970s. Such approaches that draw from many sources have been until very recently called *eclectic*, but are now more likely to be called *integrative*. There has been some debate on the different nuances of meaning of the two terms:

Eclectic

In general it seems that the term eclectic may be taken to mean a number of things including assembling a collection of techniques on an *ad hoc* basis according to the requirements of the situation as seen by the helper. So if a person seeking help seemed to require a bit of active listening, then having a defence mechanism or two explained to them, followed by instructions on how to defeat negative self-talk, you would have a sort of individually designed 'client-centred' approach for each person you were trying to help. The trouble with this approach is that it has no theoretical integrity, no underlying philosophy or theoretical framework on which to base therapeutic or helping decisions. So, there is no basis on which to really judge the needs of the person being helped other than the hunch of the helper - there is no theory to back up the helper's hunch.

It is like trying to make a soup by putting all the ingredients in a bowl and serving it up without making any attempt to integrate them through preparation and cooking.

Integrative

The term integrative is chosen for two reasons, firstly it tries to give 'theoretical integrity' back to eclectic practice, since integrative approaches attempt to provide an underlying theoretical framework for helping decisions. Secondly they attempt to integrate the elements of different approaches into a coherent method producing something qualitatively different than just assembling the techniques in an *ad hoc* manner.

Here the hope is that we have a bowl of steaming soup where all of the ingredients have been blended so that none can be detected as separate. They have become a new entity, different from its constituents. A recipe (*theory*) has been followed and so the product can be replicated according to rules.

NOTE *The term integrative is also used by some to include the search for common elements in therapeutic approaches on the assumption that any such common elements must be the most universally effective.*

The best known and one of the most highly developed approaches of this kind was developed by Gerard Egan in 1975. In Egan's seminal book *'The Skilled Helper'* he set out the framework within which the helping process could be enacted. Egan has revised and refined his model many times since *The Skilled Helper* was first published. Some practitioners think that the model is now over complicated and too cumbersome for easy use. Many prefer to use a version of the model published in 1986. In this version, Egan divided the helping process up into three stages. The division of the helping process into stages remains the subject of vigorous debate (revolving around the appropriateness of such a framework) that lies outside any debate about its complexity.

We can get a glimpse of the debate by briefly considering the part played by human personality in integrative approaches. In the previous sections on other approaches to helping, it is clear that the theorists have had a view of human personality which clearly underpins the approach and from which the various helping methods, techniques and skills spring. Beyond the structure of personality, each approach makes some assumptions about human nature. Sometimes these appear to be embedded in a philosophical position such as humanism.

It has to be said that integrative approaches which assemble elements of other approaches can have little to say about human personality. It may be that as we assemble an approach from many sources, we should bring with the various elements the appropriate bit of personality theory to accompany it. This does lead to the general perception that integrative models are either light on theory or have

theory constructed after the event to explain the selection of therapeutic elements.

REBT, for example, is an approach which offers no real personality structure, but this is because behavioural theorists see no need for one since they believe that psychological processes do not need a structure in which to reside. So it could be argued that it isn't necessary to have a theory about the nature of human personality at all. However, integrative approaches do not embody a similar philosophical view of the inappropriateness or lack of need for a personality structure, they have been assembled on more pragmatic and utilitarian lines. Such a view would argue that in order to be an effective helper, all that is needed is an understanding of the helping techniques that really work. Looked at from some angles, that is often what integrative practitioners seem to be asserting.

There is a similar problem when we try to locate the substantial integrative theory about mental life, or what happens inside people when they experience the need for help. To take REBT as a comparison, this is where Ellis appears to win hands down. He has an elegant explanation for the train of events which cause unhappiness. This explanation logically leads to his method for change.

Culley (1991), however, does give a very clear indication about the *basic assumptions about human nature* implicit in integrative counselling. She outlines the following values which underpin her integrative model:
  • *Individuals are deserving of acceptance and understanding because they are human.*

- *Individuals are capable of change.*
- *Individuals create their own meaning.*
- *Individuals are expert on themselves.*
- *Individuals want to realise their potential.*
- *The behaviour of individuals is purposeful.*
- *Individuals will work harder to achieve goals which they have set for themselves.*

These values are largely humanistic since there is an emphasis on the individual, the primacy of their experience and their responsibility, motivation and power to change. This view also has phenomenological undertones and both features seem to link it with the person-centred approach. The source for this framework seems to be recent developments in social psychology, since Culley cites Deaux and Wrightsman (1981), a popular undergraduate psychology text.

We say a little more about integrative approaches in the *'Final Thoughts on Theory'* section following this. You will have noticed that we have not described any one approach in detail. This is because we do not think that any integrative approach could be seen as contributing ideas that form a foundation for contemporary helping theory. It may be that Egan, for example, has marshalled other people's fundamental ideas into a new shape, but those fundamental ideas have been covered elsewhere.

Some final thoughts on theory

Our intention in this section was to continue your exploration of the wider theoretical context of helping by looking at what we consider to be the main influences on helping skill development in the 1990s. There may be some who would recommend a different or wider selection, but we wanted to stick to ideas that were the foundation stones of helping behaviour in our culture.

The integrative approaches section is not there to suggest that integrative *models* are a good thing, rather to suggest that an integrative *way of thinking might be a good thing*. We pursue this idea further below.

One problem with integrative models, Egan's in particular, is that they can be aligned too easily with the view that the helping process follows a number of set stages. Whether or not this is true, we find it unhelpful to see helping processes in this way at this point. In the first place, Egan's stages get more and more complex as each version of his approach is published. Secondly there is a sort of 'battle of the stages' developing in the world of integrative counselling wherein theorists struggle to think up catchy acronyms to hook the reader, viz DASIE (Nelson-Jones 1993) or Six Category Intervention Analysis, (Heron 1990).

We would prefer counselling skills practitioners to be more open, less structured and more client-centred in their helping than a stage-by-stage method permits. We prefer Culley's simple and, in our view,

quite obvious assertion that counselling (helping) relationships have three stages - the beginning, the middle and the end. Although this is, of course, not a new idea(!)

Your own explanations of how you use counselling skills in helping and why they work.
So, if Culley demonstrates that it is possible to move towards a philosophical-value framework for an integrative model, what about you? What do you think and how do you explain your helping skills?

It must be true that we are all integrative helpers at one very fundamental level - we each draw our final mix of helping attitudes and skills from a number of sources:
- our experiences of being helped from childhood onwards,
- our personal morals and values,
- our spiritual path,
- literature, art and media,
- books on counselling and helping,
- courses and training.

We have tried to give our wider experience some recognition throughout this book as well as inform it through excursions into theory. We wish to encourage readers to continue to examine their personal sources, experiential and theoretical. Neither are there to be slavishly followed, but to be added to your personal mix. At the same time we expect that readers will be drawn towards one approach rather than others. It may be because that approach to helping fits in with your personal values, or maybe you have been helped that way yourself in the past. We would like to make two points, firstly beware becoming a 'true disciple' as Carl Rogers put it in an interview towards the end of his life. Secondly, do remember that these are *counselling approaches,* whereas we have tried to compose a book about helping using *counselling skills.* We think we have assembled the skills we think are useful and necessary, and explained where they come from. Now it's over to you to do the same in your practice as helpers.

A note on jargon and the use of terms

We have tried to keep this to a minimum, but on reflection we realise that this section might still be a bit dense for some readers. We also feel quite strongly that helpers wanting to learn counselling skills at this level do need to understand where ideas come from. Not so that you can quote sources or blind others with your knowledge, but simply so that you can feel secure in your understanding that most helping skills have not just dropped out of thin air. Someone, somewhere has thought long and hard about why they might be good ideas. You will need to do the same if your helping is to be of substance rather than thin and groundless or 'just being nice'.

Some ideas run through a number of approaches and can create some confusing cross-currents, so in order to help you understand how some terms may be used, we offer the following:

• *Humanism*

Humanism is a philosophical outlook or system of thought which places prime value on human interests and dignity, putting them at the centre of importance rather than divine or supernatural matters. Although the Person-Centred approach was developed alongside other humanistic psychology initiatives, other approaches have humanistic foundations too, e.g. REBT; Ellis wrote several articles stating his own atheism and criticising religiosity for its absolute notions of right and wrong (irrational), also Culley's list of assumptions summarised on pages 87 & 88 is largely humanistic.

• *Phenomenology*

As we have already explained, phenomenology is the belief that our knowledge is based on our own experience, on attending to phenomena as they are *subjectively* experienced. One way of looking at it is to say that each person is the centre of their own unique and perfectly valid reality. What is real to me is real and what is real to you is real, but our experiences may be different, so there is no *objective* reality. The Person-Centred approach is clearly phenomenological in both theory and practice, but some approaches appear to contradict themselves by having a principled position on the validity of a client's reality, yet wanting to get the client to do some 'reality checking' to see what *really* happened. Both REBT and some integrative approaches do this.

• *Client-Centred*

This term was coined by Carl Rogers in 1951 as the 'title' of his new approach. It indicated a particular philosophy, theory, set of helper attitudes and practice skills. Now, however, the term is often used by any approach wanting to indicate that the client and their experience is at the centre of the helping process. This is rather an easy claim to make since it doesn't mean that the client's experience will be valued, respected or not interpreted according to another theoretical framework.

•*Person-Centred*

Again coined by Carl Rogers, this time in the 70s when he wanted to emphasise the people-centredness of his helping approach. It was effectively a re-titling of the Client-Centred approach. Again the phrase has been appropriated by others in a much weaker sense to mean putting the person at the centre of the process - without saying quite what process they've been put at the centre of. I suppose that there could be someone who calls themselves a person-centred interrogator working for the secret service. They may not use empathy, respect and genuineness as their interrogation equipment.

•*Active listening*

This term is used a lot when trying to capture the special kind of empathic listening required by almost all helping models. It is not specific to any one approach and is probably seen as a core skill by all helping practitioners.

Chapter 7 Summary

1. Although we believe that Person-centred concepts are central to all helping interactions, we also believe that understanding the roots of contemporary helping ideas helps us place our own personal theories of helping and why certain activities are helpful and some are not.

2. Psychodynamic approaches, cognitive behavioural approaches and the so-called *third force* in American post-war psychology, humanistic approaches are briefly outlined.

3. Each approach is illuminated by looking at a substantive example, namely, Freudian Psychoanalysis, Rational Emotive Behaviour Therapy and Person-Centred Therapy respectively.

4. Each approach is examined in terms of views on:
   • The development and structure of human personality.
   • How we organise and explain our experiences or our mental life.
   • The role of the helper, the nature of the helping process and the best ways of helping people in psychological distress.

5. The tendency to draw influences from many sources is examined by looking at integrative approaches to helping.

Section III
Practising Counselling Skills

Setting Up and Getting Started
Page 95

Listening and Exploring
Page107

To Question or Not to Question?
Page 123

New Perspectives
Page 133

Challenge
Page 143

Action and Ending
Page 147

Helping Skills in Action: Karen's Story
Page 155

Vignettes

Ashley: 102, 128, 153.
Charlie: 98, 101.
Karen: 155-161.

Setting Up and Getting Started

8

Relationships in which counselling skills are used, whether they are helping relationships or not, all have to start sometime. Either we start the relationship knowing that we are going to try to help using counselling skills from the word go, or we find ourselves in an established relationship where we wish to begin to use counselling skills.

Earlier in this book, in Chapter 6, we looked at the conditions which Carl Rogers thought were necessary and sufficient for helping to take place. The first of these conditions deals with the *roles* of helper and the person being helped, then there is the question of being in *psychological contact*. In other words, in order for a relationship to be experienced as helpful, the people involved have to:

- know who needs, is asking for, or is receiving, help,
- know who is offering, or providing help, and
- be in contact with each other, be in touch, or have a sense of shared purpose.

As we have suggested, this is more complicated than just saying *'Me helper, you helped'*, and being in the same room as the other person. Making the *right kind* of psychological contact for helping using counselling skills doesn't happen by accident. It is the product of a series of deliberate actions:

- Your offer of help has to be sensitive to who the other person is and how they might be feeling.

- The other person has to hear or receive your offer in a way that gives you permission to help.
- You both have to '*agree*' that it is a helping relationship that you are having, rather than some other sort of relationship, e.g. friendship.
- You both have to '*agree*' that a helping relationship has started.

Structuring

This 'setting up and getting started' part of helping is absolutely crucial if the helping we offer is to be of any use. It is rather like making sure that the train is on the right tracks at the beginning of a journey. If the tracks are not '*helping relationship tracks*', then the relationship will not be seen as helping and will simply end up somewhere else. If, however, the relationship is put on the right tracks at the start, then it will take some effort to knock it off its helping course.

Structuring is the act of aligning the expectations of the helper and the person being helped. It is a feature of *all human relationships*, not just helping ones. We know that the structuring has gone wrong in a particular relationship when we realise that the other person wants something different from the relationship than what we are offering. This misalignment of expectations can be:

- a nuisance - a friend stops in the street and wants simply to say *'Hi, how are you today,'* and quickly pass on when I wanted to tell them

all my exciting news.
• embarrassing - I wanted a leaflet giving information about vasectomy for my friend but the receptionist wanted to offer me lots of friendly advice about the operation itself.
• non-productive - I was offering counselling skills to the young woman at the drop-in centre but she wanted to talk to someone else who had suffered post-natal depression.
• tragic - I wanted comfort and a cuddle because I was upset, but my friend was offering sex and thought that I was asking for it.

Activity
• *Can you call to mind a time when your expectations about a relationship were out of alignment with the other person?*
• *What feelings were you both left with?*
• *What could you have done to avoid the particular mis-perceptions that arose on that occasion?*

It is important that we get our expectations aligned in relationships since getting our relationship structuring wrong nearly always leads to negative feelings such as frustration, disappointment or embarrassment. In helping relationships, the effects of getting our expectations and offers muddled will almost certainly wreck our efforts to offer help and the chances of our offer being received. It is difficult enough for the *helpers* to deal with these feelings when the expectations of a helping relationship are not met. It can be the proverbial straw that breaks the camel's back for the *person seeking help*.

If some kind of structuring happens in all human relationships anyway, the only decision we have to make in helping relationships is whether we are *actively* going to shape the setting up and getting started process, or whether we are *passively* going to stand by with our fingers crossed and hope for the best. It is our view that helpers wishing to practise counselling skills must take an active position on the structuring of a helping relationship. It is through structuring that the solid foundations are built on which the remaining core conditions for helping can be offered. Counselling skills are most effective when they have the foundation of a well-structured relationship; the question is, how do we go about deliberately structuring a relationship for helping?

Structuring for helping
Throughout this book we have consciously chosen a wide spread of backgrounds to our characters to show that the use of counselling skills does not rely on a 'professional' setting. This point is equally true of structuring and we hope that you can follow our characters' stories as they, or the people around them, try to structure helping relationships that are effective. You will note that in some cases the characters have to form new helping relationships, whilst in others the characters have to add or integrate counselling skills into an existing relationship. When an existing relationship changes in some way, we call it *re-structuring*.

In order for us to feel comfortable in a relationship we will need to establish certain limits to the relationship. It is our expectations of these limits that structuring is concerned with. The limits that we *require* in order to feel comfortable and safe will depend upon the situation, so we will limit our attention to helping relationships in which counselling skills may be practised.

The 'What' and 'How' of structuring

The questions any helper must ask themselves are:

- *'What expectations might the person I am trying to help arrive with?'*
- *'What kind of helping am I offering?'*
- *'What must I do in order to make sure that their expectations of help match what I am offering?'*
- *'How must I behave in order to ensure their expectations of my helping are in line with what I am offering?'*

The words that most fit the overall *effect* we are after here are 'trustworthy', 'genuine' and 'authentic'. The person we are trying to help will surely want to know that the offering *is* genuine, trustworthy and safe. That it lives up to its billing. It is, therefore, vital that any information we give about our helping is as accurate as possible. We have identified two features of structuring, *content* and *presentation*.

Activity
Write down your answers to the following questions.
- *What sort of information do we need to get across to the person we are helping in order that their expectations are reasonable.*
- *How should we present it?*

Whilst there are no right or wrong answers to the questions in the activity above, the following points might raise some issues for discussion:

- Does the person you are trying to help know what counselling skills are?

- Do they know understand the boundaries of the helping relationship such as confidentiality?
- Do they know how much time you can give them and what your commitment is?
- Do they know what commitment you expect from them?

We will continue to explore these issues in detail in the section below, since successful structuring depends upon good timing as much as content and presentation.

The 'When' of structuring

There are four time periods in a helping relationship when the alignment of expectations happens, so if we wish to be active in shaping this relationship and getting it on the right tracks we will have to be involved in each of these time periods as is appropriate to our circumstances. It will become clear to readers that these time periods do not apply equally to all possible situations in which counselling skills can be used. You will have to adapt the general principles of structuring to fit your personal circumstances.

Expectations are set at the following times:
1. **Before** the helping relationship starts.
2. In the **first few moments** of helping.
3. **During** the helping relationship.
4. When the nature of **the relationship changes.**

Activity
Read the vignettes on pages 98 and 101 and see if you can identify the moments when expectations may have been set or when they might be changed or aligned.

Charlie

In the end, Charlie's first stop is not the counsellor at his GP practice. Instead he succumbs to gentle persuasion by Zack that the Neighbourhood Centre may be able to help (although Zack isn't really sure, he thought that they might give advice about benefits.)

At the Neighbourhood Centre, Janet has just left a meeting to discuss the leaflet advertising the new debt counselling service. She was not happy with the way the leaflet described the new service. She wanted debt counselling to be presented as supportive and caring yet professional and focused. The leaflet had made it sound as supportive as a trip to the bank manager!

Janet walked back to the interview room thinking that a plant or two or even a nice framed poster would brighten the place up. She liked to spend a minute or two just clearing her mind and focusing on listening to other peoples' problems and helping before each client arrived. She was a little nervous, as always before seeing someone new; all she knew was that his name was Charlie. There was a knock at the half open door as a nervous-looking man peeped into the room...

'Er.. is this the right room?' he asked.

'Yes, hello my name's Janet. You must be Charlie'. Janet promptly stood up and smiling, offered her hand to shake as Charlie took a couple of steps into the room. He visibly relaxed.

'Please, do sit down wherever you like.' Janet closed the door firmly behind Charlie and offered him a choice of two chairs set side-by-side at a table. Janet turned her chair round so that she almost faced Charlie. When they were both settled, Janet caught Charlie's eye with a steady, reassuring look and said,

'As I said before Charlie, my name is Janet. I'm an advice worker here. We've got around half an hour together today, and we can meet again for a couple more sessions if you need to. I don't know why you have come to the Neighbourhood Centre, but it would help me if you could tell me why you are here and how you hope I might help.'

'Erm...yes, well, my friend said I should come and that you were good. I was given a card about this by the receptionist just now and er, is it true that you won't tell anyone about what I've said?'

As we mentioned before the vignette, there are four time periods during which we can actively structure our helping relationships:

1. Before the helping relationship starts.

You may be thinking '*How can structuring happen before I have even met the person I am hoping to help?*' This is where the **setting up** bit in the *setting up and getting started* comes from. This can mean different things in different situations.

- if you work for a service or agency:
  - the structuring of your helping relationships started when your clients saw your agency's publicity,
  - carried on when they walked into your agency's premises,
  - continued when they were greeted by your receptionist,
  - progressed further as they walked through the door into your room....
- if you know the person you are wanting to help in another capacity:
  - their previous experiences of you will have structured their expectations,
  - they will carry these expectations with them into the helping relationship unless...

• if you have a title such as 'doctor', or a role such as 'nurse' or 'teacher':
  • their expectations of the type or style of helping you can offer will be set,
  • if you are hoping to offer counselling skills, you will need to structure their expectations so that they are not disappointed or confused when you fail to behave like a 'regular' nurse or teacher.

The people you are offering help to will have formed a distinct impression of the kind of help you will be offering from all of this pre-relationship structuring and as we have pointed out, you will have to do something to align what they are expecting with what you are offering.

If we are working for an agency or institution, or if we have a professional role, we may find that we are almost battling against people's pre-formed expectations of what to expect. Cold, uninviting publicity, an office located in an 'unsafe' part of town and dingy decor can create a set of expectations that run against our best efforts to structure for the caring use of counselling skills. If we are stuck with a situation like this or a professional role such as 'nurse' we will have to become active at the next opportunity for structuring.

Activity
• *How would you go about reducing the effect of expectations people might have before they meet you for help?*
• *Do you have control over publicity or policy, e.g. do people know that you are offering counselling skills help?*

Activity...continued
• *How do you make your counselling skills helping feel welcoming?*
• *Is there good and equal access to your counselling skills helping for disabled men and women, people of different races, religions etc?*
• *If you are targeting your counselling skills helping, are they getting your message, e.g. do you publish leaflets in the right language?*
• *Write down a plan to improve your pre-meeting structuring.*

---

2. In the first few moments of helping.

One important feature of structuring or the alignment of expectations is that it will be different for each person being helped and different in each situation in which help is offered. Even so, the point at which each helper is most effective in setting appropriate expectations in the client and making a clear and unambiguous offer of help, is the moment the two people meet for the first time. (This applies equally to helping relationships formed over the telephone.)

We suggested that you look at the vignette on the previous page and write down the moments when structuring was possible. It should be clear from the script that Janet, for example, did a number of things when her client arrived that whilst being and looking quite natural, were also quite deliberate. She was skilled in her use of structuring. What impressions do you think were created when she:
  • left the door to her room open?
  • introduced herself by her first name?
  • offered her hand for Charlie to shake?

(Example continued on next page)

• closed the door behind him?
• told him how much time was available?
• explained her commitment to helping him over a number of sessions?
• said that she didn't have any background information on the reason for visit?

What expectations of help might Charlie have formed after only a few brief seconds in Janet's room? What *didn't* Janet talk about as far as expectations of helping are concerned?

Janet's behaviour at the beginning of the session is not, by the way, held up as a model of good practice. It is presented as a focal point for discussion. Let's take just two points for discussion one from the vignette and one from another setting, e.g:

• Do you feel that confidentiality is best dealt with by handing out printed leaflets or cards? Of course Janet may have mentioned it later if Charlie hadn't brought it up - what do you think *should* happen when you're setting up a counselling skills relationship?

• What do you think of the role of notes and records passed on to the helper at the point of referral? Should a helper look at, e.g. a client's medical records? There are points to be made on both sides of this argument.

The question is, how do you feel it would be appropriate for *you* to behave at the beginning of a helping relationship involving counselling skills. What impression do you want the other person to form about you and the helping you are offering? What would you do?

Activity
• *Taking the situation in which you are most likely to practise counselling skills, how would you start a helping relationship?*

• *How would you meet and greet someone you were trying to help in order to give them just the right impression and create just the right expectations of the helping you really can offer?*

---

3. During the helping relationship.

Structuring doesn't stop after the first few minutes of any given episode in a relationship. Expectations regarding what is on offer are constantly being checked out, refined and re-affirmed throughout the relationship. Once again, our decision is whether to be active or passive in this process, since it is a natural relationship process that will happen anyway.

Read through the vignette on the next page where we re-join Janet, ten minutes into her session with Charlie. The relationship is now under way, yet there is still some structuring going on.

People come to a helping relationship with a variety of expectations, sometimes these expectations are based on helping they have received in the past, sometimes based on their immediate needs. From the vignette on the next page, we can see that sometimes the person we are helping will want reassurance:
• reassurance that everything will be OK,
• reassurance that their 'problem' is big enough,
• reassurance that they're not wasting our time.

Charlie

After around 10 minutes, Charlie had begun to relax and had told Janet that he had been made redundant. Janet had been listening attentively and Charlie began to loosen up. He took a deep breath and launched into another part of his story.

'I don't know what to do about anything really. Everything's fallen apart. No job, no money; Maria, my wife left me 'cos I was a disaster area. No friends, nothing.'

'You look awful when you say that,' said Janet. 'Almost as though there's no reason to do anything anymore, no reason even to get up in the morning.'

'Yeah, that's right, I even thought of topping myself, but I hadn't got the guts. Anyway, my mate came round the other day and he made me see what a mess I was in and that I was drinking all my money away. I need a drink to get through the day.....all I really need to do is get some money so that I can sort myself out.' Charlie seemed to brighten at the thought of money.

'You must have felt desperate if you thought of killing yourself. Your drinking seems to be worrying you too, yet it seems as though all of these problems would go away if only you had more money.'
Charlie thought for a while.

'That's stupid, isn't it. I mean, nothing will change if I get more money. What I really want is a job. That'll mean I'm worth something.'

Sometimes they will want advice or instructions:
- how to stop something from hurting,
- how to get things back to normal,
- how to make the problem go away.

In fact they may want us to behave in any way at all which will make them feel better. Most of the time, however, we will have no sensible, respectful reassurance to give and we may not have much useful advice or instructions. What we *do* have is the idea that the self healing process within each person can be activated by the *core conditions*. At times like this we will need to be *authentic, respectful* and *reaffirming* in our responses.

Janet continued to structure her helping relationship with Charlie by acting out a way of helping that didn't jump in and give advice straight away. The *messages* behind her words were:
- I am going to listen to your point of view and make sure that I understand what you're saying.
- I am not simply going to give you advice.
- The helping I offer is centred around *you* and *your* experience.
- You can expect me to listen respectfully to what you are saying, trying to sense the tangled feelings.

4. When the nature of the relationship changes.
As we have pointed out above, this is called *restructuring*. Our notions of what the relationship is all about will be renegotiated so-to-speak, at intervals. Sometimes this will be a formal event:
- *everyday example:* a proposal of marriage, or
- *helping example:* the signing of a consent form for a surgical procedure.
Sometimes it happens informally:
- *everyday example:* deciding to become lovers rather than just good friends, or

• *helping example:* offering counselling skills in addition to being a disciplinarian teacher.

There are several situations in which we might wish to do some re-structuring of a helping relationship:

   • Perhaps we wish to move a relationship from being a workplace relationship as colleagues to being a helping relationship in which counselling skills are used.

   • Or perhaps we might want to move between helping styles in a relationship, such as moving from information and advice giving to using more formal counselling skills.

Wendy West tries to change the nature of her relationship with Ashley in the vignette below. Read the vignette through then move to the following activity.

Activity
• *What leftovers of poor structuring and relationship-building does Wendy have to deal with in the session described below?*

• *Wendy West is trying to change the nature of the relationship:*
   • *What old expectations is she trying to get rid of?*
   • *What new expectations is she trying to establish?*
   • *What does she do in order to achieve this?*

• *What would you do in a similar situation if you were trying to change the nature of a relationship in the middle of the relationship?*

Ashley

When we left Wendy West in her room with Ashley, she was trying hard to step away from her role as a disciplinarian teacher and towards a more supportive teacher role. She realises that Ashley might be helped if she can only listen to him in a supportive way, but she fears that her first rather clumsy attempts have made him angry and more defensive.

Later that week at the end of the year assembly, before the morning break, Wendy West notices that Ashley is hanging back from the rest of the group. She waits until they are alone in the classroom and as he is about to leave the room she quietly asks him if he had a moment to spare...

'I've been thinking about what happened in my room the other day, Ashley, and I was wondering if we could try and make a fresh start. You made it clear that you didn't want to talk about your Gran, yet you still seem troubled at school.' He looked at the floor as she continued. 'I can suggest some things we could do, like meet in private one lunchtime or after school. I'd make sure we would not be disturbed. But I'm more interested in what you would find helpful.'

'I've said already that I don't want to talk about it,' Ash said quietly. He let out a big sigh.

'Please don't go on pretending that you're not upset, I really do want to listen to what's bothering you.'

Wendy has realised that her relationship with Ashley is going nowhere. As far as helping is concerned, she's got to think again and make a fresh start. The trouble is that each time she and Ashley even bump into each other, the weight of their previous meetings bears down on the relationship in a number of ways. Here are three 'leftovers' from previous meetings - can you add any more?

- Ashley, quite reasonably, thinks he might get reprimanded.
- Ashley thinks he will get put on the spot over his gran - this makes him feel very uncomfortable.
- Wendy feels the pressure of having to get it right this time, it feels so fragile that there might not be another chance.

In order to make a fresh start, Wendy needs to be:

- *Empathic and Non-judgemental*: she needs to understand why Ashley is so upset, not only in general but with her too. She has got to stop prying, thinking she 'knows' what Ashley's 'real' problem is (she reckons it's got a lot to do with grief for his Gran), and wait for him to tell her in is own words in his own time.
- *Warm and Congruent* : she has got to look at how to soften her disciplinarian edge a little for helping to begin, without compromising her role as a teacher.   One way of doing this will be to tell Ashley honestly how she feels.

Wendy tried hard to get things right this time. The 'messages' behind her words were:

- I care about you and what happens between us so much that I am prepared to put myself out.
- I want to make a fresh start.
- *You,* what you want and find helpful will be at the centre of the proceedings.
- I understand that your feelings are still raw from before.
- I know that it's difficult to find a good place to meet at school, but I can make sure we get quality private space and time.

Making contracts for counselling skills helping
Since both helper and helped will have expectations about the helping that is on offer regardless, some people prefer to make a more formal agreement about the nature of the helping. This can take the form of a *contract*. There is, however, plenty of room for negotiation between the extreme positions on this matter:

'The person I am helping is an adult person, quite capable of understanding what's on offer without having it all put in little pictures.'

and

'I'm not moving a muscle until it's all down on paper and signed by both parties.'

You may feel that some more formal agreement is needed if:

- You are not clear how you came to be using counselling skills with this person.
- Helping sessions are ad hoc and have no time limits, and you wonder whether you should have planned, regular meetings.
- The person you are helping seems to expect help which you are unwilling, unqualified or unable to give.
- You are not clear what your role as a helper actually is with this person - are you using counselling skills, some other helping skills or are you a friend?

A more formal agreement brings with it responsibility on the part of the helper too. This is a promise or commitment to help the other person in a particular way for a particular time, etc. It means that the person being helped is given *rights* in the relationship is a more formal way.

Some helpers find this way of making arrangements useful because they believe that:

- making and keeping agreements is an important part of social behaviour anyway,
- it protects the help-seeker from unwanted, unasked for helping, and
- it helps the person seeking help to focus on what's really bothering them.

Some helpers prefer not to make formal arrangements because they believe that:

- it takes the essential trust and humanness out of helping relationships,
- it *forces* the person being helped to have a good reason for wanting help when they might not be too clear, and
- it makes it more like a business agreement about providers and suppliers than helping between persons.

Activity
- *What do you think about contracts, agreements and the nature of helping?*
  - *Do contracts improve helping when counselling skills are used or not?*
  - *What is your experience of contracts in other helping professions?*
    - *Are they used?*
    - *Are the benefits as advertised?*

If you decide that making formal agreements or contracts is a good idea for you and the people to whom you are offering counselling skills, then you may find the following helpful:

- Don't delay making an agreement or contract. Mention it as soon as you meet. Some helpers have a 'pre-helping' meeting or session to talk about contracts.

At the first meeting:

- Ask the person you are helping what they expect from you.
- Explain what you expect from them - fees, to maintain medication, to stop drinking alcohol or taking other drugs, to arrive on time, etc.
- Explain as clearly as you can the helping you are qualified, willing and able to offer.
- Explain your limits regarding confidentiality, supervision arrangements, whether you are still in training, etc.
- Make clear arrangements about:
  - when the meetings will take place,
  - where the meetings will take place,
  - how many meetings there will be,
  - if there is to be a case review and when.
- Summarise the points at the end of the first meeting and put it in writing to bring to the next meeting if you or the other person wishes.

In subsequent meetings:

- Always be clear about how much time you have, or re-state arrangements regarding starting and finishing times.
- Be vigilant - listen out for the other person's changing expectations or them expecting something that wasn't agreed.
- Be prepared to renegotiate the agreement.

Chapter 8 Summary

1. Helping relationships need structuring to ensure they get on and stay on the right tracks. There are four times when structuring occurs:
   • before the relationship starts,
   • at the beginning of the relationship,
   • during the relationship,
   • when the relationship changes.
2. Careful attention to the alignment of expectations of the helper and help-seeker will reduce the possibility of misunderstanding.
3. Contracts are one way of helping this alignment process, although not all helpers want, or see the need for, contracts.

Listening and Exploring

9

Without exception, all counselling methods, approaches and 'schools' put an emphasis on the skills of *listening* and helping the client to *explore* their experience. Most readers will have come across these skills already as 'active listening'. To many of us these skills do not come naturally, we need to practise them for quite a while before they feel natural to us rather than wooden and artificial.

In some settings, listening means catching just enough of what someone says to be able to answer a question or give an opinion. In a helping relationship where counselling skills are used, listening is an active process through which we hope to be allowed to see into the other person's world and help them explore it. In Chapter 5 we referred to this viewpoint as the *internal frame of reference*. We also defined empathy as looking at the other person's world from their point of view. Both empathy and adopting the internal frame of reference are complex attitudes; not just one skill, but a constellation of several interrelated skills. We will look at these skills both individually and how they might fit together in a counselling skills-based, helping relationship.

It will be clear from the previous chapter, that how a helping relationship starts is crucial to the quality of the helping that can be offered and received. All of the skills we shall be looking at will be much more effective in a well-structured helping relationship rather than one that 'just happens'.

Discrimination and Communication

One of the reasons active listening is called *active* listening, is because the listener is expected to *do something*, to *respond* in some way to what the talker is saying. Just being there is not enough. It helps to think of the process of active listening in two parts or phases, *discrimination* and *communication*.

Discrimination:
> This is the *listening* part, the picking up of the relevant information. Not just the words, but picking up all of the subtle nuances between the words, the non-verbal communication, the feelings that go along with the *story*.

It doesn't matter how good I am at discriminating sensitively between elements of the other person's experience if they don't know I'm doing it. Discrimination means listening to and understanding the subtle differences between the elements of what is being said. Empathy is only an active core condition if it is experienced by the person receiving help, and it is the *communication* of my effort to be in their frame of reference that is now of paramount importance.

Communication:
> This is *reflecting back* to the other person that they have been 'heard' and accurately understood. It involves *checking out* that your understanding is complete, accurate and appropriate.

In our experience it is the communication, or reflection, element of the skills that are most difficult to perform with confidence. When starting to look at counselling skills training and trying to practise active listening, many people attend only to the discriminating bit of the skills. They do a lot of head nodding and 'Mmm Hmm' - ing, but fail to get to grips with the feedback stage of the skills.

Basic listening skills

Following extract adapted from 'First Steps in Counselling 2nd Ed.' by Pete Sanders, pp 77 & 78.

Active listening and communicating empathy:
1. Identifying, acknowledging and reflecting thoughts, behaviours and feelings.

Active listening is one of the key ingredients in any helping relationship. It is impossible to be helpful if you are not actively listening. Active listening means that you have to attend to all of the signals given off by a person - not only the sounds, but using your sight to pick up the non-verbal signals. It should really be called 'active attention' because we are actively trying to pay the most detailed and special attention to the other person using all our senses.

The purpose of this active listening is to pay attention to, and try to understand, the thoughts, feelings and behaviour of the other person. How do we do this? If you were the helper, what would you be paying attention to in the speech and behaviour of the other person?

Activity
• *If the purpose of active listening is to understand the thoughts, feelings and behaviour of the other person, how do we do this?*
• *Write down what you think is important in the speech, behaviour and appearance of the other person.*

There are three stages to the skill of active listening (the arrows indicate the flow of information):

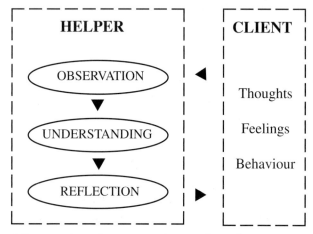

After paying close attention to the other person, comes understanding the meaning of what you are seeing and hearing. In order to do this you need to have achieved some degree of self-awareness. We find it easier to understand another person if we:

• Suspend our judgement of the other person.
• Put our own feelings and experiences to one side while we are trying to understand theirs.
• Try to put ourselves in their shoes and see their world from their point of view.

The final test to see if we do really understand the world of meanings of the other person in all its subtlety, is to check with them. We do this by *reflection, paraphrasing and clarifying*. Reflection is the basic skill and at its most simple involves reflecting the content of the other person's utterances back to them. The purpose is to give the message :

I am listening carefully to what you're saying and I am trying to understand. I will demonstrate this to you by letting you know that I heard what you just said. Did I get it right?'

The ability to give good reflections without sounding like a parrot is a matter of practice until the activity becomes natural to *you*.

Active listening and communicating empathy:
2. Paraphrasing,
3. Clarifying.

Paraphrasing and clarifying come hot on the heels of reflection and constitute the three basic skills of the core condition of empathy. When used together they become a powerful method of communicating your care and attention for the person you are trying to help.

Paraphrasing: is summarising in a few words what the speaker is saying. Depending upon the circumstances, it may be best to use the other person's own words or use your own words. It is a matter of judgement to know how best to paraphrase depending upon the situation. In order to paraphrase effectively we need a reasonable vocabulary, especially when it comes to putting feelings into words. For this reason, it is helpful to develop a 'feelings vocabulary' as suggested on page 79 of *First Steps in Counselling 2nd Ed.*.

Clarifying: is not quite as obvious as it sounds. It doesn't mean that you clarify the other person's muddled thinking, or can see more sense in the client's world than they can. Both of these are rather arrogant positions to be in and would probably be experienced by them as very unaccepting and superior. Rather, it means seeking clarification of your own understanding of the other's world. This can have a number of helpful effects:

1. They will feel that you're trying really hard to understand.
2. You will get a better, more accurate understanding of the help-seeker's world.
3. They may come to understand themselves better as a consequence of having to explain something in more detail, or in a different way to you.
4. Sometimes when a person is in a muddle or fog, you may pick this up by feeling muddled yourself. If you ask for clarification *for yourself*, it can help your help-seeker clarify their own thoughts and feelings.

Activity
• *Try practising these skills in pairs with a friend or fellow student. One person should be the 'talker', the other the 'listener'. Try talking about a current issue of mild concern for ten minutes rather than playing a role (role plays soon run out of steam).*
• *Remember to give feedback to your partner on their performance.*
   • *Was their reflection, paraphrasing and clarification*
      i) **accurate** *and* ii) **complete?**

Non-judgemental active listening

The word *active* is again the key here, since the communication part of the active listening process is as important as the discrimination part. So it is vital that you are not simply sitting there being silently non-judgemental, you have to somehow let the other person know that you're being non-judgemental. The other extreme is no more satisfactory - you could hardly expect to announce 'I am being non-judgementally warm' to the person you are trying to help and retain credibility!

The core condition usually referred to as Unconditional Positive Regard, or UPR has two components:

- being non-judgemental - this means accepting the other person's worth as a human being. It does not mean condoning all their behaviour, regardless of how antisocial it may be.
- warmth - this means positively valuing the other person as a fellow human being. It does not mean saying that they're wonderful or even that you like them.

It is sometimes assumed that if we are interested in counselling, we are probably OK at being non-judgemental and therefore we don't have to monitor our performance or try to improve our responses. This is nonsense of course. The question is how do we look out for ways to improve when we are all trying our very best to be non-judgementally warm? Helping skills are often most vulnerable when we feel emotionally compromised by the person we are trying to help or the issues they are bringing. If, for example:

- We have had to deal with similar life situations.
- We feel strongly about a moral issue concerning the other person.

- They remind us of somebody we know - our parents, friends or children.
- We find ourselves drawn into debate over a political or social issue they might bring.

Activity
- *What are the circumstances in which you are tempted to judge others and their behaviour?*
- *Make you own list - what can you add to the list above?*

Under such circumstances there are several ways in which we might slip into a judgemental way of listening:

- Labelling the other person whether from your own ideas or from another theoretical viewpoint, e.g. saying *'You're depressed'*, or *'You have low self-esteem'*.
- Moralizing is not helpful, e.g. telling the person you are trying to help how they should live their life.
- Blaming either them or someone else for what has happened, e.g. *'You asked for it.'*
- Interpreting and diagnosing the other person's behaviour, Offering an explanation for someone's behaviour is not only judgemental but arrogant. E.g. *'You are depressed and need cheering up'*, or *'You are showing typical signs of grief, you should let your feelings out.'*
- Taking sides, even taking the side of the person you are trying to help means that you are making a judgement, e.g. agreeing with the other person. E.g. *'Yes, I agree you have*

been treated very badly' or *'You have every reason to feel angry, I would too.'*

• Reassuring or trying to make the other person feel better is tantamount to saying that in your opinion it is bad for them to continue to feel upset or that you know more about their situation than they do, e.g. *'You mustn't worry, it won't solve anything'*, or *'I'm sure everything will turn out for the best; just think positively.'*

Activity
• *With a fellow student, give each other feedback on these issues:*
  • *Look at your own helping skills, do you sometimes do these things?*
  • *What are you trying to achieve at these moments?*
  • *Is there a way of achieving the same ends without being judgemental?*

The *Internal Frame of Reference Activity* on page 114 should help develop the idea of making non-judgemental responses further. It might help you increase your repertoire of non-judgemental responses as well as develop a sense of working from the internal frame of reference.

When thinking about judgement and counselling skills, we often worry about 'bogey-people' whom we just couldn't stand to be in the same room with. Rapists, murderers and child abusers figure highly on lists of such people whom we could feel obliged to judge. It is a useful self-awareness exercise to talk through your feelings about these 'bogey-people' and how you feel emotionally charged by even the thought of them. This feeling of being emotionally involved can be quite disabling to our efforts to be non-judgemental. Talking through the feelings may help clarify the issues without leaving us feeling that we have to change our moral outlook so that we can accept all people and all behaviour. We should always remember that we do not have to help everyone and we should not expect ourselves to be able to. Furthermore, these 'bogey-people' crop up more often in our imagination that they do in real life. We can take some control over who we offer help to, e.g. if you believe that murder is vile and evil and that murderers should be locked up for life, you should not volunteer for a scheme to help rehabilitate life-term prisoners.

Feedback from others is one of the best ways to improve your helping skills. In particular, when trying to get an idea of how warm you are being in a relationship, try concentrating on your voice quality, facial expression and posture. Warmth is a quality that we pick up more from how something is said than from what is said.

Activity
• *In pairs try acting out some helping responses:*
  • *First act them out in a cold way,*
  • *then say the same words as warmly as possible.*
• *What are the differences:*
  • *in the tone of voice,*
  • *in the volume of speech,*
  • *in the pace of speech,*
  • *in the facial expressions,*
  • *in the posture.*

Authentic active listening

The skills involved in authentic active listening are almost entirely those involved with the *communication* element of helping skills. Authenticity is a quality of response to the person being helped. It is appropriate to pick up the issues we left on the previous page under the sub-heading of *non-judgemental warmth*. In many ways these two qualities are flip sides of the same coin. The problem is to reconcile the apparent contradiction of being non-judgemental on the one hand whilst saying what you really feel on the other.

The dilemma comes to life when:
- we are helping someone we don't really like,
- we are offended or repulsed by the personal habits of the person we are helping,
- the person we are helping does something that irritates us,
- the person we are helping tell us they have done something which we don't approve of.

What should we do under these circumstances? Tell them we don't like it/them (which would be judgemental but authentic) or cover up our feelings and say nothing (which would appear to be non-judgemental but not authentic)?

Activity (linked to the next two activities)
- *Make a list of things that really irritate you in the behaviour of other people. Think generally, not just in a helping situation. Here are two examples to get started:*
    - *people that eat noisily*
    - *people that stare.*

I know my own list of things people do that I find irritating or distressing would include driving too fast or erratically for me, empty breakfast cereal boxes being put back in the cupboard and making sexist or racist comments. I also have clear pictures of times when this has happened to me recently.

Activity (linked to the previous and next two activities)
- *Look at the list you made in the previous activity and beside each irritation write down what you do whenever you are in that situation:*
    - *Do you do nothing?*
    - *Do you say or do something about it?*
- *Next, think about the feelings you are left with in these situations:*
    - *Are the feelings different when you say or do something?*
    - *Do you feel better or worse if you say or do something?*
- *If you do nothing:*
    - *Can you ignore the feelings?*
    - *How long do the feelings last?*

The problem with being authentic is that not only is it apparent to the other person that we are being inauthentic (do you think you can spot it if someone is not being honest?), but the feeling of being inauthentic or holding back, continues to eat away at us, distracting us from whatever we are doing. In a family setting it might lead to raised tempers, in a social occasion it can spoil our enjoyment and in a helping situation it stops us attending to and effectively offering our helping skills. In short we are disabled as effective helpers.

Of course, it is not only negative feelings caused by irritating behaviours in the people we are trying to help that challenge our willingness and ability to be authentic. Positive feelings bubbling up inside us can also be difficult to express. We may feel embarrassed or that the feelings are inappropriate to the helping relationship. The energy we are diverting to keep track of such feelings is at best distracting and we must quickly decide to either put the feelings aside or find a way of expressing them to the benefit of the helping relationship we are in.

Activity (linked to the last two activities)
• *Try the two exercises above again, this time using positive feelings which you think might get in the way of helping, liking or admiring the person you are trying to help, for example.*

Effective authentic responses

It enhances our helping relationships if we can make authentic responses when the people we are trying to help bring up feelings within us that challenge our ability to help, or interfere with the other person's ability to receive the help we are offering. Each set of circumstances demands different responses, so there is no such thing as a 'formula' response. The very thought of creating formula responses would, in itself, automatically, and necessarily, lead to inauthentic responses. We can however, try out some ways of responding, based on the activities in this section. Authentic responses need to have a number of components in order to be effective. There is no 'magic blend' but the following list is intended to:

1. Help you express your feelings so that you can concentrate on active listening.

2. Enable you to be congruent and 'transparent' by disclosing some information about your feelings.

3. Give the person you are trying to help some feedback about how they come across, or their behaviour.

There are also some by-products of this process, such as enabling the person you are helping to see that talking about yourself is a good thing and that talking about feelings doesn't mean that the world will end.

In order to achieve effective authenticity, you will need to do some or all of the following:

• Say something about how you feel, both about the issue itself and how you feel about addressing the issue right now, e.g. *'I've been uncomfortable for a little while, and to be honest I'm embarrassed bringing this up now.'*

• Acknowledge that it may be painful or embarrassing for the other person if you address the issue, e.g. *'I realise that it's difficult to have someone say that they don't like something about you.'*

• Explain how what you're doing is actually an investment in the relationship, e.g. give the message: *'This relationship is so important that I'm prepared to be embarrassed for it.'*

• Make a direct, no-nonsense statement about the issue at hand; don't apologise for it, e.g. *'You have a very strong body odour, I would be obliged if you to have a good wash, shower or bath before we meet so that I can give you my full attention.'*

Activity (linked to previous activities)
• *Go back to some of the difficult situations on your list and put together some authentic responses that have a chance of being effective.*

The other person's point of view.
(*Internal Frame of Reference activity*)

On page 42 we explained the idea of the *internal frame of reference*, a term used by Carl Rogers to indicate the point of view of the client. When helping using counselling skills, we want to try to enter into the world of the client by looking at their world from their point of view, in other words we want to see things and make our responses from the internal frame of reference. This exercise helps us identify the internal frame of reference (the other person's point of view) from all others (called the external frame of reference).

Read the following statements and helper responses. For each statement there are three possible helper responses, your task is to decide whether the responses are from the internal (IN) or external (EX) frame of reference.

Statement: *'I heard on the phone that my son was ill. He was in hospital a hundred miles away so I got straight into the car and drove down. I felt sick with worry all the way there, imagining things, you know.'*

Helper: **1** 'Do you think it was wise to drive when you were in that state? Perhaps you should have got a friend to go with you.'   *IN EX*

        2 'How awful! What was wrong with your son, nothing serious I hope?'   *IN EX*

        3 'That must have been really upsetting; you were worried sick about him.'   *IN EX*

Statement: *'When I got there they wouldn't let me see him straight away, just put me in this waiting room. They didn't even give me a cup of tea and I'd been driving for two hours. I said I'd come down from the North. I just blew up at the nurses...gave them a real mouthful. I didn't mean it, I was just stressed out.'*

Helper: **1** 'I know, I waited for three hours in casualty once, so I know how you feel.'   *IN EX*

        2 'Any reasonable person would have been angry by then; don't be hard on yourself.'   *IN EX*

        3 'You were angry as well as worried and with all the stress; you just lost your temper.   *IN EX*

Statement: *'They showed me to this ward where he was in like a cot thing with sides. He looked really ill, grey, you know. He just said....'Dad'....and I...I just (starts crying)....couldn't....handle.....'(tails off sobbing).*

Helper: **1** 'Oh ..there now, don't upset yourself,' (puts arm round shoulder and pats back).   *IN EX*

        2 'When you saw him lots of feelings came up, your love and concern too. You just couldn't handle seeing him in that cot. And you're feeling them again now.'   *IN EX*

        3 'Yes, its terrible seeing someone really ill, don't worry, its quite natural to be upset'.   *IN EX*

Statement: *'I couldn't let him see me get upset. I didn't cry then, just bottled it up, you know.'*

Helper: **1** 'You bottled up your feelings because you couldn't bear to let him see you upset.'   *IN EX*

        2 'It does you no good to bottle things up, you should let feelings out.'   *IN EX*

        3 'Yes, that was a good idea, you could have made him feel worse by getting upset.'   *IN EX*

Statement: *'When I had to go...(gets upset again)...I...I couldn't hold on anymore...I just put my arms around him and... held him tight. I cried and cried...then he got upset and cried and said...'I'll be OK Dad...'(cries more).*

Helper: **1** 'So he ended up looking after you.'   *IN EX*

        2 'You finally let him see how upset you were and he got upset too, you even felt that maybe he tried to comfort you by saying that he'd be alright and that upset you more'.   *IN EX*

        3 'It's good to let your children see you cry. What a precious moment for you both.'   *IN EX*

Content and process

When we think of the basic techniques of active listening - summarising, reflecting and clarifying, more often than not we think of listening to a person's *story*. That is to say, the *content* of their world:

    what is happening,
    who said what to whom,
    what ideas they've got about it,
    how they felt then,
    how they're feeling now.

The story or content consists of lists of activities, thoughts about them and the feelings that go along with them, (and it is easy to get caught up with the list).

This is familiar territory for most of us. We are used to listening to these stories and sometimes it is helpful, if not essential for our stories to be heard, using counselling skills, in a respectful and genuine way. We can sometimes be almost bursting to tell our story, or we could be afraid or ashamed of our story and may not want to tell anyone, even though we know somehow that telling it will help us feel better.

If the content is our story, then the *process* is our *way of telling* it. Some readers may be familiar with the television programme 'Whose Line Is It Anyway' in which celebrities improvise comic routines. One game in the show is where the celebrities are given a topic such as 'vegetable gardening' and they have to talk about it *in the style of*, for example, a Shakespearian play or sports commentator. Our process or way of telling our story is rather like telling it *in a style*. Of course, it is true to say that I will always tell my story in the style of Pete Sanders, but sometimes it will be Pete Sanders the hurt little boy, or Pete Sanders the confident man or Pete Sanders knight in shining armour!

It is important that my process is attended to since it will help me understand myself better. Listening respectfully and genuinely to someone's process is a very difficult thing to do, yet we should aim to improve our skills in this area. The big problem for most of us is that our own process tends to get in the way of us being able to see the other person's process, or may even interact with the other person's process. My process doesn't stop when I'm using counselling skills, even though I might be trying to be more aware of it. It would be a difficult tangle to unravel if the process of the person I was listening to was that of a victim wanting to be rescued, whilst I'm busy being Pete Sanders the knight in shining armour! More detailed understanding of process is a part of counsellor training.

Listening to and exploring content 1: thoughts

This is more familiar territory, since most of us are happy to listen to other people's thoughts and we will probably be quite good at catching the general points. When using counselling skills, however, we will be wanting to achieve a degree of accuracy and completeness of understanding that would be unusual in everyday conversation. We will be trying to discriminate between the subtle distinctions the other person makes, trying to capture the detail and nuances of ideas in our communicating of our understanding.

This attention to the detail of someone's world of thoughts needs practice at both the discrimination and communication phases: we need to listen hard and develop a vocabulary that does justice to the richness and complexity of the other person's thoughts. This means paraphrasing and reflecting in the language that the other person is used to. So, we would need to use colloquial and slang words rather than, for example, technical or medical terms.

Activity
• *Following the suggestions to work in a pair in the activity on page 111, this time the talker should talk about a decision they are having difficulty making. The listener should pay particular attention to the talker's thoughts, the pros and cons of the decision, the details of the issue.*
• *Again remember to give feedback on your partner's performance.*
  • *Were they able to discriminate between the details of your thinking?*
  • *Was their reflection, summarising and clarification accurate and complete?*

Listening to and exploring content 2: feelings

Listening to another person's thoughts is one thing, but many people feel distinctly uncomfortable when the world of feelings of the other person makes itself known. British culture is infamous for its rigid and limited ways of dealing with the expression of feelings. Most of us have very clear ideas about the 'suitable' times and places for the 'appropriate' expressions of joy, anger, fear, sadness or whatever. If we have a problem expressing feelings ourselves, we are likely to also have problems being around when strong feelings are expressed. These limits on our 'range' of expressions will cramp our ability *genuinely* to listen to a wide range of feelings with *respect*. We may not even be able to recognise the feelings present in the person we are trying to help.

At this point it may be useful to read page 47 and look at the exercise on page 79 of *First Steps in Counselling 2nd Ed.* if you have not already done so.

Activity

Identifying Feelings

• *Read through the following statements and make a list of the possible feelings involved in each one.*

'After they told me that my mum was dead I walked back from the hospital in a daze. It was over three miles, and I don't remember it at all. I was gone...cried all the way, I think'

'Nobody takes me seriously. I can say something serious, perhaps about something in the news, but they treat it as though I'm just joking.'

'When he said he'd like to go out for a drink, inside I had a grin from ear to ear and inside I was saying, 'Yes! Yes!' But I stayed cool.'

'When she said that she was having an affair with him I wanted to kill them both! My heart was pounding and I thought I'd go round to his house and just punch him over and over again! I had loads of dreams about it.'

'If they expect more out of me at work they'd better think again. Something's got to give and it's not going to be me!'

'Nothing seems worth struggling for anymore, I just don't think I can make it, just don't want to go on.'

It may appear obvious that helping someone by using counselling skills will involve feelings, yet we need to both *prepare* for discriminating between feelings and communicating our understanding, and *practice* the discrimination and communicating of feelings. The activity above is a warm-up to get us ready to sense feelings and express them. Most counselling skills training will spend some time on the discrimination and communication of feelings (although these particular terms may not be used).

In trying to be empathic we are making our best attempt to enter into the world of the other person as completely as possible. This will inevitably involve an effort to understand their feelings and the reasons for them. We can start to communicate this effort to understand by recognising, naming and reflecting the feeling. However, it is not enough to simply recognise and name a feeling. Feelings come not only in different shapes, but very different sizes. Some are small and some are *very BIG*. It would be neither accurate nor complete to follow:

> 'After they told me that my mum was dead I walked back from the hospital in a daze. It was over three miles, and I don't remember it at all. I was gone...cried all the way, I think.'

with

> 'So you felt sad and upset when your mother died.'

It might be experienced as disrespectful. Even saying

> 'So you felt **very** sad and upset when your mother died.'

is no improvement since it in no way captures the breadth and depth of the emotions experienced. So, in order to empathise with another person we must be able to sense and reflect the degree of emotion as well as the type of emotion being experienced. You might like to go back to the last activity and use the same statements to generate some helping responses; reflections which attempt to capture the degree or *size* of the feeling as well as naming the feeling.

At this point you will probably realise that it's not only the choice of words we use that indicates the breadth and depth of feelings, its also the way we say them. What dramatic effect we use when we speak, how we emphasise words, raise or lower the tone and volume of our voice, etc. Skilled use of summarising and reflection involves the use of a wide range of expressions. In recognition of this some counselling training includes voice work - speaking, singing, shouting, crying. Some people do feel (and sound) very wooden when reflecting emotions although with practice things do improve.

Activity
- *Working in a pair as before, try focusing exclusively on the feeling content of your partner's world. You could even try ignoring the rest of the storyline, just reflecting the feelings. The talker could talk for around fifteen minutes about a recent experience when they felt strongly about something.*
- *Don't forget to give feedback to your partner.*
  - *Was their reflection of feelings accurate?*
  - *Did they name your feeling correctly?*
  - *Did they gauge the depth of your feeling accurately?*

- *Look at page 121 of this book and pages 42 &43 of 'First Steps in Counselling 2nd Ed.' for help with giving and receiving feedback.*

Listening to and exploring process

On page 115 we briefly defined the notion of *process* as the *style* a person is acting out. We also pointed out that getting a good idea of another person's process is a very difficult thing to do, but there is a sense in which picking up, or being sensitive to, another person's process is a very natural thing to do. We recognise certain more obvious elements of another's process as a part of everyday relationships, and this is evidenced by comments such as:

- 'Mum's doing her martyrdom thing again.'
- 'Stop being the victim!'
- 'There he goes with his little boy lost routine.'
- 'Pete Sanders, knight in shining armour.'

Of course, such labels as 'martyr', 'victim', 'little boy lost' and 'knight in shining armour' are simplistic to the point of being offensive when used loosely in a helping relationship. Their use implies an ability to make accurate judgements about others which, in everyday relationships we may have the depth of understanding to make, but which in relatively brief helping relationships are inappropriate and unhelpful. How, then, can the idea of *process* be useful to those wishing to improve their counselling skills?

Again we find a natural relationship process (the ability to recognise process) which needs to be used with sensitivity, discretion and respect if it is to be at all useful in a helping relationship. There is a way in which such observations can be presented for the other person to take on board if they choose, or reject as unhelpful if they wish. It is more a case of:

> *'I think I've noticed a pattern in the way you've been talking. It sounds like this......, does it ring any bells?'*

Rather than:

> *'I am an expert in (armchair) psychology and I'll name your process in one!'*

Attempts to reflect a person's process require a number of qualities and abilities in the helper:
- the ability to practise counselling skills at a high level with patience and a keen sense of good timing,
- a high degree of self-awareness in the helper,
- a clearly non-judgemental attitude,
- a well developed ability to be authentic or congruent,
- a well established helping relationship in which the core conditions have been consistently experienced by the person being helped.

Because of the qualities required, working at the level of process is often seen as the province of professional counsellors, rather than helpers using counselling skills, yet it is our view that such a natural part of human relating should be acknowledged as a valid component of helping someone increase their self awareness, even at the level of counselling skills. In a long-standing helping relationship the process of the helped person will become evident to the helper *if the helped person is making it visible* and *the helper is attending well enough*. It could be argued that not to reflect what you are shown under these circumstances would be disrespectful.

Sensing and respectfully reflecting another person's process is not magical or mysterious, nor does it involve working with 'unconscious' material. We can only reflect what we have been shown, and those

we are helping will only show us what it is wise to show us. Any problems are likely to stem from:
- muddling our own process with that of the other person,
- poor timing,
- lack of skill in reflecting this process respectfully.

These problems can be overcome in part by:

i) Preparation

Commitment to self-development on your counselling skills course, either through the personal growth course component or personal therapy. This will help you understand elements of your own process so that you have a better chance of spotting when you might get your own process muddled up with the other person's.

ii) Practise

In skills development sessions with fellow students, try using your own personal material instead of role-plays and tape-record the sessions for later review with a tutor if at all possible. When you have become proficient at reflecting content, you could try some tentative process reflections, but remember: *you can't reflect what isn't there*. If the person you are helping doesn't show you their process or if you can't pick it up, you can't reflect it. Don't force it. Just listen patiently, summarise, reflect, and restate what you see and hear. You might even capture some elements of process without even realising it.

Listening to and exploring the whole world of the other person

When you have got the hang of the separate components of reflection and exploration, the next task is to do more than one at once, to build and integrate these skills into a well-rounded ability to reflect and explore the world of another person. This is often experienced as two separate problems:

- *Problem No.1.*

It becomes increasingly difficult to remember the growing number of things that have to be done *and* do them at the same time. So when in training to learn counselling skills, it is not uncommon to 'clog up' after the first few moments of a practice interview. Your head is filled with a list of things to do; your thinking goes something like this:

'Don't forget structuring, empathy...let's see reflect, active listening....er... congruence...yes, must be genuine, what did the client just say?...er...remember structuring... and feelings of course, was that a feeling just then?... did I introduce myself?...what did they say their name was?...HELP!'

This can seem a daunting if not impossible proposition at first, rather like the apparent impossibility of steering a car in traffic whilst changing gear when first learning to drive. We all know that most of us are soon happily driving along, listening to the radio and holding a conversation at the same time; the 'secret' is practise.

• *Problem No.2.*

This is the feeling of awkwardness and unnaturalness that leads to a wooden performance. You sound like a sports personality trying some Shakespeare, but less convincing. This can lead trainees to throw up their hands in frustration declaring that active listening is artificial and unnatural. Elsewhere (Sanders 1996) I suggest that such dismissal of active listening may be premature and could be approached in a similar way to the learning of ballroom dancing.

It could be said that ballroom dancing is simply a matter of putting one foot after the other. That's all Ginger Rogers and Fred Astaire did, after all. After trying it for five minutes it would be easy to come to the conclusion that ballroom dancing is unnatural, impossible and looks stupid. The real dancing starts only when you have practised the steps sufficiently so that you can blend technique and your own personal qualities. Then you can appear to float effortlessly across the floor - and it feels like that too! The same goes for counselling skills. The 'secret' again is practice.

Learning skills - a word about how it happens

Acquiring skills can be painful and our progress might be occasionally discouraging. Many writers have identified a distinct phase in the learning of counselling skills in which the trainee becomes de-skilled. Sometimes this de-skilling is something that happens inside us, i.e. it is a question of our own confidence, and how we see our own competence, rather than any deficit that is observable by others.

On counselling skills courses, there are usually opportunities for each of us to look in detail at our own learning process. Personal growth opportunities, keeping a personal journal, and support from staff and fellow students will all help get us through the difficult times.

As we have pointed out above, when learning counselling skills the task is to combine the technical ability to do the skill with our own unique way of performing it. Our personal style is what makes the skills in counselling come to life. Receiving feedback on our abilities in counselling is therefore more personally involving than feedback on our ability to, say, ride a bike. We are getting feedback on our *selves*.

When learning any skill we start off from a position of:

unconscious incompetence - we don't know what skills are needed, nor do we know what skills we have or don't have. We move on to;

conscious incompetence - when we start recognising skills that we need but we don't have. This is the frustrating and sometimes soul-destroying phase. Next comes;

conscious competence - when we have to concentrate like crazy in order keep the skill going and it feels really awkward and artificial. Finally we arrive at;

unconscious competence - when we can take our hands off the handlebars and whistle as we go along! The activity which once felt variously impossible, or just possible but very awkward and wooden, now becomes second nature.

Progress through this learning path is repeated for each separate skill and maybe even again when the skills are integrated. So be prepared for the moment when you find you cannot do the basics that you thought were really easy and that you had mastered once.

Activity
• *Make a list of the counselling skills you have been shown so far and against each one note where in the cycle you are:*
  • *unconscious incompetence,*
  • *conscious incompetence,*
  • *conscious competence,*
  • *unconscious competence.*
• *Check this out with colleagues - get some feedback.*

Much of the success or failure of skills development depends upon the ability of ourselves and others to give and receive feedback. In *First Steps in Counselling 2nd Ed. pp 42 & 43,* I gave some ideas on how to manage the feedback process. It is important to balance the challenge and support aspects of any feedback, but particularly when someone invests an activity with so much of themselves as we expect in counselling skills. To be told that your skills are not up to scratch can be a very personal comment reaching right to the heart of how we feel about ourselves.

In a recent conversation Alan showed me the following *feedback hieroglyph* a sort of picture or symbol which explains how to give good feedback. It's a graphic reminder of a good way of making sure our feedback is balanced and therefore easier to take in.

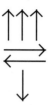

The arrows mean that you make:
• **three** positive comments or things that you like or appreciate about the person's skills,
• **two** alternative ways of trying something, or ways to do things differently, and
• **one** negative comment; a *'I didn't like this bit,'* or *'Don't do that.'*

I realised that I usually do do something like that, but the *hieroglyph* will help me remember.

Chapter 9 Summary

1. Active listening has two elements: discrimination (the listening part) and communication (the *'I am listening'* and checking that you understand what you have heard part).

2. Non-judgemental active listening is not the same as *liking* someone, it involves understanding yourself well enough to positively value the other person as a human being. It does not permit labelling, blaming interpreting and diagnosing, taking sides or reassuring in the *'there there'* fashion.

3. Authentic active listening means being able to be yourself whilst listening. Making authentic responses which speak of your feelings, explain your motives, make an investment in the relationship and are said in a direct, no-nonsense way.

4. We can pay attention to the content of a person's story (what they are saying), or the process of their story (how they are saying it). Content can be in the domain of thoughts or feelings and we must be able to listen openly and attentively to either or both of these domains.

5. Learning skills can be a demanding and sometimes troubling activity. Feeling de-skilled is a common experience as we move from *unconscious incompetence, through conscious incompetence and conscious competence, to unconscious competence.*

6. Successful skill acquisition involves being able to receive constructive feedback.

To Question or Not to Question?

10

The sensitive and sensible use of questions

There is often much discussion on counselling skills courses over the thorny issue of questions. This is mirrored in the literature too. The point at issue is whether to ask questions or not, and if we do, what sort of questions are useful and when should they be asked? Some counselling skills users and trainers take the view that the sensitive and sensible use of questions is an essential skill when helping people explore their concerns further. Others, including your authors, disagree with this view.

We put the argument against questions on the following two pages, followed by a section on the sensible and sensitive use of questions so that you can debate whether and how questions *can* be used constructively. One of the points we wish to emphasise is that the timing of questions, if used, is vital. The general view seems to be that once a relationship is well established, questions may be used sensitively to probe the other person's deeper understanding, to elicit more detail and to prompt them to explore possible experiences that may be on the edge of their awareness. In order to help you fully exploit the potential of questions whilst avoiding the pitfalls, we will briefly consider types of questions on pages 126 & 127. This is followed by a similarly brief appreciation of the uses of questions in counselling skills helping in pages 128 & 129.

We have delayed looking at questions until this point in skills development so as to emphasise the point that *timing* of probes and prompts is of the essence and to encourage a considered approach to using questions. Questions are best used in an established helping relationship when the possibility of questions seeming too intrusive has lessened somewhat. The issue of whether and how to use questions is also linked to *structuring* covered in Chapter 8 since it is concerned with the setting up of patterns in relationships. This point is also discussed more fully on the following pages.

Some arguments against the use of questions

Pete writes, as a Person-Centred counsellor, I can find no useful purpose for questions in the usual run of helping. I find questions intrusive, even in everyday social interaction - something that causes some irritation at home - and I am sometimes accused of not being interested in other people because I don't ask questions. I also tend to not respond very well to questions and sometimes even my family think this is rude. I, on the other hand, do not like the 'culture of the question', in which the question rules over all and, however well-meant, almost demands an answer. Sometimes I would like to say, *'I didn't ask you to ask me.'*

There are also some 'technical' problems with questions which I think are best dealt with by avoiding questions as far as possible. It is not at all difficult to avoid questions constructively, by turning the few questions we might be tempted to use into statements.

Problem 1.

Most of us are familiar with a style of helping session in which a wise person (a physician perhaps or a lawyer) asks us wise questions and then dispenses a solution. As we have already discussed in Chapter 8 when we looked at structuring, such patterns in relationships are very powerful. I have an expectation that a physician or lawyer will behave in a certain way and I am confused and disoriented if they don't. A visit to my G.P. might go something like this:

GP: *'What's troubling you?'*
Pete: *'I've a pain in my chest.'*
GP: *'I see.'* *She then shines a light in my ears.*
GP: *'Does this hurt?'* *She gently prods my stomach.*
Pete: *'Not really, it's a little tender just there.'*
GP: *'Have you had any headaches recently?'*
Pete: *'No.'*
GP: *'Do you get the pain just after you've eaten a meal?*
Pete: *'Yes.'*
GP: *'Well, you seem to be suffering from dyspepsia, take this prescription to the chemist. Chew two tablets after each meal. If the pain hasn't eased by the end of the week, come back and we'll have another look.'*

When I go to my GP I feel ill and I am slightly nervous. Now as a patient, I am familiar and comfortable with this question-and-answer helping. The GP asks me wise questions based on some (I assume) wise, scientifically proven, theory about people's insides. I don't understand the mysterious links between my chest pain, my ears, my stomach and my head, but I trust that the GP does. I also trust that the wise questions will lead to a diagnosis and that the diagnosis will lead to a medicine, even though I understand none of the ins and outs of the theory. To my relief the GP delivered my expectations.

Now think about a helping session in which counselling skills are used. If questions are used early on in a session, as the person being helped I would be forgiven for thinking

'Aha, I know what's happening here. This is question-and-answer helping; just like my GP.'

I then sit back and relax, expecting a series of wise questions leading to a solution to my problem. Now here is the difficulty: when using counselling skills in helping with human distress, there are no *wise* questions we can ask, because there is no consolidated theory about human distress that will lead us to a diagnosis and a prescribed medicine. My helper trying to use counselling skills might ask a few disjointed questions and then run out of steam. They will have started a pattern that they cannot finish and I will be at least confused, definitely disappointed and probably angry that they have not delivered what they promised.

Solution

Don't set up a question-and-answer pattern. Avoid questions in the first few minutes of the first session and think carefully before asking questions at all. Instead ask yourself, *'Why do I want to know this?'* Will it really help the other person, or *is it just getting me out of a sticky situation?'*

Problem 2

Since counselling skills keep the focus on the person being helped; their values, their world, their view of their problems anything that moves another view into the centre of the process would be automatically seen as running contrary to the ethos of counselling skills. Any device that shifted the focus so definitely away from the person being helped might even be thought of as harmful to the helping process.

Asking questions is, in my view, such a device. It stops being 'client-centred helping' and becomes 'helper-centred helping' as soon as the helper moves their agenda; what *they're* interested in, where *they* think the session ought to be going, what *they* think is important, to the centre of the relationship. The person being helped loses control of the helping process and takes second place to the helper who directs proceedings by asking questions. The tail has started to wag the dog.

Solution

Don't ask questions unless you find yourself in one of the few situations when using counselling skills in which you will need to genuinely gather information. Instead ask yourself, 'Why am I tempted to ask this question? Is there any useful information needed here or *am I trying to control the helping process*?' Get feedback from fellow students on your use of questions.

Problem 3.

Remember that being a helper is a position of power. If the other person is needy or vulnerable, almost anything you do will be invested with authority and expertise. If you ask questions they will feel obliged or beholden to answer. They may even feel that you could withhold your help if they do not answer. Questions demand answers. They can be instruments of interpersonal oppression.

Solutions

• Unless you are filling in a form or have to collect details for records, there is really no need to ask:
'How old are you?' or *'How old are they (e.g. relatives)?'*
'Are you married?' or *'Do you have children?'*
• Some questions give *you* control and could be just left out. The other person will tell you if *they* think it is important:
'Why did you do that?'
'Did that frighten/annoy/please you?'
'How did that make you feel?'
• Try rephrasing some questions as statements, for example:
'How do you feel now?' could become *'You seem to be feeling.....'* or *'I can't really tell how you feel right now.'*

• *'Good' Questions* are any that do not take the emphasis away from the other person. For example, checking that you understand something the other person has said, or that you have got a subtle nuance of feeling right:
'I heard you say...is that right?' or *'Did you mean this...?'*

Closed questions

These limit possible answers to 'Yes' or 'No', or to a limited set of multiple-choice options. They do not facilitate exploration and can only be of use in restricted information gathering since you have to know what information you want to gather before you can ask a closed question:

'Are you heterosexual?'
'What birthsign are you?'
Would you say that you are an anxious person?'

Inexperienced helpers could, in their anxiety, put together a string of closed questions. We all know that this sort of interrogation is unhelpful and do not enjoy being subjected to such a 'barrage' of questions.

Helper: *'Hello I'm Pete, What's your name?'*
Other: *'Dave.'*
Helper: *'Do you have a problem I can help with?'*
Other: *'Yes.'*
Helper: *'Would you like to tell me what it is?'*
Other: *'Er...Yes...I think I'm gay and I'm scared to tell my parents.'*
Helper: *'I see, do you get on well with your parents?'*
Other: *'Yes, alright I suppose.'*
Helper: *'Do you think that they'll go mad at you?'*
Other: *'I don't know really, that's the trouble.'*

And so the barrage continues. Closed questions will not help you listen actively, nor will they help someone explore their problem. If used at the beginning of a helping session they set up a question-and-answer pattern that is hard to break later. Closed questions are also of no real use further on in a

helping relationship:

Helper: *'Do you think it would help to get another viewpoint on this problem of telling your folks that you're gay?'*
Other: *'I suppose it could be helpful, yes.'*
Helper: *'Have you tried looking at it from their point of view?'*
Other: *'No not really. I'm not interested in their point of view. It's been a struggle to build up my confidence and get this far.'*
Helper: *'Do you think both your parents will go mad, just your mum or just your dad?'*
Other: *'I've already said I don't really know if they'll go mad or not. My dad might be OK though, but my mum's very religious you see...she thinks it's evil....I'm evil.'*
Other: *'I see. Does your mother belong to a strict religious order then?'*

Here we can see a closed question that gives options is of no real use either and the focus of the session has shifted away from the person being helped to their parents and their beliefs. The helper is also ignoring the parts of each answer that are related directly to the person being helped. If the helper did focus more specifically upon the experiences of the other person, the session might sound even more like an interrogation.

Leading and loaded questions

Favoured for different reasons by teachers, journalists and television interviewers, leading questions do as their title suggests, they lead the respondent to a particular answer. This leading is done either by putting together a series of questions that lead to one conclusion or by individual questions which bias the possible answers in favour or a logical, reasonable or socially acceptable one. For example:

Helper: *'Have you made your mind up to talk to your parents about your sexuality?*
Other: *'No, I haven't.'*
Helper: *'I see. It's obvious that you love your parents and you wouldn't want to upset them by springing it upon them would you?'*
Other: *'No, I suppose I wouldn't want to do that.'*

Teachers use sequences of questions to lead pupils to a particular point or conclusion by a series of small, logical steps. The logic of each step may be indisputable, but the end-point may not be logically linked to the start. Furthermore, we have already established that the process of helping using counselling skills is not educational, instructional, or leading those we are trying to help to a conclusion we have prepared earlier. It is a process directed and led by the person seeking help. We are their servants and companions not experts or, worse still, moral guides.

Open questions
It is possible to ask questions that do not lead, direct or limit the options of the person being helped. These are called *open questions*. They leave the options for answers wide open, giving the person being helped the opportunity, and even the encouragement they might need, to explore their experience. When asked an open question, it is not possible to give a 'yes' or 'no' answer. An open question demands a fuller, more considered response. Open questions usually start with 'why', 'how', 'what', 'where', 'when' or 'who' although there has been much written about the inadvisability of asking 'why' questions. So rather than asking the closed question:
> *'Do you think your parents will go mad when you tell them?'*

Try asking an open question version:
> *'What do you think your parents' reaction will be when you tell them?'*

Open questions, then, can be used judiciously to help someone explore their experience. It is still important to use them only in a well established relationship so as to avoid setting up a question-and-answer pattern early on. Some writers, e.g. Culley (1991) and Trower et al (1988) recommend the avoidance of using 'why' questions for a number of reasons:
- they invite 'I don't know' responses,
- they invite respondents to move away from feelings towards intellectualising,
- they invite respondents to search for reasons and causes (thereby increasing the likelihood of putting the focus for change outside the respondent),
- some people seeking help do not want to understand *why* things happen, they want solutions.

Others would assert the positive value of 'why' questions, e.g. Nelson-Jones (1993) and Dryden (1990) for more-or-less the same reasons, but opposite explanations:
- the search for reasons and causes is not a bad thing if the person wants to do it,
- intellectualising is OK, thinking and reason are helpful problem-solving processes,
- problem solving requires self-awareness and so the person being helped must accept greater self awareness and understanding whether they want it or not, if they are to tackle their problems successfully.

Ashley

Wendy must have read the signs right in Ashley and her declaration of authentic caring struck a chord. He agreed to meet up with her during lunch break on Fridays. Wendy was determined to get things right at these meetings and things did indeed seem to be going well. She decided to strike a reasonably formal note in the sessions so that Ashley could see that whilst she did care about him, she might also offer the same care to any school pupil in need. We join them in the second of their Friday lunchtime sessions.

'Last week I asked you when you thought things started to go wrong at school, Ash, and you said that you thought it was around the time your Gran died. How do you feel about that now?' Wendy decided to start the session off in the deep-end.

'I've thought about that a lot since then Mrs West,' said Ash. 'I think my Gran dying has had a lot to do with me getting so short tempered with everyone.'

'So your gran's death affected you more than you bargained for. Can you think of any other ways it affected you apart from affecting your school work and being on a short fuse?'

'I don't think it has really, erm... I suppose I spend a lot of time at home just sitting, you know...sort of blank. Not doing anything. I'm supposed to be doing something like homework, but I just sit and...well...look at the wall.'

'That sounds as though it could be very lonely. What do you think about when you go blank like that Ash?'

'Lonely...yes I miss Gran....I think about my Gran... and about how she used to look after me...and when I was little she used to tell us stories about when she was a girl. She would just laugh and laugh. She was famous for it; always had a smile on her face. She wasn't like other old people...she had a life, you know, an exciting life.' Ash was suddenly involved and excited himself.

'I can see that you're right there now, reliving those memories. What do you feel at these times when you're thinking about your Gran?'

'Oh, happy!' Ash's eyes suddenly clouded over and filled with tears. 'And at the same time....sad.' He started to sob. 'Really sad.'

In the vignette above, we see an example of questions being used in a way that helps Ashley explore his feelings without feeling interrogated. Wendy West takes a risk by diving in to the deep end at the beginning of the session, but there is obviously enough of a foundation in their relationship for Ashley to take a risk too. He accepts the gentle probes and finds that there are more feelings about his Gran, just at the edge of his awareness, and that these feeling are sometimes conflicting. Whilst the session is meant to illustrate how questions can be used constructively without being oppressive, we still generally recommend leaning towards summarising and reflection on the one hand, and away from exploration using questions on the other.

Questions and the core conditions
Empathy

We have defined empathic responses as those coming from the internal frame of reference, or the help-seeker's point of view. There can be little doubt that a question comes from the helper's point of view. This means that generally speaking questions, almost by definition, cannot be empathic. This is one of the reasons why many Person-Centred counsellors tend to not ask questions. However, there are some questions which do fall within the spirit of empathy.

- Firstly, there are checking questions of the *'Is that what you meant?'* which are used to follow up a reflective response.
- Secondly some questions invite the other person to explore under their own steam, at their own pace, or at least are tentative enough to be turned down. For example, *'Would you like to say more about that?'*
- Thirdly, it is perfectly acceptable to repeat a question that the other person has asked of themselves, or life in general, e.g. *'Why did it have to happen to me?'*
- Sometimes we are just bursting to ask a question, and then the issue is one of congruence.

Authenticity or congruence

There is nothing secret or mysterious about the helping process. None of it has to be kept back or with held from those we are trying to help. It is always essential that we are transparent, authentic and congruent. This applies equally to questions, indeed, you may well be asked, *'Why did you ask me that?'* Always share your reasons for asking a question, if the opportunity arises. Be ready to explain the purpose of a question, e.g.

'I didn't really follow you there, was is your sister or your mother that said that to you?'
or,
'I think it might help me if you could talk about one thing at a time, which would you like to talk about first?'
or even
'What happened next?...I'm really curious.'

Do remember though, that questions are not always necessary. Some of these questions can be turned into statements, especially when congruence is the issue, since a question often conceals something about ourselves. We can nearly always just come straight out with whatever is bothering us, for example,

'I'm really curious to know what happened to you after that if you would like to tell me.'

Non-judgemental warmth

Since this core condition is expressed as much through tone of voice, quality of facial expression and eye contact, we might well think there is no connection between questions and warmth. However, there is a need for caution since leading and loaded questions are clearly judgemental. Also certain styles of questioning will seem calculated and cold. Get feedback from fellow students on your performance when asking questions in helping sessions.

Activity
- *Think about times when you have been aware of being questioned.*
  - *What sort of occasions were they?*
  - *Were they helpful or not?*
- *Think about times you have been helped.*
  - *Did questions figure highly in the skills repertoire of the helper?*
  - *If so, what sort of questions were they?*
- *In threes set up a helping relationship in a pair with the third person observing.*
  - *Get the observer to write down the questions used in the session (you could use a tape recorder).*
  - *Put them in categories; 'open' or 'closed', then try 'helpful' or 'unhelpful' after getting feedback from the person being helped.*

The dos and don'ts of asking questions

In order to summarise the points we have been trying to make about the use of questions as a counselling skill, we present the following list of uses for questions in helping. You will notice that the list of 'don'ts' is longer than the list of 'dos'. This simply reflects our feeling that questions can be a hindrance as much as a help and need to be used judiciously and skilfully. Do try out your question-asking skills with fellow students and get feedback from them.

Don't use questions:

- to lead the other person to a conclusion you have already prepared, possibly according to your own notions of what's good for them.
- too frequently or the other person will feel hounded and interrogated by your barrage.
- that limit the possible answers to 'yes', 'no' or a few named options.
- to take control of the session.
- to break into a silence (see page 174).
- to rescue the other person by diverting their attention away from a painful issue or feeling.
- to satisfy your curiosity or to be nosey.
- in an effort to be more intimate or in an attempt to build trust. These aims are not achieved through questioning.

Do use questions:

- to help people explore; either familiar or new territory:
  'How do these experiences of loss affect you?
- to help people elaborate their experience, or give more detail:
  'Would you like to talk more about that?'

- to help someone move into feelings:
  'How do you feel right now?'
- to help someone bring into focus an experience on the edge of their awareness:
  'You mentioned your mother just fleetingly then and a troubled look came over your face. What feelings do you think you might have about her?'
- to help someone explore their fantasies or imaginations:
  'What do you imagine might happen if your wife left you?'

Finally, always use questions sparingly and in conjunction with summaries, restatement and reflection.

Chapter 10 Summary

1. The use of questions in a helping relationship needs to be given lots of thought. They can be intrusive, judgemental or controlling and can take the focus of the relationship away from the person being helped to the helper. This then becomes helper-centred helping.

2. Closed questions and loaded questions are the least helpful of all, whilst some counsellors and helpers advocate the sensitive use of open questions.

3. If there is a need for questions, then they should be:
   • few and designed to either check that the helper has understood correctly what is being said or felt, and
   • designed to facilitate the exploration of the other person's world.

New Perspectives

11

The nature of problems and how to help

We have suggested in earlier chapters that there could be a level at which helping takes the form of helping someone to solve problems in their life. Everyday experience of problems would suggest that there is some value in trying to break out of our own rather limited point of view of the problem. In fact we have an everyday phrase *'The problem as I see it is...'* which acknowledges that, for some of us a problem:

- is experienced as an inconvenient or unpleasant *external* force in our lives,
- can be thought of as having some *objective* validity,
- therefore it will be helpful to look at it from different points of view.

[If we were to incorporate these observations into a set of helping skills, we would come very close to the model that Gerard Egan developed in his first three editions of *'The Skilled Helper'*.]

Another everyday perception of human problems is that they can be very difficult to 'solve'. We have also explained in earlier chapters that some human problems are more to do with the systems within which humans live, rather than something to do with the individual human experiencing the problem. This leads us to the view that although we might think we have simplified the issues by talking about *'Problem Solving'*, we have to understand that there are catalogues upon catalogues of human problems and their sources. It would also seem from our own experience of problems that if they were that simple to *solve* we would all have solved our own problems long before we sought help from someone else. The task is to find a set of generic skills specifically aimed at helping humans with problems. This would relieve us of the burden of having to try to understand the ins and outs of different types of problems. Egan's model of helping is an attempt to do just that. He suggested that if problems cannot be *solved* we might at least develop a set of skills to help people *manage* them better.

This view is not held by everyone involved in helping and using counselling skills. Both the ideas that problems can be seen as external to our selves, and that another point of view might be helpful, are variously challenged by, for example, psychodynamic and person-centred practitioners. Whilst neither approach would argue that systemic problems do not exist, nor would they argue that problems cannot be ameliorated at a practical level, they would suggest that our system is a reflection of and product of our internal system or personality. Therefore, individual internal 'health' will eventually lead to external or systemic 'health', whether we see the system as our family, our workplace or 'society'.

Further more, as we have seen in Chapter 5, the person-centred approach would suggest that the only helpful viewpoint is that of the person seeking help (known as the *internal frame of reference.*). Other viewpoints at best will provide a superficial short term patch-up job of a solution rather than a lasting solution. The effect would be rather like using hypnotism to help with a toothache. The hypnosis would help you to anaesthetise the tooth by effectively giving you another viewpoint on the matter. Your original limited viewpoint was 'My tooth hurts.' The hypnotist suggests that on the contrary, 'Your tooth doesn't hurt'. The difficulty is that the problem of the toothache hasn't been *solved,* i.e. cured; it has been *managed.* The hypnosis might make you more comfortable until you can get to a dentist for treatment, but it cannot be seen as a lasting cure.

NOTE: I am not suggesting that an ethical hypnotherapist would do anything other than refer such a case to the dentist!

Activity
* *Think back to times when you have needed help or offered help.*
  * *Was problem solving effective?*
  * *Were there certain categories of problem that benefited from this type of helping?*

It might be then, that a problem solving approach could be a stop-gap, tide-you-over sort of helping, or there could be categories of problems which will genuinely be helped by a problem-solving approach. The skills involving new perspectives that are associated with problem solving have been identified by a number of practitioners as those involved with:
* helping a person to get a wider and different perspective on their problem and,
* challenging the person's limited view of their situation.

We will look at each of these in turn below. If a problem-solving method is being applied, then we might also include the following skills:
* sorting the elements of the problem into those that can be changed from those that can't and
* dealing with feelings which might be blocking clear decisions.

Both of these helper activities have a place in a person-centred way of helping if they are generated, asked-for, or driven by the help-seeker. The first is looked at, at least in spirit, in Chapter 13; whilst the second idea is touched on later in this chapter and emerges as an occasional theme throughout the book. It is linked to the general issue of how a person's feelings fit into the whole helping picture, and the relationship between thoughts and feelings. Sometimes feelings get in the way of coming to a personally meaningful decision because they 'fog-up' or block our thought processes. The fog clears when the feeling are ventilated, let out or expressed. Sometimes this ventilation is all that is needed to unblock a decision-making process that seemed well and truly stuck.

New perspectives
The first stage of helping a person with their problem is to identify the problem through understanding the person and their point of view in their world. Sometimes this means helping them to identify the problem because in the initial stages of seeking help, they may not have a clear understanding of what's wrong themselves. The skills needed for this stage involve active listening and helping the person explore their experience. This perspective on the problem is called the internal frame of reference and for some offers limited opportunity for helping unless

other perspectives are used. So the next stage of helping involves firstly discovering and establishing new and different perspectives, then generating new information from other perspectives and finally identifying those perspectives and particular information that may be helpful.

Discovering new perspectives and assembling new information needs to be handled with skill and care in a one-to-one helping situation. A common mistake is to liken the process to 'brainstorming' activities in groups when everyone chips in with their ideas, in any order. If handled insensitively this can have the effect of:
- diminishing the person's problem through apparent oversimplification,
- making it seem as though the person with the problem is inadequate for not finding their own solution,
- being disrespectful to the person and their life situation,
- failing to put the *person* and *their world* and *their values* at the centre of the solution.

The prime task is not to overload the person being helped with piles of possibly spurious information. Rather the first objective is to mobilise the resources of the person being helped to enable them to discover different perspectives for themselves.

Egan's approach is most often described in terms of skills. Usually the skills of the counsellor or helper are in the foreground. However, Egan also puts an emphasis on the problem-solving and problem-management skills of the *client* or *person being helped*. Some people do not have very highly developed problem solving skills, and this could

account for them seeking help from you. This then sets the scene for our first objective in this stage of helping, namely helping the other person develop their own method for generating other points of view so that their solutions are not one-dimensional.

It may be, of course, that two heads are better than one and that the helper may have more experience of looking at problems from different points of view, but the helper should always have the clear aim of leaving the other person with an increased repertoire of perspectives, or set of options, for the next time they experience difficulties. This ensures that the experience of the help-seeker is *added to* and *enriched* as a result of helping, not diverted to a solution favoured by the helper.

What, then, are the counselling skills associated with helping people develop different ways of looking at problems?

Skills for developing new perspectives
First let us emphasise the point that as helping proceeds through the stages mentioned above, the skills associated with the first stage are not stopped and left behind, rather they are carried forward to form the foundation on which subsequent skills are based. The first stage of helping, that of establishing a good relationship, and exploring and understanding the problem from the other person's point of view is an essential re-requisite for and further progress in helping.

The skills of *active listening,* then are the first set of tools in the helper's kit when it comes to assisting someone to develop new perspectives. They help you put the other person's world and values at the heart of any new views of the problem that may be later layered over the initial internal frame of reference.

Next might come the skill of helping the person explore their experience through the *sensitive use of questions*. Questions can be used to direct the person being helped quite purposefully towards a wider view of their problem. The helper can invite the other person to take a fresh new look or to see the issues from another perspective.

Two related skills that assist the person you are helping to gain new perspectives are firstly to be able to *establish the validity of your observations* and then *make authentic statements* from your perspective. We have already looked at making authentic statements on pages 112 & 113, where we considered the components of authentic statements, namely:

  • something about how you feel,
  • acknowledge that the other person may find your viewpoint challenging,
  • explain that you are taking a risk and that you are investing in the relationship,
  • make a direct statement laying out your views clearly.

You might wonder how to go about establishing the validity of your observations. The answer is quite simple, if you haven't done it already, you probably never will. Your credibility as a source of influence in the other person's life will have been established through the relationship building that has gone on in stage one. In other words, your ability to communicate the core conditions of empathy, congruence and non-judgemental warmth will have

built a strong trusting relationship with the person you are trying to help. They will begin to see you as:

  • a caring companion who is genuinely interested in them,
  • a credible witness to their problem,
  • someone who doesn't judge them,
  • someone who can be relied upon to be honest.

So when it comes to introducing alternative or new perspectives on their problem, you are more likely to be seen as:

  • someone with a trustworthy opinion,
  • someone with something useful to say,
  • someone not having an axe to grind.

What are these new perspectives?
We could simply call all possible new perspectives 'the external frame of reference' or 'a more objective way of looking at the issues', meaning that things, including our problems, look different and sometimes not so daunting when seen from another angle. However, this would, in our view, gloss over the different aims that we might have in introducing new perspectives into the counselling skills mix for those we are trying to help. We have summarised these aims as ways of looking at a problem. Sometimes we are trying to enrich a person's problem solving skills by introducing them to more than one new way of looking at things. It often occurs to us quite naturally to get a new angle on both

  • the external factors that are contributing to our problem, and
  • the part we play in our problem.

New ways of looking at the problem in general:
1. Links and patterns

Sometimes this can only be done from the 'outside', so-to-speak. I often think of a person embroiled in a problem as having their head down, toiling through dense jungle, keeping their eyes focused only on the next few yards ahead. The helper on the other hand, can get a wider view and take the time to do two important things:

• See patterns or themes in what the other person is saying and doing.

Sometimes the person you are helping says the same thing two or three times, or maybe they repeatedly overstate or understate a feeling.

• Make links or connections between thoughts, feelings, behaviours or events in the other person's world.

Sometimes you will remember a reference made at some point in the past, maybe last session or the one before. Sometimes these links reinforce each other, sometimes they are contradictory.

The person seeking help is far too busy just coping and living with the problem to do either of these activities in a systematic way. It's not that the helper is more clever or is more of an expert, but just that they have a different view and more time to ponder because they are not beset with the problems themselves.

If, as the helper, you are able to make links or see patterns, in the other person's world, you should briefly check to make sure it is not a pattern or link of your own making. Sometimes we want to help so badly that we see solutions and connections where none exists! Then your task is to present what you

see to the person you are helping. Making such statements should embody the skills of communicating both *authenticity* and *non-judgemental warmth*. It should be done with the following in mind:

• Be tentative - you could still be wrong. Say something like:

'How does this sound to you...'
'This might ring bells for you, if not, ignore it.'

• Don't present your ideas as a 'scientific' hypothesis, make sure the other person understands that it's just your view. Say something like:

'I think I've noticed a pattern...'
'There may be a link here, let me explain so that you can judge for yourself.'

• Make a clear, simple statement. Don't make it sound complicated or confused.

• Do not insist that you are right, be ready to let go of the pattern or link you think you see if the other person cannot see it too. Don't try to persuade them. It will only be helpful if they can also see it simply and easily.

You may well find that they will say 'No, it doesn't ring any bells for me,' when you first present your observations. Do not be surprised if they announce that they found your suggestion very helpful at the next session, even though they dismissed it at first. Sometimes people need a little time for the meaning of a new perspective to sink in.

The links and patterns that we might see as helpers can assist our clients to gain a new insight into a number of issues relating not only to their current situation, but to their lives in general. It is possible to look at some general types of patterns and links as they surface in particular problems. We take a brief look at some of these types of patterns and links below

New ways of looking at the problem in general: 2. Reality testing

One of the common feelings experienced by people who are distressed or in need of help is that they realise that their natural abilities to handle difficult situations might be going a bit askew. We often want to check that what we're saying is reasonable, sane and based in reality. Sometimes we directly ask those that are helping us to give us a raincheck which goes something like; *'Does this sound mad to you or what?'*

Being able to dispense such 'reality checks' is not really part of counselling skills, since we would have to answer the question *'Whose reality?'* before we could give an answer. The skill that would be part of the counselling skills repertoire, however, is enabling the person we are helping *to do their own reality testing.*

Some of the topics below show how we can encourage those we are helping to develop a new perspective that grounds their problem in reality. Looking at resources and their availability; getting specific, concrete information and improving problem-solving skills are all ways of bringing reality to bear on a problem if the other person wishes it.

New ways of looking at the problem in general: 3. Problem-solving strategies.

As we have already explained, one of Gerard Egan's stated aims is to help the client develop better problem-solving strategies themselves so that they

are not so dependent upon helpers in the future.

All of the skills mentioned in this chapter, this book, and counselling in general are good strategies for solving problems. There are a couple of mechanisms by which people will learn new strategies for good helpers:

- by observation - they will see how we do it and try to copy this in their own lives. This is often called 'modelling'.
- we will actively encourage them to extend their problem-solving capabilities by suggesting they try to do some of the things mentioned in this and the next chapters. The most highly developed form of this is practised by cognitive behavioural counsellors and REBT practitioners when they set 'homework' for their clients to complete between sessions. *We definitely do not recommend setting homework as a counselling skill to be practised at this level*, but it is acceptable to encourage those we are helping to try out new strategies and, if they find them helpful to add them to their repertoire for use on future occasions.

We might encourage the person we are helping to improve their problem-solving skills in the following ways:

- identify the problem,
- establish priorities,
- look at and enhance where appropriate any existing coping strategies (see below),
- assess the personal resource implications of the problem and its solution, (see below),
- explore and express any accompanying feelings, (see below); not forgetting that the

ventilation of feelings may be sufficient in itself.

• look at and change any self-defeating ways of thinking, (see below),

• be generally more creative in tackling problems.

New ways of looking at the problem in particular: 1. Behaviour

Here for example, we might be able to shed light on certain patterns of behaviour that may help the other person change:

• How the other person might be avoiding tackling the problem:

Throwing myself into my work to avoid dealing with the grief of a failed relationship.

• How a problem may be used as an escape from something even more painful:

Drinking to excess in order to avoid looking at the unhappiness of my marriage.

• How certain behaviours are repeated in certain circumstances:

Every time I have an important project at work, I get a stomach upset.

Sometimes just seeing a pattern of behaviour from another point of view is revelation enough to produce a fundamental and lasting change in that behaviour.

New ways of looking at the problem in particular: 2. Thinking

Albert Ellis developed RET specifically to help people see the self-defeating ways we have of thinking about ourselves and our lives. For more detail on the particular contribution made by Ellis, see Chapter 7 pages 75 - 79.

There are other common ways of thinking about problems that block progress towards useful solutions:

• Locating the problem outside ourselves:

Blaming other people when things go wrong in my life, or blaming a weak constitution for my many bouts of nausea before important meetings.

• Being vague in my thinking about problems or believing that human problems and their solution are somehow mysterious:

Not being able to pin down the general feeling of unhappiness and dissatisfaction with my life even though I'm drinking nearly a bottle of spirits a day. Ah well, I guess it's just my mid-life crisis.

New ways of looking at the problem in particular: 3. Feelings

There are many ways that our discomfort with feelings impacts upon our lives.

• Sometimes we bottle feelings up that are better expressed and we feel tense, excitable or overburdened and depressed as a result.

• Sometimes we avoid feelings because they are too extreme or painful, sometimes we almost become addicted to certain feelings and lose the sense of balance in our emotional lives.

Noticing such patterns in other people's experience and feeding such observations to them can be experienced as both very helpful and very challenging, (see Chapter 12).

New ways of looking at the problem in particular: 4. Resources

Sometimes we need to look at the sort of resources that a person needs in order to tackle a problem successfully. Once again, rather than lead a person to resources or provide them with resources, a better way of helping them might be to get them to identify the resources they need, locate the resources and then obtain them.

Simply looking at a problem from a resource point of view can sometimes be such a breath of fresh air that the person being helped feels much more optimistic very quickly. This is often due to the fact that looking at resources puts the problem into a perspective that seems to make it manageable, actionable or do-able.

It is important to not give false hope by using such perspectives, so it is essential to include both the:
- external resources and
- internal resources

a person might need in order to tackle a problem successfully. Internal resources would include:
- How *personally strong* someone feels.
- Do they value themselves and have high self-esteem?
- Do they have negative thoughts about themselves or self-defeating patterns of thinking?

New ways of looking at the problem in particular: 5. Coping strategies

For many years, psychiatrists and others trying to help very disturbed people noticed that, for example, people who 'hear voices' do things like play loud music, hit their head against the wall, shout back at the voices, and a whole range of other apparently bizarre behaviours. Psychiatrists spent a lot of time and effort, largely unsuccessfully, trying to get people to stop doing these things.

It has now become clear that far from being the stylised bizarre behaviour of the deranged psychotic, these behaviours all helped people cope with the symptom of hearing voices. Now psychologists are busy helping people enhance these coping strategies, or adapt them to help alleviate the symptoms whilst being socially acceptable or less injurious to the individual concerned. We could see that coping strategy enhancement (as it is now called) is a belated acknowledgement of Carl Rogers' assertion of the fundamental self-protection and self-healing wisdom of the organism.

Rather than catalogue occasions when it might be possible to help someone enhance or adapt their coping strategies, we would rather suggest that helpers using counselling skills, develop a deep respect for the wisdom of the people they are trying to help:
- try to find out what might be helpful in the other person's behaviour, no matter how bizarre it may appear to you,
- do not assume that behaviour that *appears to you* to have no purpose, *actually* has no purpose,
- develop an attitude of mind in which you seek the meaning in someone's behaviour in terms of *how it helps them* rather than how weird it is,
- remember to share your observations with the person you are trying to help.

Chapter 11 Summary

1. Even if it were possible, solving people's problems *for* them would be disrespectful.

2. Rather than steering people towards helper-generated solutions, some helpers use skills to enable their clients to *manage* their problems. This can include developing new perspectives for viewing their difficulties, trying new ways of looking at the same tired situations.

3. These new perspectives might enable the help-seeker to ventilate their feelings, or make new links and patterns in their thoughts and behaviour.

4. A key part of this strategy is to help the other person to develop and enhance their own existing repertoire of problem-solving strategies and techniques which they use to constructively cope with distress.

Challenge

12

There are two fundamentally different ways to look at the dynamics of challenge in helping relationships.

Firstly:

We could understand challenge as something the helper does deliberately and consciously as a strategy. It is seen as a skill which needs to be implemented with great sensitivity since there is a fine line between helpful challenge and destructive challenge. Such a view of challenge often carries with it the idea of a balance between support and challenge. In *'First Steps in Counselling 2nd Ed.'*, the following diagram was used to demonstrate the nature of this balance (read pages 39 - 42 of *First Steps* for more coverage):

High Challenge

Too scary, we get too frightened, defensive or hostile.	*The right balance for active participation in self-exploration. Exciting stuff!*

Low Support ———————————— High Support

Too dull, we become bored, disinterested and lose heart.	*Too comfortable and cosy, we don't get much work done.*

Low Challenge

This view would suggest that there are some things that the helper could do that are challenging in an absolute sense, i.e. in their own right, regardless of the circumstance, problem or person. Some writers go so far as to give guidance on *how to challenge* or *how to be constructively challenging* as a specific set of skills. This view of challenge is held particularly by integrative counsellors, who are likely to see challenge as an essential skill for managing the second stage or middle phase of problem-solving.

Secondly

We could, on the other hand, see challenge as a response in the person being helped. Something that happens inside them as a result of a particular behaviour of the helper. Consider the following examples:
• One individual might find it particularly challenging to be confronted by the helper's irritation at their persistent lateness. This is close to the meaning of challenge presented above.
• Another individual might be most challenged by the effort the helper makes to be non-judgemental, since they may have only had experience of harsh judgement at the hands of others in all their previous relationships. This is sometimes described as being challenged by love.

• Yet another individual may not find confrontation particularly challenging having been brought up in a family atmosphere of belligerent exchanges of views. This person may, however, be deeply challenged by the care someone evidences through their attempts at empathic listening, again, because it is something that their fragile self-concept has had little experience of, i.e. being *listened* to and *cared* for.

So in these examples we can see that challenge is defined from the internal frame of reference of the person being helped, not by the theoretical framework of the helper. Person-Centred counsellors are more likely to hold this view.

Which of these views of challenging you subscribe to as a helper will have a further profound influence; namely if you favour the first view, you will see challenge as a counselling skill, practised by the helper; whereas if you favour the second view, you will not see challenge as a counselling skill at all, but as something the person being helped experiences as a consequence of the normal process of experiencing empathy, non-judgemental warmth and congruence.

Challenge as a skill
The aim of challenge as a skill is to encourage the person being helped to:
• look at other viewpoints and
• accept the value of some other viewpoints although (and here's where the challenge comes in) :
• they may not agree at first,
• they may find other viewpoints painful,

• they may not want to leave the comfort of their own point of view.

The helper may not know whether certain observations or statements will be challenging or not, but it is best to:
• consider whether the person you are helping is up to it,
• be specific not vague,
• do not make it the other person's fault or blame them,
• set a good example by accepting challenges from the person you are trying to help, and finally,
• always be tentative.

Because challenging is seen, even by its advocates, as a risk to the helping relationship, some emphasis is put on deciding what to challenge in order to be maximally helpful rather than inadvisedly challenging and spoiling the helping relationship altogether. The penalties for clumsy or injudicious challenging are the loss of trust and possible breakdown of the relationship. [Challenge can also be an affirmation of the strength of a relationship when it's OK to challenge.]

At the level of using counselling skills in helping relationships, challenge must be used with extra discretion, since those being helped may not expect helping relationships to be challenging at all! (And yet it clearly isn't the helper's job just to make people feel more comfortable in the short term by saying soothing, pleasing things that they would like to hear.) Counselling skills must support and complement other helping skills, not cause the people seeking our help to walk out of the door in tears or a blazing temper.

We will look at some typical areas of challenge and would always emphasise that challenges must be always tentative, gentle but firm and specific:

• *Discrepancies and contradictions*: between accounts of events, between what someone says and what they seem to be feelings (e.g. *'You say you're sad but you're smiling'*), between beliefs, between the experience of the helper and the person being helped (e.g. *'You say you cannot hold your own in an argument, but you argued with me in our last session.'*), and so on.

• *Ways of thinking:* high on the list of acceptable challenge for cognitive-behavioural counsellors are the many ways we have of defeating ourselves with irrational thoughts, e.g. *'if you treat me badly it means that I am completely and utterly worthless'* and *'if I am late for work it will be the end of the world'*.

• *Vagueness or apparent confusion:* can sometimes be a real block to moving on, e.g. *'I never seem to be able to figure anything out when it comes to my parents, I'm so confused about it all.'*

• *Making someone or something else responsible for the problem:* a popular and effective way of preventing us from owning and therefore having the power over our problems.

Challenge as a response

If you subscribe to the view that challenge is not a valid or acceptable helper skill, you will not seek to develop it as such. Some people who hold this view strongly, feel that deliberate, helper-initiated challenge is unacceptable, offensive and unhelpful. They prefer to continue offering the core conditions keeping a sharp lookout for the effects the core conditions are having on the other person and feeding this back. In many people's experience this is challenging enough. An extension to this view is that even if the helper challenges in a conscious, deliberate way, good challenge should add up to nothing more than deliberate congruence or authenticity, or even high levels of empathy.

Activity

• *Think back to times when you have been challenged. Did you experience it as helpful?*

• *Think back to times when you have been helped. Was challenge a part of the repertoire of skills that your helper used?*

• *After reading the arguments for and against and considering you own experience of challenge, which do you hold?*

• *For you, what is the difference between helpful challenge and unhelpful challenge?*

Chapter 12 Summary

1. There are two views of challenge that can be held by counselling skills practitioners:
 • that it is a deliberate and consciously used strategy or skill of the helper, *(you are being challenging), or*
 • that challenge is the other person's response to our actions, whether we are being accepting or empathically reflecting discrepancies in their story *(I feel challenged by your behaviour).*
2. The aim of challenge as a skill is to move the help-seeker forward by confronting them with some aspect of their thoughts feelings or behaviour, for example:
 • discrepancies or contradictions,
 • illogical over-reactive ways of thinking,
 • vagueness or confusion
 • blaming others.
3. Those holding the view that challenge is a response would expect the person to feel challenged in ways that would have unique meaning for that person, rather than expect everyone to feel challenged by having contradictions brought to their attention. (An individual brought up in an argumentative and belligerent environment may relish or feel comforted by such confrontation rather than feel challenged by it.)

Action and Ending

13

Action, what action?

Many helping models and approaches take some time to look at 'action'. The idea that the helper should somehow need different skills for different phases or stages in the helping process has been suggested by many writers, including Carkhuff (1969) who saw the change process as having two phases:

> •The downward and inward phase where the client explored and elaborated their experience.
> • The upward and outward phase where the client moved towards resolution and changed behaviour.

This idea was built upon by Egan who developed the idea of three stages, first came relationship building, and exploration, next came developing new perspectives. He called the last of his stages 'Action' (Egan 1981).

It is often suggested that at a certain stage of helping, the helper understands the process well enough to know when and how to move on to some kind of planning, action-oriented, behaviour-changing phase. There is no shortage of books explaining how this is to be done, see for example, Culley (1991), Egan (1981) or Nelson-Jones (1993). These problem-management or skills-based models of helping are accepted by many as useful frameworks within which to understand problems and the process necessary to bring resolution.

Not all helpers share this view. Those coming from a Psychodynamic or Person-Centred background do not understand the process in terms of stages or phases. In particular, the Person-Centred approach would suggest that it is the person being helped that directs and determines the action and anything else would be helper-centred helping. We share this latter view. There is an interesting debate to be had here and we would encourage you to look at both sides through your own experience. First we will present both arguments briefly (and we admit to weighting it slightly in favour of a person-centred view), then invite you to take part in an activity to help crystallise your views.

Two views of action

Action as the helper's agenda

As a helping relationship proceeds, the needs of the person being helped change. We could say there is a beginning, middle and end to all relationships and that the helper needs firstly to be aware of the different needs at each stage and secondly to have different skills for each stage.

> • At the beginning of helping:
> > • the person being helped needs to build trust in the helper and explore the problem,
> > • the helper has to establish contact, build the relationship and help focus on the problem.

- In the middle of helping:
    - the person being helped needs to reassess the problem in the light of new perspectives and feel empowered,
    - the helper has to maintain contact and challenge the person they are helping to see things differently.
- At the end of helping:
    - the person being helped needs to change their behaviour and move on,
    - the helper has to help the other person plan and evaluate strategies of action.

At each stage, client needs must be met by appropriate helper skills. It's no good trying to build a relationship when a help-seeker wants to reassess a problem or to plan strategies of action too soon. This model pursues what many believe is a 'common-sense' view of managing a problem which goes roughly like this:

Explore general issues.

Identify the particular problem.

Get more information from as many sources as possible on how to solve it.

Sort the ideas out.

Make a plan based on one of the ideas.

Carry out the plan and evaluate the outcome.

It is easy see how action, the activity and action skills fit into the overall pattern of helping. The person being helped will want to change their behaviour and the helper must help them do it using concrete action-oriented skills.

Action as client movement

The problem with the argument laid out above is that it emphasises the helper role at the expense of the person being helped. The model concentrates too much skill-based expertise in the helper. In a person-centred model, the energy and 'expertise' is located in the person being helped. Their own self-healing energy is released and facilitated by the helper. The helper is relieved of the burden of having to be an expert on human problems or some sort of technician diagnosing and responding selectively to stages in the helping process. This is helper-centred helping.

The idea that action is an expression of movement within the client rather than something that the helper thinks would be a good idea lies at the heart of person-centred helping. There are some further key points that help define the helping process as being located with the person being helped:

- Everyone will have their own idea of 'useful action' in any given situation.
- All situations are different.
- Many people being helped wish to take no action at all.
- Sometimes action-planning can sound like advice, which:
    - if it goes wrong can lead to the helper being blamed for failure,
    - if it succeeds can lead to the credit being taken by the helper,
    Note: in both cases the person being

helped can only take control of the helping process if they are given responsibility for it.

At the heart of our argument is the same issue that we considered on pages 143-146 when we looked at the nature of challenge, namely whether a helping event is best seen as a helper skill or a client response. This view has implications for practice since it helps you decide what you will be doing as a helper towards the end of a helping relationship.

Special 'action skills'?

So what of the idea that special skills are needed to help people in the latter parts of a helping relationship? The answer for each helper will be different depending upon where you position yourself in the debate above. The argument for a separate, or different, set of helper skills puts emphasis on such things as:
• being able to help the other person focus on one problem at a time,
• encouraging them to be specific rather than vague,
• being able to help the other person brainstorm ideas.

And later:
• helping them to set realistic goals,
• helping them to take reasonable action,
• helping them to evaluate their actions and sustain useful change,
• help them transfer their learning to other situations.

There is a clearly identified path that helping takes and the skills required to move the client from stage to stage, or task to task.

We, as authors, have nailed our colours to the mast on this one - since it is our view that action is defined as client movement rather than the helper's agenda, we do not think there are any *different skills* needed in the latter parts of a helping relationship. We see it more in terms of doing the same things in a different place. Take the analogy of eating a meal; the same things happen - we put food in our mouth, we talk with other people present - regardless of the setting. Yet we know that the purpose and overall experience of eating the meal will be very different depending upon the setting; a meal at home compared with a meal in a restaurant, or a meal on holiday compared with a meal in the works' canteen.

If we now think of a helping relationship we hope it is clear that although the activities and ingredients (the core conditions) remain the same, the purpose, experience and outcome will be different depending upon where in the relationship they occur (beginning, middle or end). The same core conditions will feel different when helping is well underway or at the end of helping because:
• The person being helped has changed and so will:
  • look at their world and their problems differently,
  • have different needs.
• The helper themselves will have changed a little too, perhaps as a result of being a helper to the other person.
• The helping relationship itself will have changed as the helper and person being helped have got to know each other.

The helper's task in the latter stages of helping using counselling skills is to be aware that the helping is continually changing and may soon be ending. This requires a developing awareness and flexible attitudes to the helping process. Though the core conditions are the same, we have to develop different attitudes about how we might offer them, including what we think will happen when we do offer them in a changing relationship.

The core conditions are *fundamental relationship tools* and *fundamental healing tools*. They release and facilitate positive change in people at all stages of a relationship:

  • At the beginning of a relationship they help build the relationship.
  • In the middle of a relationship they help keep it going and deepen it where necessary.
  • At the end of a relationship they help bring it appropriately to a positive and fulfilling close.

So, in our view there is no reason why the core conditions shouldn't help the person do all of the things mentioned above [i.e. Help the other person to focus on one problem at a time, to be specific rather than vague and to brainstorm ideas. Then later, helping them to set realistic goals, to take reasonable action, to evaluate their actions and sustain useful change and to transfer their learning to other situations.] This has the added bonus of making sure we are doing them only if the person being helped brings them up as useful strategies. The core conditions follow the other person rather than lead them. This means of course, that whilst it might be helpful to *our* thinking on how to help to consider what might be helpful at different stages of helping, it still leaves us open to the idea that the particular person we are helping *right now* doesn't have to follow that pattern, or indeed any pattern that has meaning to us. (It only has to have meaning for

them.) *We suggest that helpers cultivate the attitude which re-invents the helping process each time we meet someone new.* It is for this reason that we have tried to encourage mental and emotional flexibility throughout the book.

Throughout the relationship the core conditions put control and responsibility in the hands of the person being helped, so that they can take *just as much* as is helpful and *only* that which is helpful at any stage. I often think of the core conditions as a vitamin-rich broth that contain all the essential nutrients for healthy growth. Your body takes just enough of what it wants from such broth; you cannot overdose on anything, nor can it make you ill. You and your body are in control, you take what is needed and heal yourself as a result.

In a helping process driven and directed by the person being helped, it is likely (though not certain) that their needs will change. Action or behaviour change may well be something they want. As helping progresses to the point at which the person being helped decides to change their behaviour or take some action on some issues, they might want you to:

  • be a *witness* to any action or change in behaviour,
  • *monitor* the effects of any action or behaviour,
  • help them debrief or *review* the experience and consider further changes.

These are not new skills. Empathy, respect and genuineness will enable you to follow the other person's efforts at putting together useful strategies without direction, advice or prompting from you. You will be a respectful witness, a congruent companion as they monitor their efforts, and an empathic listener as they seek new understanding in their review of their experiences. Through your offering of the core conditions in this way the person you are helping will be able to transfer their learning to other areas of their life if they choose. They will not be dependent upon you for your 'expert' interventions in the future. They will have been empowered by your continued efforts to let the control and responsibility for helping process reside with them.

Ending

The last bit of change in a helping relationship that the helper might have to facilitate is the *ending*. The vast majority of helping relationships where counselling skills are used will be temporary. Many will be 'contractual' relationships, limited by time, professional responsibilities or other boundaries. Regardless of the circumstances, once again we suggest that the decisions about how and when to end helping are best left to the person being helped.

You may also have guessed that we don't think there are any different *helper skills* required for ending, just continued provision of the core conditions in a manner that is sensitive to the ending of a relationship. It is at this time in training groups that I like to say '*the ending is in the beginning*' (which I think of as being vaguely biblical or T.S. Eliot), to indicate that structuring a relationship well at the beginning will facilitate a 'good' ending. This is done by suggesting to the person you are helping roughly how long you are prepared to help them for.

Any limit on your helping may be there for a number of reasons, including:

- external factors, e.g. guidelines at work.
- what the other person wants,
- negotiated between you, i.e. what seems reasonable to you both,
- your personal requirements, i.e. what you think you can cope with.

If you are offering helping in a professional or voluntary setting that has built-in limits in the form of guidelines or time-limited relationships, these boundaries are best incorporated to any helping contract you make with the person you are helping. (See contract setting, pp 103 & 104.) If there are guidelines or rules saying that clients can only expect x number of helping sessions, it is essential that they know this at the start of the relationship. A good end can be made if they know it's coming.

Some people come for help with a rough idea of what they want. This will also include how long they expect the help to last. When beginning a helping relationship, letting the person being helped know what to expect in terms of the length of the relationship, is a part of the initial structuring. We looked at this in Chapter 8. Sometimes this structuring becomes more formal contract setting where the person being helped and the helper actually write down the limits of the helping and the timing of any reviews of the contract that they might plan. Sometimes this structuring is a time when commitment, service provision and resource allocation are negotiated by both parties, i.e. how badly it's needed, where and for how long the helping will be offered. It is best to be as specific as possible and actually set times and dates rather than say something general like:

'Until you feel better.'

Which is as long as the proverbial piece of string. It is much easier to end well if you can remind the person you are helping of the agreement you both made:

'We agreed to meet like this for x weeks, and that time will be shortly up. Now that we are here, does it still seem like a good time to finish?'

Never overlook your personal requirements when offering help. These will fit in somewhere between what your agency or service expect of you, and what the current client wants from you. The question is, *What are you prepared to give?* Helpers are notorious for forgetting to attend to their own needs when offering help. A good ending will be more likely if you can finish feeling as though you have given enough and not been exploited, nor been exhausted by your own collusion through over-enthusiasm.

Real-life endings

Many books write about endings that are carefully planned and perfectly worked through by both the helper and the person being helped. They also tell of the pitfalls and disasters, but rarely do they help with the stuff in between those two extremes; what happens in real life.

We have looked at preparing for good endings but in real life, however carefully you prepare through initial structuring, contracting and reviewing, helpers have to deal with the following sorts of endings:

• When the person being helped is forced to end the relationship before they want to and the helper knows this is going to happen.

• When the person being helped just stops coming after helping is well under way and 'disappears' without giving any reasons.

• When someone comes for just one session and leaves saying you've been a tremendous help (even though you can't work out what you've done!) and they don't need any more, thank you.

• When you have to refer the person on to another helper.

• When the person you are helping thinks you are no help at all, gets disgruntled and leaves.

• When the person you are helping dies.

Our message throughout this book has been that the only skills you need are those associated with the core conditions. It should, therefore, come as no surprise that we are saying the same thing now. The difference with endings is that the helper is made more immediately aware that *they have feelings and personal issues too.* The scenarios outlined above are all ones in which the helper is left with a problem. The person being helped has gone away, thus ending the relationship, and because the helper had no control, possibly because the ending broke the 'contract' or was outside the limits envisaged during the initial structuring, the helper is left to deal with some uncomfortable feelings. These could include anger, sadness, hurt, relief or disappointment associated with feeling:

• bereaved,
• left or abandoned,
• under-valued,
• used,
• lost and purposeless.

Dealing with feelings of this type at the end of (or even on some occasions during) a helping relationship is a matter of both personal development and support for the helper, it is not a matter of developing skills. We will look at support for helpers in Chapter 16.

Ashley

Wendy West was feeling pleased with the second lunchtime session she had with Ashley. He had talked mostly about his Grandma and how much he missed her and, although he got upset at a couple of points during the time they spent together, he seemed, to Wendy at least, lighter and more settled when he left.

It was all the more disturbing, then, when he Ash failed to show on the next Friday lunchtime. Wendy sat there in her office with a succession of thoughts and feelings washing over her in waves. She knew that he was in school because she had seen him. Her churned over, 'Is he alright? Should I go and find him? Perhaps he has forgotten. Well, if that's all he thinks of my efforts to help, sod him! Perhaps he...' and then she remembered the last session and the thought crossed her mind that maybe Ashley was avoiding her because he revealed too much of himself then. Maybe he had been frightened off, embarrassed by showing his feelings to her, a teacher, and a woman to boot! Now she really was in a turmoil. What on earth should she do?

Wendy is in a difficult situation. She would like to continue to let Ashley take responsibility for himself and his actions, gaining a sense of his own personal power, but she doesn't know whether he had quit and ended their 'helping' relationship, since he cannot quit and end their teacher-pupil relationship. It would be awkward and embarrassing to not acknowledge this new development, and after all, Ashley might have genuinely forgotten or have gone home. She knows that since she has gone some way to draw a line carefully between her 'disciplinarian' teacher role and her 'helper' teacher role she must not go charging out

to find Ashley. That would betray the trust he had put in her as a helper.

In the end, Wendy 'decided' to wait and do nothing. She actually spent half an hour alternatively angry with Ash and upset with herself, and before she knew it lunchtime was over.

At the beginning of the next week, she saw Ashley around school as usual, and even given that she might be over-sensitive to their paths crossing, she did feel that he was avoiding her. Friday was approaching and she was still no nearer deciding what to do. She couldn't work out how to let Ashley know that she was still there for him as a 'helper' as well as a teacher without him thinking he *had* to go out of a sense of guilt because she had given up her time, or duty because she was a teacher and should be obeyed. Then she knew what to do.

Again she chose the end of the year assembly to ask if he could stay behind for a moment.
    'Listen Ashley, I wanted to say a couple of things, firstly, that if you want to see me on Friday, I'll be there at lunchtime like before.' Ash looked sheepish but she went on, 'Secondly, I was disappointed that you didn't let me know why you didn't show up. I don't want you to come just because you think you have to. I'm happy to help in any way I can, but only if you want. It's really important to me to know that you really want to be there. So, have a think about it and if you don't show again I'll know that you don't want to come, unless you let me know otherwise. OK?'

Activity
• *What would you have done in Wendy West's shoes?*

• *If you planned an ending that you and the person you are helping agreed on, what messages would you like to convey? What words would you use?*

Chapter 13 Summary

1. Some helpers see the helping process as having different stages as it runs its course from beginning, through the middle, to the end. This raises the question of whether different helper skills are required at these different times or stages. Both sides of the argument are presented.

2. Where you position yourself will depend upon your own experience and whether you lean towards an unstructured model of helping such as person-centred or psychodynamic, or a structured model such as REBT or an integrative model.

3. Endings are best planned for by incorporating at least the idea of reviewing the helping and ending into the initial structuring of the relationship. However, life doesn't present us with neat helping relationships which end on cue. Helpers are often left with some personal development work to do at the end of helping relationships that finish abruptly or unexpectedly.

Helping Skills in Action: Karen's Story

This extended vignette is our attempt to show how the different waves of helping activity based on the core conditions might fit together in real life. The left-hand column on each page is the story, the right hand column in italics is our commentary. We suggest that you read the story first and try answering the following questions:

- At what times is Karen offered:
  - practical help,
  - personal help,
  - developmental support,
  - problem-solving counselling,
  - therapeutic counselling?
- Can you detect the core conditions in the helping she receives?

Karen is a District Sales Manager for a Midlands leisure and sportswear company. Although now mainly occupied in a managerial role at Head Office she still needs to drive several hundred miles a week to support her sales staff, meet occasional important customers and generally keep an eye on growth opportunities. One Friday morning she is pushing on up the motorway in poor weather conditions when a lorry sways out from the middle lane, physically nudging her car into the central reservation, where it rebounds in a full spin from the crash barrier across all three lanes to end up facing oncoming traffic banged up against a sign support, partly on the hard shoulder and partly on the inside lane. Karen has

In common with most people, Karen's life is going well until she has a crisis. This road accident knocks her usually well-ordered life off balance. As we shall see, Karen reacts in a particular and understandable way to this crisis.

*We have demonstrated, in Chapter 4 and the other vignettes, that you don't **have** to be in a crisis situation in order to benefit from the use of counselling skills. We shall see what different types of help Karen gets along the way.*

been briefly knocked out by the buffeting and has some cuts on her face and from flying glass but is not badly hurt considering the drama of the crash and the state of her car.

While she is being cut out of her car by the Fire Brigade Karen is surprised how calm and collected she is and she shows little distress for the first hour or so, even when she is told that she will have to be admitted for observation because it is not clear how bad the head injury might be and because she had been unconscious this needs to be carefully monitored. It is not until she is lying in a strange bed in a hospital ward two hundred miles from home that she realises that she hasn't let anybody know where she is yet, the company does not know why she is late for the appointment, her partner, Kim, does not know what's happened to her, she has no idea where her things are, or when she'll get home and it's then that she starts to get frightened and tearful.

The first help she needs and gets is predominantly practical, the Fire Brigade have to be called to cut her out of the car because both doors are so battered she cannot be reached, and then the ambulance staff take her to A & E, treating her for the cuts and bruises, helping her to manage the physical shock and monitoring the potential seriousness of the cuts and the head injury.

It's the tea-lady who first comes to Karen's assistance now, leaving aside the practical issues of one lump or two, she collects some tissues from a bedside locker and quietly offers the wisdom of ages.

    "That's right, you have a good cry love, what was it then? Did you get knocked down or what?' She just sits and waits for a bit, concentrating hard on Karen's attempts to communicate through tears and pain-killers and a swollen lip. Karen tries to describe what happened, but finds she is crying too much to talk.

    'Oh my, that must have been right upsetting, and now you're here miles away from home and all. Have the police been yet for your statement? Has Sister rung your family or did they do that in casualty?'

This isn't formal professional helping, its just ordinary human concern and kindness, expressed informally and directly, but there are the rudiments of the core conditions, lots of **warmth**, *some* **respect** *and a good bit of* **natural empathic feedback***. Alongside the practical care she is getting, what Karen seems to need most right now is this kind of warm* **personal support.***

And in the next day or two she gets quite a lot of that, from her partner, other members of her family, her immediate boss and other friends. They visit, listen to her telling the story of the crash (several times over) and, when she is discharged forty eight hours later, they create a rota and provide both company and more practical aid like food and ironing.

As Karen realises that for her all her calmness she actually doesn't know what's happening; the shock and fear begin to take hold and she starts shaking.

'Oh dear there you go love, you are feeling rotten aren't you. Look, I'll just leave you a mug of tea and go and tell Staff and she'll come and have a word with you.'

Two days later

It's Karen's Mother who first realises that Karen is trying a bit too hard to push on her recovery, when she overhears a 'phone call where Karen seems to be suggesting that she will be back to work next week, just as soon as the contract hire people can deliver the new car. Mrs Preston is not the interfering kind, but she does ask whether Karen is pushing on a bit fast. She waits quietly when Karen snaps that *of course she's alright* - she remembers the little girl who was always cross when she hurt herself. But now Karen knows that her mum knows, and a day or two later Karen asks, apropos of nothing:

'Mum do you remember what Dad was like after he had to go for that scan last year?'

'Course I do love. I remember what I felt like too.'

'I never understood it. It must have been such a relief to discover that it wasn't malignant and could be cleared up with the laser treatment, but he seemed dead miserable about it.'

'He certainly was miserable love, took him weeks to get his old self back again.'

'But why Mum? You were both quite down. I'd had thought you would have been really pleased. All the worries gone about it. No big deal. Life back to normal.'

'But it was such a shock you see Karen. Your Dad's never had more than the odd dose of flu in his life, doesn't smoke, watches his weight, takes a bit of exercise. Planning on thirty years retirement he always said. Then he finds this lump; bang, that's it

*Sporadic conversations like this over the next few days gradually help Karen to accept that what she is feeling is natural and understandable and that it may not be pleasant, but there is something to **learn** in all this, greater knowledge of self and of how the world is. Mrs Preston clearly isn't counselling, she*

in his head. He's back with Grandad Preston dying on him when he was a lad. Of course it was daft to get so worried about it without checking, going to the doctor and that. But to your Dad it was like a death sentence. Do you see?'

'But when he was better, why wouldn't it go away? Why does the fear last so long when everything's all right and you should be recovering and getting on with life? Why do I feel so gloomy and miserable as if I've lost something really important, not just had a really lucky escape. Why Mum, what's happening?'

'Is that what you are really feeling love? It's bad isn't it? And it does seem so unfair. I don't understand it all that well myself. But your Dad read up about it when he began to feel a bit more positive and one idea was that a thing like that is like grief, because even through you are all right really you have lost something in the process - the old certainties, peace of mind, call it what you will. So you feel sad, and scared and even guilty at times.'

'Yes because you ought to feel grateful, but you just feel miserable or irritable. I keep going on at Kim, for no real reason. But it's got to go soon hasn't it? I've just got to pull myself together and get back to work, haven't I?'

'I can see you want to pack it all away and move on love, but I'm not sure life's like that. It's hard, but if it's anything like your Dad and me after that business we're talking weeks, not days, you know. Do give it time love.'

After rather longer than first intended Karen starts to feel more like her old self and is ready to get back to work. Because her neck is still painful she is advised not to drive for a while in case she needs to claim for a whiplash injury, so she works from the office for three weeks and then she and Kim take a couple of weeks' holiday.

*would just see herself as being a good Mum. She is being **empathic**, trying to see Karen's world, and **authentically** sharing some of her own experiences in a way that doesn't take away from Karen's experience. In terms of our levels from Chapter 4 this is more than personal support - Karen is being given help to grow in knowledge and understanding and this could be characterised as **Developmental Support**.*

The day comes to collect her new car and Karen is not altogether surprised to find that she feels a bit nervous. She has not actually driven for nearly three months. It's a lovely car though and she goes quietly for a few days expecting her confidence to come back. The journey to the office is O.K., but she still feels apprehensive about longer trips. She and Kim talk about this fear and arrange to go out to one of their favourite places for Sunday lunch some fifty odd miles away, they'll take the new car and Karen can practise a longer journey. It goes well and they have a great day. Problem cracked! Karen makes plans to resume normal working. She feels some of her staff (and some of the men) at work are beginning to think she's been making too much of the crash.

She sets off quite confidently on Tuesday, it's a bright day and the planned journey is not a long one. And then it happens. As she turns out onto the dual carriageway the anxiety starts, as the first lorry comes up behind she starts to sweat and feel sick and then she can feel the panic and the world closing in. She feels ill, unreal, as if she was watching herself: she is scared that she will just close her eyes and accelerate into oblivion: somehow she pulls over and into a lay-by where she can phone Kim. Talking helps a bit and she decides that if she's sensible she can at least get home again - perhaps it's the time of the month or something she ate. She drives home somewhat shakily and 'phones in sick. It'll be alright tomorrow.

Any of us who have had anxiety or panic attacks will know that it isn't necessarily all right tomorrow, and although it takes another couple of episodes Karen gradually realises she needs help. She talks to her G.P., who arranges for her to see Paul, the Community Psychiatric Nurse attached to the

This is more helping of an everyday almost 'common-sense' variety, but where does it fit and what skills are being used? Talking about the fear, is helping using the **counselling skills** *of* **active listening**, *including;* **empathy.** *They also decide to practice driving to get back into the swing of things. So this can be thought of as an informal attempt at* **problem-solving counselling.** *Although neither Karen nor Kim would dream of calling it that. This demonstrates that counselling skills can be used quite naturally in all kinds of non-professional relationships where no-one even mentions the word counselling.*

practice. When they meet he explains that they have a maximum of eight sessions;

'Doctor Williamson told me that you had a lucky escape from a bad road accident. You've also had an unpleasant experience whilst driving, is that right?' Karen nods. 'Well I really hope we can improve matters. It would help me if you could put it all in your own word. Where would you like to start?'

Two months later

It rather surprises Karen when about a month after finishing with the CPN she realises that she really rather misses their sessions, and the opportunity they gave her to think about what makes her tick.

She rather thought before the accident that she was sharp and pretty street-wise, that she knew what motivated her and other people and that she had good people skills. She'd thought of herself as a bit of a natural psychologist, but working with Paul she had come to realise that often she pushed down emotions, got on with practical issues rather than attending to what was going on inside, and that she rather expected the world to respond to that. At work it usually did. She could make the system work, until it all went haywire. Although she has got a lot of her confidence back she now realises that some of it was based on a mixture of immature optimism and an unwillingness to look at uncomfortable feelings. Now she feels unwilling to let this go - she tries to read about it. Rather uncharacteristically she calls the surgery and asks for a further appointment to try and figure out what to do next.

Paul listens carefully and reflectively to what Karen pours out - and recognises that this is no longer part of his brief. Karen clearly has real issues to take up. It had been very tempting when they were working together to take up the issue about suppressed emotions, but Paul knew that would take them

*The CPN is very open and initially works in a person-centred way, helping Karen identify issues and feelings from whatever she brings for the first few sessions. It helps her to explore what's happened, what she feels and to decide what **her** priorities are. It's not hard for Karen to be specific; she wants to stop the anxiety and to get back to normal working.*

Gradually she is assisted both to relax and manage the anxiety, which makes the driving easier, and to discover that she is really very angry about the accident, and that this part of her grief has not been expressed. As she gets in touch with the anger about the lorry she also begins to have dreams and flashbacks of the incident which disturb and frighten her, but she feels safe telling Paul about it.

Paul also helps her manage her medications by checking whether she really does need to keep taking the sleeping tablets she's been on since she left hospital. He consults with Dr Williamson, who, after talking to Karen, reduces the dosage until she is able to get a reasonable night's sleep without medication.

At the end of eight sessions Karen is beginning to accept that it may be years before she gets to feel completely relaxed about driving again, if ever, but she has pretty much come to terms with that. She has developed a few successful strategies and techniques for getting into driving without panicking and for managing her anxiety if it starts to rise.

*This is **problem solving counselling** and Paul has used a variety of techniques and maintained a pretty fixed focus on the agreed problems. Clearly **active listening**, **empathy**, and **acceptance** are very important throughout the sessions. These **counselling skills** are added to the other skills which Paul's CPN training equips him to use.*

beyond their contract in terms of focus and time. His work in the practice is specifically problem focused and short term, and besides he knows that he is not trained for the sort of work that Karen wants right now. Fortunately for Karen Paul's referral network is sound, and he knows someone who he thinks would really be ready to work with Karen on all of this. She works in private practice, but is still not fully established so she has space and her fees are pretty reasonable. She originally trained in community theatre, but realised a few years ago that she wanted to work with individuals, she uses a lot of creative methods like drawing and story-telling. She is a well qualified counsellor who can offer Karen the therapeutic counselling she needs to understand herself better, to heal if she discovers hurts and to make positive choices for change if that is what seems right. Feel free to write your own happy ending.

*Paul knows where **problem-solving counselling** ends and **therapeutic counselling begins**. He is not a trained counsellor, but a CPN who uses **counselling skills**. Part of his skill, though, is not only to know when to refer Karen on, but to have well developed resources including a referral network. His last contact with Karen is to give her the details of the counsellor so that she can make contact herself. This is an important step for Karen to make and Paul can't make it with her, she must make the next move on her own.*

Section IV
Counselling Skills Issues and Settings

Counselling Skills for Difficult Situations
Page 165

Ethics for Counselling Skills
Page 185

Helper Support
Page 195

Vignettes

Ashley: *179.*
Charlie: *178.*

Counselling Skills for Difficult Situations

14

Learning about difficult situations

We had a problem or two when trying to write this chapter. Firstly, it was not easy to identify what readers might find difficult, since many readers will already be working routinely in a situation which others would find difficult if not impossible. Working with intoxicated people will be familiar ground for some, as will working with someone in great distress, shock or someone who is very disturbed.

The message then is clear. Find out what experiences other people are bringing to your course. Ask them what they have found useful.

Note Not all routine working practices are really helpful, nor have they been designed to be. Look out for some ways of 'helping' that are really more to do with managing people and their problems or distributing limited resources, rather than actually helping the individuals concerned. For example, some medication regimes, some time-limited helping and some rules of assessment for, e.g. self-harm, could be seen as examples of people or resource management.

Secondly, we didn't want it to be come a list of 'pitfalls' with 'solutions' that could be treated like a list of essential techniques. We wanted to keep in mind that effective helping is mostly done through relationships which emphasise the uniqueness of each situation, person, their needs and the person of the helper. If we lose sight of this and begin to put those we are helping into 'categories' which set us on a track to a particular 'solution', we will be not all that far removed from diagnosing and prescription-writing. It is no part of our intention to do this. What we feel is important though, is to encourage ourselves to ask questions about these difficult situations. What is happening in this situation? Do we need the same skills or different skills? Are we prepared to help people with different experiences? We believe that counselling skills give us some of the essentials to work in these and other difficult situations, if only we use them wisely.

The responsibility lies with you, the reader to keep you mind focused on:

- Central counselling values and their worth, i.e. the value of empathy, respect and acceptance in enabling people gain self-acceptance and positive change.
- The uniqueness of the relationship between you and the person you are trying to help. There may be some useful points in the next few pages that help you keep your head or help remind you to look at your priorities.

Note It is our experience that difficult situations do not require different skills. We just need to be reminded that the skills we already have will do just fine - if we can deliver them without getting flustered. When the going gets tough we sometimes throw our counselling skills out of the window, roll our sleeves up and get well and truly stuck in. Only rarely is this a helpful thing to do. Rather like when in deep water, a disciplined swimming stroke will be of more use than panicky thrashing around - even if you feel most inclined to splash madly, a disciplined approach to helping is of more use than a frenzied doing for the sake of it.

Feeling safe to help someone

We have put this first in our list of difficult situations because it helps us lay the foundations of good helping in the way you must lay your own foundations for good helping, *whatever* the situation. Effective helping at the practical helping level relies on the helper feeling in a position to help. This means that the helper themselves must feel safe to do the practical helping. Other levels of helping require the establishment of a good relationship between the helper and the person being helped. Once again an essential pre-requisite is that the helper themselves must feel safe. Feeling unsafe is one of the ways we can get flustered when trying to help. We forget our skills and if we're not careful we can make the situation worse rather than better. There are different ways in which we can make sure we feel safe enough to help, we present these under the following headings:

Confidence in your competence

An important but underrated kind of safety is feeling confident that you have the skills and qualities necessary to deal with the situation in hand. A couple of points can be made here, firstly that there is a balance to be struck between a keen and accurate appreciation of your capabilities (and the understanding that in some circumstances, people surpass themselves), and complacency when confidence hardens and acts like a shield between you and the person you are trying to help.

Secondly that having confidence in your competence is something that will grow throughout your training. You will have listened to feedback from tutors and fellow students on your skills. How does their feedback square up with your own view of your skills and qualities? You should aim to finish your training with the capacity not only to offer counselling skills in helping relationships, but also to monitor your own ability and performance accurately.

Both of these points boil down to getting feedback from others, listening to it, evaluating it, dealing with the feelings it brings up and acting upon it. Your course should provide you with opportunities for doing this, probably in the skills-training sessions, but also during personal-growth time. There will be further chances to monitor your own feeling through your personal journal or self-evaluation assignments. We also believe that it is important for helpers using counselling skills to develop their own methods of accurate self assessment. When you can make a confident assessment of your competence, you will have a better chance of trusting your judgement.

Confidence in your physical safety

Your workplace may already have rules and regulations regarding personal safety, although some do not. Do make sure you are familiar with these guidelines or regulations, or you may compound physical risks with disciplinary ones if you have not followed thought-out procedures. You may end up putting yourself *and others* at risk. If there are no regulations, why not devise your own code and see if you can get it adopted by the agency or service you work for?

Make sure that you have a safe place in which to offer your help. There are many circumstances under which we might feel unsafe - sometimes we don't feel safe with a particular person, in a particular room, or helping with particular problems.

If you are worried about your physical safety, you will be spending energy on worry that could be used for better attention to your helping. Helping should not be done in an atmosphere resembling a scene from 'MASH' with bombs going off and the surgeons operating regardless. Simply yelling louder than the patients will inevitably detract from anyone's capacity to help. Your ability to help will be distorted, if not fatally impaired, if you do not feel safe because it will interfere with your ability to be congruent, to offer non-judgemental warmth and to be empathic. The sense of danger that you feel may then 'leak' into the relationship with the person you are trying to help. This muddle can be very difficult to sort out.

Do try to ensure that your agency or service has guidelines for helping practice which are specifically aimed at making the workers/helpers/volunteers feel safe. This will need to include the social control and oppression issues around sexist and racist language and behaviour, and recruitment policies for the organisation, e.g. one way to make black helpers feel safe is to make sure that there is not just one black person employed as a helper.

Confident that you're supported and backed-up.
Whilst support and back-up would be hollow if it paid no attention to the issues of personal safety mentioned above, this section is not about those sorts of protection. Here we are considering support and back-up for our helping. This most usually happens

when we set up backup systems and resources, and through on-going training, supervision and cover arrangements. *These issues are covered more fully in Chapter 16.*

Helping someone within your limits
Knowing the limits of your competence and qualifications as a helper is one of the key learnings at this level of counselling skills courses. It is also one of the most difficult competencies to get a handle on. This may be because it is not easy to define quite where helping using *counselling skills* ends and *counselling* begins. Another complication is that many students on counselling skills courses will already have qualifications and experiences that have prepared them to work with clients in very difficult circumstances indeed.

When you do feel that you are at or beyond your limits, you will then have to decide what to do. This will usually involve *referring* the person you are trying to help to someone who is better placed to give the help that they need. Many readers will already have developed referral skills in connection with other helping jobs or activities, for example:
- Nurses should know when to refer someone on for specialised treatment.
- Social Workers should know when to refer someone on to another agency for help.
- Teachers should know when to refer a pupil or student on for more specific academic support or discipline.

In addition to these specific specialist referral skills we all have a *sense* of when we are out of our depth in a helping relationship. It can be difficult to put your finger on precisely why we feel uncomfortable

when using counselling skills:
- We might think that we lack crucial information or skills.
- We get anxious and we do not know what to do next.
- We might fear for our safety or the safety of the other person.
- We might be aware of regulations or guidelines for work held by our employer or agency.
- Sometimes we don't know who or where to refer someone for particular help.
- Sometimes we might not know *how* to refer someone on to another person or place for help.

When it comes to knowing our limits as helpers using counselling skills, the first thing we have to do is decide where our feeling of discomfort is coming from, and whether or not it should lead us to referring the other person on. In his book *'An Incomplete Guide to Referral Issues for Counsellors' (1993)*, Steve Williams notes that referrals can be made for many reasons and although he is writing for counsellors the issues are very similar. He suggests the following reasons:
- Because of:
  - your personal limits,
  - your professional limits,
  - the limits of your experience.
- Because the person you are helping:
  - needs another kind of helper,
  - needs other kinds of help.
- Because of:
  - agency policies.

Behind each of these reasons lies a difficult decision. For counselling skills situations we suggest following the series of steps set out below to help find your position regarding these difficult decisions. This,

or a similar series of steps should be followed whenever helpers are considering making a referral.

Activity
You could try following the steps now as an activity.
- *It will help if you do this activity with someone else to help you crystallise your thoughts.*
- *Use some imaginary case material if necessary.*
- *Consider your thoughts and feelings at each step.*
- *Make notes on your thoughts and feelings in this activity as you go along. (It is also useful to make notes in real-life situations too in case you have to justify your actions to anyone.)*

---

1. Decide whether referral is appropriate. You must ask yourself:
   - Are you just trying to get rid of an awkward person, or whether they would be better off being helped by someone else?
   - Are you hanging on to help this person when they would be better off being helped by someone different?
2. Prepare yourself.
   - Are you prepared for the feelings that might come up when you let go of this person?
   - Will you feel bereaved or relieved?
3. Prepare the person you are helping.
   - How do they feel about the possibility of referral?
   - Have you mentioned it to them?

• Have you explained why you think referral might be a good idea?

4. Make the referral through appropriate public channels, personal contacts or professional liaison.

• Do you have a list of possible agencies or helping professionals?

• Do you know where to get such information?

• Would it be a good idea to get the person you are helping to sort this out for themselves?

5. Follow up if necessary.

• Would it be a good idea to follow up your actions to see if the person you are helping has successfully made contact with the new helper or agency?

The skills required to effect a sensitive referral are largely those counselling skills we have been talking about throughout this book:

• Active listening skills, which help ensure that the referral flows from the needs of the person being helped.

• Differentiation: being able to separate the issues, in particular any needs the helper might have to hang on to, or get rid of someone, rather than make a principled referral.

• Reflecting on your own practice, to enable you as a helper who uses counselling skills to evaluate your own part in the referral process.

You might also need to consider what resources you need in order to make a fully informed referral. An important part of referral is knowing what services are available in your area. Information of this kind is kept by, for example, the Citizens Advice Bureau, so even if you are only interested in informal or community helping, you should know where to start looking. On further investigation you will find a whole network of local agencies and people who are dedicated to providing various kinds of help either professionally or voluntarily. If you are already involved in the helping professions through your job or as a volunteer, you may already know how to access networks such as these. You will also have to consider services specially provided for and by disabled people, black people, people with different cultural or religious needs and sexual orientations.

Helping someone in great distress

We could have started this chapter off with an activity in which we invite readers to think up some difficult situations where they feel their ability to help is in some way compromised or made more difficult. High up on such a list would be what to do if someone gets very distressed during a helping session. By distress we mean crying, shaking, wailing, shouting or behaving in ways that we recognise as the very active expression of emotions such as fear, sadness, anger, rage, etc. It is interesting to note that people who are in great distress are often very distressing for us to be around and this seems to one of the roots of the problem.

It is possible that these situations are difficult for us because unless we are quite experienced, we simply may not be used to people expressing very strong emotions in our presence. In everyday life, we are probably more accustomed to people keeping such feelings to themselves or only letting them out in private. The point is that when we use counselling skills we create a very safe, 'private' space through our relationship building efforts, so it is to be expected that if we are successful, people will begin to behave in more 'private' ways when we help them in this way. It is a matter of cultural norms that many of us think that feelings should be private things. It is also a matter of common understanding that helping someone in a counselling way will more than likely involve feelings at some time or another. If we are guided by the principles of letting the person we are helping take control of the helping process, we would be trying to facilitate their expression of emotion without either encouraging them, or discouraging them. The effect we are after is one where they feel neither pushed into deeper feelings than they want, nor feel pulled away from deep feeling because we can't cope with their feelings or our own.

Activity
- *Think back to times when you have been helped by someone. Focus on the following points:*
    - *Did you feel safe to express your feelings?*
        - *How did that safe feeling come about?*
    - *Was it important for you to feel that you could express your feelings freely?*
    - *If you did express your feelings, what were they?*
    - *What effect did this expression of feelings have?*

When I try this exercise I know from my own experience that:
- Just knowing that it's OK to express myself is sometimes enough. I like to feel safe to express myself and sometimes I need someone to say that it's OK.
- At other times just being able to get my feelings out like blowing off steam is all that it takes to feel better. I don't need to understand the feelings - it is enough to express them.
- On yet other occasions I need to feel the feelings and then try to understand them or make the experience fit into some sort of pattern before I can get any sense of resolution or relief.
- I know that it's been important to express feelings when trying to resolve personal issues since if I don't I sometimes can't think straight. Actually getting angry, sad or frightened rather than cutting off from it seems to get rid of the fog.
- I think I have learned that feelings, for example tears, are not part of the problem - they are part of the solution.

Whatever message we give in words and actions when things are calm in a relationship need to be backed up by congruent authentic actions when someone is upset or distressed. It is at those moments when those we are helping will be most sensitive to our behaviour as helpers. The only way to ensure a helpful response is for us to have prepared as fully as possible by increasing our self-awareness through personal growth activities. Having said this, we can still be left feeling unprepared for florid expressions of feelings, and so those that we are trying to help may feel less than helped by our lack of preparedness:
- They may feel ashamed if they detect embarrassment in us.
- They may feel judged if we are shocked or uncomfortable.

• They may feel that they have to shut up in order to rescue us from discomfort and embarrassment.

Good initial structuring of a helping relationship could include an acknowledgement that helping often engages us on a feelings level. This could happen at the beginning of the relationship or during the relationship by giving explicit permission to get upset. This might allay fears that too much expressed emotion will embarrass the helper. We want to give the message *'It's OK to get upset here,'* or, *'Feel free to explore your feelings whatever they are.'*

Helping someone who is very disturbing

We might have many worries about quite how best to help people who are disturbed. If I had set this sub-title as 'Helping Someone Who is Very Disturbed' it would imply that we could easily judge the level of disturbance in other people. It is, however a very difficult thing to judge how disturbed someone is. Since making such judgements is, by and large beyond the competence of most helpers who use counselling skills, it is better once again to focus on ourselves and our experience. Many of us may share the experience of finding certain behaviour very disturbing. If other people's behaviour seems very bizarre to us we might be frightened. We might fear for our own sanity, our physical safety or our lives.

Activity
• *Think of a recent incident when you were disturbed by someone's behaviour.*
   • *What was it that disturbed you?*
   • *What particular fears did the incidents trigger?, For example,*

• *Did you worry that they might harm you?*
   • *Did you worry that they might harm themselves?*

• *Did you worry that it might trigger the same response in you; that such behaviour might be 'catching'?*

We have focused on the helper's feelings and reactions because it is clear that if the helper is disturbed to the point of being frightened or suspicious, then their capacity to help has been critically impaired. If I am worrying that I might 'catch' bizarre behaviour from someone, there is no more effective barrier to me offering empathy since the last thing I want to do is to see the world from their point of view!

If you find yourself disabled in this way you will need to get support for yourself. This is looked at in more detail in Chapter 16. Such support may be not available immediately and we will look at what immediate steps you might wish to take on the next page.

• Sometimes getting support is enough to clear away your fears so that you can in turn support the person whose behaviour is causing you problems.

• Sometimes through this support you will decide that you haven't got the personal resources necessary to help this person any more - you are just too disturbed by their behaviour. You have come to the limit of your personal or emotional capacity.

• Sometimes such support will lead you to the conclusion that the person you are helping needs a different kind of care (see page 167) and that you will have to refer them on to someone who can give them this kind of care. You have come to the limit of your helping skills.

Sometimes the person you are trying to help is behaving in aggressive or violent ways, either towards someone else, you, or themselves. The latter two cases are dealt with more fully on pages 180 and below respectively. If you are worried that the person you are trying to help might hurt someone else, you may find the section on *'Helping someone who isn't there'* useful. There are some logical as well as ethical dilemmas to come to grips with in such situations. We would emphasise that since you are the person involved in the situation, you will have to use all of the information to hand, including your gut reactions. If you do not feel safe, make the situation safe for yourself as soon as possible. You cannot be an effective helper if you feel at risk yourself. The following steps might be useful *when you are disturbed by someone's behaviour*:

1. Try to relax and stay at least outwardly calm.
2. Take some time to assess the situation, including you feelings.
3. Decide whether you need professional support. You might want help if, for example, you feel cannot make any real contact with the person, or they are not making any sense, i.e. they are talking in sentences but they don't mean anything, or they feel out of control.
  • If you do, you must decide whether it is urgent or not.
  • You may need to hold on to the situation

for long enough for help to arrive. If this happens, make sure the other person knows what you are doing and at all times try to get their consent before doing anything on their behalf like, calling their GP.
4. You will probably feel as though you're 'flying by the seat of your pants', but remember:
  • The core conditions are the most effective helping tools you have. Continue to use them.
  • The other person is probably very frightened by their own thoughts, feelings and behaviour.
5. Do not offer platitudes if the other person is frightened or depressed. Try not to add to nor take away from their experience, help them stay with it.
6. When it's over, get support for yourself. You may well feel shaky.
7. Follow up what has happened if you have promised to do so. It's nice for someone to know that the helping relationship is still intact even if they have behaved in a bizarre or disturbing way.
8. Finally, review your handling of the situation. Give yourself the chance to learn by looking at what went well, what you might do differently and what you don't want to repeat.

Helping someone who threatens to harm themselves

The prospect of someone harming themselves, or worse still committing suicide, will not fail to arouse strong emotions in most people interested in helping.

Such urges and needs in others challenge us in several ways:

- We might worry about the professional and legal implications of our involvement.
- Our feelings about our own mortality might be aroused, making us feel upset and uncomfortable. We might not have worked out our own feelings about dying very well, so we could get overwhelmed by fear or other upset.
- We might be reminded of times when we have been hurt ourselves or times when we have been bereaved. This could lead us to over identify with those who might be left to grieve for this person.
- We might get very upset at the thought of someone injuring themselves in our presence or shortly afterwards.
- We might have strong moral or religious feelings about self-harm and suicide.

Some helpers work in settings where there are regulations or guidelines indicating how employees or volunteers should firstly assess the risk of self-harm and suicide, and secondly what action should be taken if the risk seems high. Nurses, for example, are required to take action to prevent patients harming themselves or taking their own lives.

The use of counselling skills, however, does not specifically indicate any course of action. Helpers using counselling skills are expected to make judgements based on what they believe to be the other person's best interests, within the helper's moral framework and professional ethical code. If you are a nurse using counselling skills, this will mean that you follow the nursing code of practice on the matter.

If you are a teacher using counselling skills, you will follow the guidelines laid down by the school or local education authority.

We do not advocate simply saying, *'It's up to you to do whatever you want, just follow your own moral code'* to helpers trying to understand how to form a helping relationship with people threatening self-harm or suicide. This in no way prepares individuals to help in such times of great distress and crisis in a person's life. We suggest that students of counselling skills engage with the issue at both thoughts and feelings levels. The activity below offers some questions on the main issues, but individual helpers in training to use counselling skills should understand that dealing with any strong *feelings* about these dilemmas is a matter for self-awareness and personal-development. The following guidelines are also offered for your consideration:

1. Don't make any 'knee-jerk' decisions. Consider the situation carefully.

2. Continue to use the core conditions, they will help you see things from the other person's point of view, and help you to not think they're a bad person for wanting to do this.

3. If the threat seems real, you will need courage to either:
- stay with the person through the threat until they either review their plans, leave you not knowing what will happen or carry it out,
- or do everything in your power to stop them. This might include a referral to the emergency services.

4. You should always try to get the other person's consent before you do anything on their behalf.

5. You can always suggest that they contact the Samaritans, or you could insist that they telephone in your presence.

6. You will need support and comfort after your ordeal regardless of the outcome.

Activity
Consider your position on the following points and discuss them with others in your training group.
• Anyone who harms themselves must be in such great distress that they cannot make rational decisions. They should be stopped from harming themselves for their own protection.
• People should have control over their own destiny, including the right to end their own lives.
• There are no circumstances under which taking one's own life is justified. It is selfish attention-seeking and people who have been stopped are always grateful.
• Being realistic, there is no way one person can stop another from harming or killing themselves, so there's no point in taking responsibility for the other person and their actions.

Helping someone who is silent

Whenever I am asked about silences in helping relationships, I am reminded without fail of someone I was helping at an early stage in my training as a counsellor. This person remained silent for a number of sessions. After ten or so minutes of the first session my repertoire of reflective, accepting comments was exhausted, so I sat in silence with the other person until the end of the time we had agreed to spend together, whereupon I said that I would be happy to see them next week if they wished. They left without a word. My supervisor helpfully said 'Hang on in there,' even when in desperation I tape-recorded a session just to prove that it was really happening.

Through this experience I learned to be silent and comfortable for very long periods. I learned that people will talk when they're ready. I learned that if someone is offered another appointment and they willingly return for it, they must be using the time in some wise way even if they are silent. I learned to trust the self-healing energy of the other person. I learned that I may not have any idea how the other person is using the helping relationship. What was challenged in me was how I think others should use time and how I choose to spend my time. Should I require others to behave in ways that seem profitable to me? Should I expect people to change in front of my eyes?

I became very aware of posture, breathing, small movements and facial expressions in an effort to make some meaningful contact with the other person. After several silent sessions, the other person spoke. The first thing they said was, *'Please don't stare at me.'*

Activity
• What do you fear might happen or might be happening during a silence?
• Think back to silent periods during helping sessions, can you identify different sorts or qualities of silence?

• *Do you feel different during different types of silence?*

• *What leads you to break silences in helping sessions?*

• *When practising counselling skills in pairs, wait a while and sense your feelings. Try not to dive in and break the silence. Wait to see if the other person can use the silence to reflect on what has just been said or perhaps more carefully consider what they might say next.*

Helping someone very different from you

Whilst it is true to say that everyone is different, indeed, the humanistic approach to helping has it as a central principle to acknowledge our individuality, there are some differences between people which are the focus for very powerful interpersonal dynamics. In *'First Steps in Counselling 2nd Ed.'* the following dimensions of difference were highlighted as being the basis for prejudice, privilege and oppression:

Race/Ethnicity
Nationality
Religion
Class
Gender
Sexual orientation
Age
Dis/ability

It was further suggested that these dimensions were all associated with power issues, whether the power was vested in the majority, money, guns or a legal/constitutional framework. Such differences between people cannot be ignored in helping relationships. There appear to be two issues involved here, one of power and one of difference. *Difference* is something we can *learn* about, either from those we are helping, via the core condition of empathy, or by finding out about the richness and diversity of people in our community. *Power*, on the other hand is an integral element in all relationships, helping or otherwise, and we can best learn about our part in it through personal development in groups. We would, however, like to suggest that these are best considered as interwoven elements.

Firstly we want to draw attention to the role of the core conditions in helping us work with people that are very different from us. Secondly we want to be ready for those occasions when the person being helped identifies themselves as a member of an oppressed group.

At first sight it might seem that empathy holds all the answers since the essence of empathy is understanding someone else's world. This surely must mean that we therefore automatically understand their uniqueness and difference. However, unless we know that certain differences are likely to be the basis of oppression, we may miss an important element in the helping relationship itself, i.e. an exaggerated power imbalance between the helper and person being helped. Whilst there are too many possible combinations of helper-'helpee' relationship to develop any coherent strategy for action, it could be useful to think about some relationships that might have a familiar ring to them. The activity which follows overleaf provides this opportunity. As with many other activities, it will probably be more lively if done in a small group.

Activity
• *Consider the following helping relationships.
What possible implications might difference
have, leaving aside the obvious, i.e. 'everybody
is different'?*
  • *Male white nurse - female black patient.*
  • *Black female Sri Lankan doctor - white
  British male patient.*
  • *Able-bodied welfare rights worker -
  disabled client.*
  • *Male non-gay social worker - lesbian
  single parent.*

*Make notes on the key tensions and dilemmas
that are evident to you.*

The potential for the dynamics of difference and power in relationships to skew our helping towards being disrespectful are always present. The following checklist might be helpful when beginning every new helping relationship:

1. Always be prepared to identify any visible differences sensitively, at least to yourself. This can be a part of pre-meeting structuring if you work for an agency or service, e.g. the language used in publicity and equal opportunities statements.

2. Don't be tempted into guesses, e.g. guessing that someone is gay.

3. Recognise these differences when structuring the relationship. Point out that you have noticed the difference and that you realise it might have special meaning for the other person. E.g. how do they feel about the difference and would they like to see a male/female, black/white helper etc.

4. Look for points of contact that don't trivialise the differences.

5. Don't make assumptions about differences you don't understand, whether regarding race, culture, disability, sexuality or whatever.

Helping someone who wants more

Some readers will already be working in a helping setting, professional or voluntary. Others may be looking forward to such work or be hoping to help using counselling skills in their family, church or community. Wherever helping is done, there is often a fear that those we wish to help will want more from us than we are prepared to give and that we must *specially guard against this*. This is often talked about in terms of people getting *dependent* upon our helping as though helping is a drug to which poor unfortunates or inadequate persons can become addicted.

It's never quite made clear by people who hold this view whether the fault lies with the person being helped (they've got an addictive or dependent personality) or the helper (they like to rescue people and bind others to them).

Our view is that there is no fault or blame, there is just helping:

• If helping aims to emancipate people and enable them to be autonomous, free persons, then dependency is not a problem.

• If helping aims to do everything for the person seeking help through instruction or investment of expertness or special skill in the helper to which the helped must return to solve subsequent issues, then dependency will be guaranteed.

Your authors understand counselling skills as providing the former type of helping and that the use of counselling skills in helping is based on the following principles:

1. The humanistic principle of engaging and releasing potential through the self-actualising tendency.

2. Enabling people to do things for themselves using the least intrusive helper skills.

3. Giving people access to all information and opportunities which they might need in order to resolve practical issues and resource problems.

4. Giving people opportunities to develop all the necessary skills to resolve future issues and problems without assistance if they so choose.

5. Respecting and accepting others as persons and meeting them as equals.

6. Not believing we are experts or behaving as such.

7. Understanding that the process of personal change is facilitated by the core conditions, not achieved by instruction or exhortation.

8. If *enabled* and *empowered* in this way, people will decide when they have received sufficient helping and disengage voluntarily from the helping relationship.

9. Helpers are people with rights too. They can specify the limits of a helping relationship, and if they do this openly and honestly, they should expect these boundaries to be respected. This is achieved through careful structuring of the helping relationship.

Of course, as in all real-life settings, it doesn't always happen quite like this. We have much to be thankful for, since if it did we might all die of boredom. There are times, when in their distress, people do ask for more than we feel able to give. Sometimes this can be expressed as their wanting to be our friend. In very rare cases, this need can turn into an obsession in which the person being helped pursues the helper; finds out their home address, wants to know personal details, wants to meet their family etc. Rather than ask how should we protect ourselves from such unpleasant and occasionally frightening intrusions, we prefer to ask *'Should we prepare in any special way for such eventualities?'*

Many helpers will find that considerate principled helping following the guidelines suggested in this book will be sufficient to ensure that those we are helping have a clear idea of our boundaries and are, through our skilled helping, enabled to respect those boundaries. If we can stick to the principles outlined above, the helping we offer will enable the other person to feel strong enough in themselves to continue in their lives without our continued support. It might, however, take some time for them to arrive at this point and there is no real way of knowing quite how long it might take since each person will find this strength at their own pace.

There is some useful information in Chapter 15 on Ethics, since guidelines on ethical practice are intended to protect not only the person being helped, but also the helper. Of course, there is little protection available for those of us that blindly enter into helping relationships in order to meet our own needs. It might be that we 'need' people to 'need' us, in which case we would be inviting trouble if we become involved in helping relationships which do not take ethical guidelines into consideration. *Some counsellors would argue that we all become helpers to meet our own needs. Developing self-awareness on this issue is the key here. It is best to have spent some time looking at why we want to be helpers and which of our own needs we are so meeting if we want to avoid obvious ethical dilemmas.*

Careful structuring of the helping relationship (Chapter 8) and attention to balanced non-judgemental, authentic responses will help the relationship through those times when the person being helped might seek understanding of the boundaries of the relationship.

Helping someone who isn't there

It sometimes happens that a person seeks help not on their own behalf, but for someone else, and that someone else isn't present. It may be that they are worried about a friend or a relative, or that their life is being made a misery by a parent or spouse through abuse or frightening behaviour. On some occasions, the person seeking help will say straight away that they want help, not for themselves but for a friend. Whereas on other occasions, the person seeking help is after some assistance to gain relief from abuse or aggression. These two scenarios require slightly different handling, although the same principles apply to each. Read the following two vignettes from the now familiar lives of Charlie and Ashley.

Charlie

You may remember that Charlie was eventually persuaded by Zack to go to the Neighbourhood Centre for help. Zack went there himself on becoming unemployed, and remembering the sound advice, he first paid them a visit himself on Charlie's behalf.

'Do you still help people with money problems?' asked Zack.

'Yes, we do would you like to come through into the office for a confidential interview?'

'Er...well actually, it's not for me, it's for my friend' Now Janet had a problem; was Zack *really* there for himself, but too nervous or embarrassed to say so. She respectfully takes Zack at face value.

'Ah I see, well it is important that your friend comes down themselves for a private chat. Would you like to take this leaflet to give to them?'

'Yes, great...thanks', answered Zack.

Janet still wanted to give Zack the opportunity of getting help for himself if that was really what he had come for.

'OK, is there anything else you would like to talk about now?' asked Janet.

'I don't think so thanks,' smiled Zack.

'Alright. Do come back if you need more help and I hope your friend finds the information useful.'

*You may be wondering why the name **'Charlie'** is at the head of the vignette. The answer is simple, Charlie is the person that is not there. Zack is trying to get help for someone who isn't there. This is a familiar situation to Janet, she knows that she can't get the detailed information needed from Zack, nor give practical advice through a third party. She also knows that if other problems are at the root of Zack's friend's troubles, she cannot form the necessary relationship through a third party either.*

Janet needs to have the person she is helping present, either in person or on the 'phone.

Ashley

It has been a few weeks since Wendy West last saw Ashley for a lunchtime meeting when she meets up with the basket-ball coach, Bob Brooks.

'Wendy, I've been meaning to talk to you about Ashley Anderson, have you got a minute?'
'Sure, Bob - let's go in my office, it's quieter in there - what's wrong? You look terrible.'
Bob gives a resigned shrug as he starts 'I don't know, I just can't make him out, he is such a good player, but he still has an attitude problem. What's up with him?'
'I can see that it's really getting to you Bob. It sounds as though you really want to help Ash realise his potential but you get frustrated with him,' Wendy offered.
'Yes, I do - and my reward is that he's messing up the team plans through not turning up. What's wrong with the boy, do you know?'

'No, I don't know what's wrong with Ash, but it does seem that you have a problem getting wound up like this.'
'Wound up! I'll throttle him when I get hold of him! He's got to get himself sorted out or he's finished...kaput!'
'It's got to you so much that you want him out. That'll make things easier for you on the one hand, but he *is* a good player. Is there another way you could resolve it with him, asking him if there's anything wrong and really listening to what he has to say?'

Here again there is someone missing; namely Ashley. This time Wendy West refuses to be drawn in to a conversation on what's wrong with Ashley or how terrible he is. Instead she helps the person who is there, Bob, to look at his feelings and do something about it. You can't directly help someone who isn't there, but you can help the person who is there with you.

The general principle involved in 'third party helping' is ***don't try it***, since you cannot help the person who isn't there, you can only help the person that is present, because:
- You cannot form a helping relationship with an absent person.
- The core conditions cannot be offered to the person not there.
- Even if you want to give good advice, you will not get all of the relevant facts needed.
- The person who is there *has* come asking for help, so check out whether they do need the sort of help that you can offer.
- It is disrespectful to talk about someone who isn't there in a 'let's get them sorted out over coffee' sort of way.

Many helping agencies, services and organisations have policy statements about offering third party help

or even responding at all to third party requests. Sometimes this is done to avoid legal problems (supposedly 'helping' someone who isn't there is poking your nose into their business and will not be welcome), sometimes it really is a better helping strategy to work with the person present. The latter includes not only situations similar to Ashley's story, but also to the '*I've got a friend who thinks she's pregnant*' scenario. It is better to say,

'Please ask your friend to come and see me herself, and you can come too, of course.'
Followed by
'You seem a bit nervous yourself, I know it's nerve-wracking coming in here. Is there anything you would like to talk about now you've come?'

We would offer the following very general guidelines for situations in which the person you are trying to help seems determined to talk about someone who isn't there:

1. Do not get drawn in to third-party helping.
2. The only person you can help is the one you are with.
3. Focus on their feelings right now if possible.
4. If necessary, explain what you are doing:

'I know that your husband's drinking is a problem, but unless he comes here himself there is nothing we can do about it. However, you seem terribly upset about his behaviour, and since you are here why not get some support by talking about how you feel.'

Helping someone who is intoxicated

There are some situations in which we may be called upon to help someone who is under the influence of drugs of some kind. Such situations are more common than you may think and we can have very different reactions to people when they are intoxicated.

The range of situations in which people take drugs is wide:

• Taking prescribed drugs that have little or no effect upon a person's mood or psychological state.
• Taking prescribed drugs that have a marked effect upon a person's mood or psychological state.
• Taking legal 'food' substances that have a marked effect upon a person's mood or psychological state such as smoking tobacco, drinking coffee or alcohol.
• Taking illegal drugs that have an effect upon a person's mood or psychological state.

Our reactions to people under such conditions can also show a very wide range. Firstly we would need to find out whether we are reacting to

• The thought of drug taking and what it represents to us.
• Our fantasies about drug addiction, based on inaccurate information.
• The behaviour of the person we think might be under the influence of drugs.

For example, we might:

• think it's permissible for people to take drugs in order to control distressing symptoms: e.g. a person taking a prescribed drug to control anxiety or depression. Yet have a different view of someone using alcohol, cocaine or tobacco for the same purpose.
• feel uncomfortable or frightened for our safety because a person is behaving unpredictably or uncharacteristically.
• believe that somehow drugs take away our individual identity, and we respond more to what we think about the drug than what we know about the person, e.g. we say things like *'Alcoholics are manipulative,'* or *'Alcoholics are aggressive.'*

Activity
• *Take a moment to reflect upon your own experiences with drugs.*
   • *Do you have different reactions when you think about legal drugs (prescribed drugs, tobacco and alcohol) than when you think about illegal drugs, cannabis, heroine, cocaine, crack, amphetamines, ecstasy etc.*
• *Does the thought of drugs frighten you?*

> • *What do you associate with drugs?*
>> • *Do you think in terms of drugs that heal and drugs that harm?*
>> • *Do you think that people are bad or sick or inadequate if they use illegal drugs?*

Some professional helpers take the view that they cannot usefully work with someone who is intoxicated or otherwise 'out of it' because of the effects that drink and drugs have on the ability to pay attention, the experience and expression of feelings, and memory. Each worker is entitled to figure out their own policy on this (within an agency or service framework where applicable). *However you decide to use the time with someone intoxicated who is seeking your help, that person still needs you to offer the core conditions, not slip into controlling or disapproving behaviour. This will only undermine your potential to help them, both at the time and in the future.*

Drug abuse

Being able to use counselling skills effectively does not, of itself, qualify us to help someone who is addicted to, or abusing, drugs or other substances such as solvents. The best helping we can offer under such circumstances is to:

- Not panic.
- Decide whether the person is in need of medical attention:
  - Are they feeling faint or unable to stay awake?
  - Are they having trouble in breathing?
  - Are they making sense or are they delirious?
- Try to ascertain what drugs they have taken

so that the correct medical treatment can be carried out.

- If you are a qualified first aider, do whatever you think the situation demands.
- Carry on offering the core conditions, in particular:
  - Be non-judgemental, try to see the *person* not the drugs and their effects.
- Refer the person on to someone with specialised skills and knowledge. There will be a mental health or social services team that specialises in drug and substance abuse in your area.
- Follow up any medical treatment so that:
  - You know how the situation turned out and you can relax.
  - You can continue any helping relationship with the person concerned if they wish.

Intoxication

What should we do if we find ourselves with a person who is wanting help *right now* who is under the influence of drugs? When using counselling skills to help someone, the state of intoxication of the person we are trying to help might be of real concern to us, for example:

- We might simply find drug taking in all forms offensive and not wish to help someone who cannot control their habit.
- We might not feel we are making a relationship with the 'real' person if they come to us in an intoxicated state, e.g:
  - the person we are trying to help should be in touch with their real feelings rather than use drugs to dull their senses.
- We might think that it is necessary for someone to use drugs to make sufficient

contact with 'reality' for a useful helping relationship to be formed.

• We might think that it's OK for people to use prescribed drugs but not illegal drugs.

Activity
• *What do you think about this issue? Here are some examples to help your thinking and discussion. What would you do in the following situations:*
  • *The person you are helping asks you if they can smoke.*
  • *The person you are helping turns up unsteady on their feet and smelling of alcohol. It is obvious they are the worse for drink.*
  • *The person you are helping says they are taking tablets to 'help with their nerves'. They seem flat, dull and sometimes seem to have difficulty looking straight at you and keeping awake.*

The following steps might be useful in situations where someone is under the influence of drugs:

1. Take some time to assess the situation.

2. Decide whether the person intoxicated is in any danger, e.g. are they feeling faint or showing signs of exhaustion or collapse?

3. If you are worried about their physical state, get help. Let them know what is happening, what you are doing and why. If possible get their permission before doing anything on their behalf.

4. If they are intoxicated, i.e. pleasantly drowsy, or out of touch with reality, but not afraid, you will need to decide whether you want to help them whilst they are in that state. You could ask them to come back when they are 'sober' or 'clean'. You should be careful to continue to offer the core conditions, especially non-judgemental warmth.

5. If they are afraid or suffering unpleasant effects, but not in any danger, again you must decide whether you want to help them whilst they are in that state. If you do want to help them, remember that your most effective skills are the core conditions. Do not reassure them that everything will be alright. You don't know that it will.

6. If you do want to continue helping someone who is intoxicated, you need to decide how much you are going to work with the symptoms of intoxication and how much you are going to try to make contact with the person. Your ability to be present and congruent is paramount here. Neither treat them with kid gloves, nor get involved in their jokey, dreamy, nonsequential world either.

7. If you have involved others in the care of this person, you may want to follow up to find out what has happened and to give some continuity to the helping relationship.

8. Counselling skills are not specialised skills for helping people overcome drug addiction. Do not try to develop any sort of 'program' to 'cure' the person of their addiction.

Helping someone who is aggressive

Whilst you may sometimes have many fears about the safety of others and yourself, the chances are very slim that you or the person you are helping are in any real danger. People that are in great distress or very disturbed, for example, are no more likely to be violent than you or I. They are more likely to hurt themselves, and the section on *'Helping someone who threatens to harm themselves'* looks at this issue some more. They may, however *threaten* violence, which can be in itself an aggressive act. We don't want to over or under-emphasise the risk of violence. We don't advocate first looking at everyone we help as a potential aggressor, yet it is important to think about, for example, the dangerousness of the environment, i.e. hard and sharp objects to throw etc.

If someone threatens violence or behaves aggressively without actually hitting out:
- Keep calm.
- If you can successfully empathise with them, you may:
  - realise why they feel so upset,
  - get a better idea of how real the threat is,
  - be able to let them feel 'heard' which may calm things down a bit.
- If you are non-judgemental they may feel that they can express their feelings and be heard without having to make grand gestures or violent threats in order to be taken seriously.
- If you can be congruent they may realise that their behaviour is causing genuine fear and concern. Often people in such situations have no intention of hurting anyone; they just want someone to listen and take them seriously.

If the person you are helping starts hitting out at the walls, furniture, you or someone else, or starts brandishing a weapon the following guidelines might be helpful, but remember that the best form of self protection is to get out as quickly as possible and raise the alarm. You should also make sure that your working conditions are safe, with panic buttons and alarms to hand if there is any chance that you will be working alone or with violent people.

1. Stay as calm as you can, but remain alert. You will probably be very alert indeed due to adrenaline in your bloodstream.

2. Reason with someone only if they stop being violent.

3. If possible, get out and raise the alarm.

4. Do not try to reason with the violent person if they are drunk or intoxicated.

5. Do not intervene if others are fighting. This is very dangerous.

6. When the incident is over, get support or debriefing. Do not drive or walk home straight afterwards, you will probably be in shock.

7. As soon as possible write down what happened - you may want to give evidence or ask the Police to bring charges on your behalf. Only the victim of violence can bring about a prosecution.

Chapter 14 Summary

1. The main message of this chapter is that the core conditions are your best tools in any difficult situation in which you may be trying to help someone.

2. In order to feel safe enough to help someone you need to have confidence in your competence, your physical safety and your support and backup.

3. It is important to help someone only within your limits. This means that first you must know what your limits are and then develop skills in referring clients on to others who can give them more specialised help.

4. When people are distressed or disturbing to us, not only is our ability to be non-judgemental and warm challenged, but also our ability to be empathic. We also need to look to our own personal development in order to increase our 'range' in these difficult situations.

5. Sometimes the people we are helping threaten to harm themselves or commit suicide. It is a question of our personal moral position as to whether we intervene in their lives to 'prevent' this self-destructive behaviour. It is important to make clear, calm and well-informed decisions.

6. Silence in helping sessions is challenging for many helpers. There is not much to be done other than wait for the other person to speak if we wish to fulfil our role as respectful, authentic, empathic listeners.

7. The power imbalances in helping relationships need to be at least acknowledged if we are to avoid being disrespectful and unempathic towards those we are trying to help. It is important that we acknowledge and celebrate difference, not confuse 'equality' with the notion that everyone is the same or like us.

8. Person Centred helpers need not worry that the people they are helping might become dependent upon them. The aim and process of helping is to emancipate people and help them become autonomous individuals. Good helping practice does not 'cause' dependence.

9. It is necessary avoid the frequent temptation to help a third party rather than the person in front of us. We must remember that our client is the person who is with us, not their uncle, friend, parent or child.

10. Helpers need to prepare themselves for the difficult decision of whether to help someone who is intoxicated. This is not a simple issue and we encourage helpers to look at all aspects of the problem.

11. Although uncommon, aggressive help-seekers are best left to calm down. Do not intervene in someone else's fight and be prepared to make a quick exit. You can usually tell if someone is likely to become aggressive. It is very rarely the case that someone explodes totally unpredictably. Learn to trust your instincts.

Ethics for Counselling Skills

15

The need to declare our ethics when helping

We have seen in earlier chapters that helping can be practical or personal, and that one way of looking at helping activities is to see them as overlapping layers in which the core conditions of empathy, non-judgemental warmth and congruence appear in a variety of relationships which have different purposes.

Underlying all inter-personal helping is the layer that we have called *Personal Support*, where the helper seeks to show their concern for another and is willing to spend energy on their behalf, to share something of their feelings, etc.

Then we identified helping which moved beyond this basic human support, using the core conditions to help people identify and tackle new learning or understanding, we called this *Developmental Support*; it is often the type of support offered by parents and teachers.

When individuals have particular problems in their lives which seem intractable because they are repetitive, or too big to handle, or which leave them feeling that they do not have the personal resources to tackle them, they may look for, or be offered, more 'expert' help aimed at resolving this dilemma.

We have argued that whether the helper in this situation is normally a counsellor or occupies some other role in the individual's life, if the helper works primarily through a personal interaction and adopts the core conditions as they work with the person on understanding and resolving these difficulties, it is sensible to acknowledge that what they are doing is counselling - and we have called this layer *Problem Solving Counselling*.

Lastly we have seen that there is a layer that includes some elements of personal support, that is very likely to have developmental and problem solving elements but which goes beyond the specifics of a particular problem solving task to try to enable the individual to change, if they choose, on a much broader front; to help them to heal emotional wounds or bridge earlier deficits, sometimes even to deconstruct and reconstruct their self-structure so that they can come at life in a new and healthier way: we called this *Therapeutic Counselling*.

Since we are talking about a continuum of overlapping activities which starts in an approach to everyday interactions between family members, friends, neighbours and colleagues, but ends up in a process which is usually very private and to many people seems a bit strange and mysterious, it is not altogether surprising that it is sometimes difficult to know what sorts of 'rules' to expect and what form these rules could take. Yet we clearly need some sorts of guidelines to enable both the helpers and those they seek to assist to be aware of what can be offered and what should be expected.

If the help that you are getting comes from friends or family, or as an act of kindness by a stranger on a train, you probably do not expect to be able to refer to some set of *written* regulations about the relationship that exists between those who help and those who are helped, to let you know what it is reasonable to expect. There are no written rules to let you know when your helper might be considered to have acted badly or against your interests; or when you might have grounds for complaint. But that's not to say there would be *no* rules or guidelines, it's just that they would not be explicit or written down but would be part of the unwritten social rules and conventions that enable any community to operate its everyday life.

Thus in one family a daughter might choose to talk to her mother about the difficulties she is having with her bloke expecting complete privacy, from both Dad and siblings and everyone outside the family. Whereas in another family she would assume that telling Mum was also telling Dad, and that if she didn't say very clearly that Mum was not to discuss it with Aunty Jean, then Mum would not necessarily see it as confidential in that way. As another example some groups of young teenagers develop strong expectations about looking after one-another and sticking together, so in such a group a secret between two members might be shared to enable shared care. In a similar group two streets away this would feel like betrayal and the teller could end up ostracised.

Rather than leave it to chance, local agreement or convention, people who are regarded as helpers of all kinds need guidelines or rules that transcend all the variables of age, sex, culture, religion, family conventions etc. Thus helpers using counselling skills (or indeed all professionals who work with people) need to have a clear set of rules or codes that they all follow. These guidelines will define, and set boundaries to, their activities in order to protect the people they are helping, and themselves too. What follows is an example of when cultural rules were shown to be different from professional rules, and the real dilemma that that caused.

Ethics and culture
We have talked in other places about different assumptions about helping that arise in different cultures and sub-groups of society, and this stands as much for the unwritten ethical rules about such things as confidentiality, active intervention in clients' lives and responsibilities to colleagues, etc. One of the effects of professionalising some aspects of helping is that it enables the helping professions to create public systems or codes of ethics which can reduce uncertainty and difference - *although no-one can guarantee that practitioners will abide by these codes or that clients will be aware of them.* If you approach a helper knowing she or he is bound by a code of ethics and practice, but not actually knowing the details of that code, it seems most likely that you will take it for granted that what is defined in the rules as honourable and decent will very closely reflect what you think is honourable and decent.

I had a startling indication of the difficulties that arise from such assumptions several years ago when I was professionally involved in Social Work training. It was rather forcefully brought to my attention that a student of Asian origin, on learning through his work that a very young, newly married Asian woman was being mistreated by her husband, had spoken to the elders at their place of worship about what he had learned. Certain discussions and conversations had taken place, and the situation was improved for the young woman. My student felt that a good job had been done (a helpful systemic intervention!). When the agency for whom he was working had got to hear about what had happened there was uproar. Had he no understanding of ethics? What about confidentiality and the right to privacy? This was a serious breach, he had behaved in a patronising and presumptuous way, maybe the placement would have to be discontinued.

My student was genuinely hurt and mystified to be accused of being unethical. He had acted decisively to seek the resolution of an unjust situation and had been successful, how could this be unethical? How could it be more ethical to say, and do, nothing in this situation? How would that help the young woman in question to feel supported? He had been careful not to increase any risk to her. He was sure the situation for all was better now. The taken-for-granted ethics of each 'side', of what became a painful dispute for all of us, were diametrically opposed . But each had assumed the other would 'do what was right', and did not realise that this meant completely different things to them until the events took place.

I am not trying to say anything about Asian values in general here, I no more believe in pan-Asian values than I would in pan-European values. This student was clear that the prime value that he shared with others in his immediate community, and in all probability with the young woman in question, was the need for the maintenance of justice and family life and the protection of the weak. How could Social Work have ethics that were against that? The Social Workers however, had been taught a different set of values, which prioritised individual autonomy and therefore placed a premium on confidentiality and only on intervening to assist the client through agreed plans, not to take matters out of their hands; even if that appeared to meet the client's needs in the short term.

It was hard going for the student and the agency to see that this was not a disagreement about the need to be ethical, but about their taken-for-granted view of what was ethical and the basis for good practice. In the end the situation could only be resolved by agreeing to disagree on the moral issues and my student accepting pragmatically that a necessary condition of entry into the profession of Social Work was understanding and operating the specifics of its code of ethics.

For me this was a very powerful learning experience about how easy it is mistakenly to assume that people we see as decent and well motivated will share our values and thus how important it is for a professional group publicly to codify its values to reduce the trouble that such assumptions can lead us into.

Counselling and ethics

The situation in counselling and psychotherapy is more complex than this on two counts:
- firstly, there are large numbers of people who engage in counselling as part of their work who are not primarily or exclusively counsellors, and
- secondly, amongst those who do consider themselves to be primarily counsellors there is no agreement about the breadth, range or content of their work and no membership body which clearly represents all of them.

How then can we say anything much about ethics here? I think we can start by asking whether the core conditions of the counselling approach have *ethical* as well as *practical* implications for helpers. To me it is clear that a good part of the ethics of counselling at every level can be derived from these values.

I am conscious as I write this that it could all get a bit dry. It might help if you try the activity below:

Activity
• *Jot down at the top of three columns the Person-Centred Core Conditions, using your own words to describe them.*

• *Think of two or three occasions when you have asked for help or been asked for help or knew about someone needing help.*

• *Looking at each column in turn ask yourself what implications does holding this core condition have for what the helper should and should not do. Write them down.*

• *Go back over your list and cross out those elements which you see as about technique, purely about the skills and activities needed to help this person.*

What you are now left with are the ethical implications of the core conditions.

When I tried this exercise I thought about two situations. The first was when help was required from me and the second was where I was in need of help.

• Several years ago I was rather surprised that people in the area where I was living knew what I did (I was not working from home then), but one day the daughter of a local woman called on me to ask if I could help: her mother, who having been widowed a couple of months earlier, had taken to drink.

• I also thought of a time not so long ago when I was feeling really angry and upset by the behaviour of my young lodger who I felt had betrayed my trust. Whilst having a drink with a friend I started to talk about it.

Then, dividing my page into three columns, I kept these two occasions in mind and came up with the following ideas that were non-'technical' and non skills-based. (See page opposite).

Unconditional Positive Regard or non-judgemental warmth.	*Congruence, authenticity or being real and how I really want to be with you.*	*Empathy, getting on the same wavelength or seeing your world as if through your eyes.*
As a helper • *Be direct but not directive.* • *Clarify expectations.* • *The fact that I know a lot or care about them does not give me the right to boss someone around.* • *There but for grace....* • *Don't gossip or talk about them: it diminishes this person (and myself).* • *Who am I really helping here?*	**As the helper** • *What do I want?* • *Why am I going to see this woman?* • *I must be careful not to mix up my whims with what is good for this woman - especially if she is ready to defer to my expertise.*	**As a helper** • *To get something to work on I need some trust and openness from this woman. I'm not going to get that if she just feels scared or uncertain of me.*
As the person being helped • *How will I know if I've outstayed my welcome?* • *I don't want to be criticised for my feelings and wishes.* • *I'm not looking for advice, but I'd welcome some ideas, and might welcome being challenged.*	**As the person being helped** • *I don't want my outburst just to be tolerated.* • *I don't want you to pretend you like me.* • *I don't want you to pretend that you understand.*	**As the person being helped** • *I want to feel he is listening, and* • *understanding it from my position.*

In the end I only crossed off a couple of the things I had written down through identifying them as skills rather than values, although some of them (like the last one *'As the person being helped'*) I found a bit difficult to judge.

I wonder how our lists would fit together? I wonder if it would have made a whole lot of difference if I had chosen situations where there was specifically a counsellor and client rather than neighbours or friends? I am pretty sure that the list would have been different if I was a woman, or black or disabled, and looking back over my listing now I am anxious that I may have overlooked issues to do with oppression from my two examples, let alone if I was to change my perceived gender, race or physical capacities.

For me the central ethical values of the counselling approach are to do with the way power is handled in the relationship (and so they will have implications both interpersonally and socially). Because of power issues I would see that it is really important for any helper to be open and honest with people they are seeking to help about what is on offer, what sorts of things might happen, what kind of guarantees of success can be offered.

Thus we are talking about clients having a right to clear information about the help that is on offer, about the direct costs in time and money, etc. and perhaps even the indirect costs of taking risks, etc. They have a right to clear discussions leading to some sort of contract. We are talking, too, about 'client self-determination' so that the helper's power is not used to push a help-seeker towards any particular course of action, so that a client can get information without having to have advice, and so that such a person feels valued not criticised.

Putting these together in a wider context we might want to identify the need for help to be offered with an awareness of oppression issues. I think all of these stem to some degree from the core value of **respect**, [and I don't think it is just a matter of opinion - because as we have seen there is a long tradition, from Rogers himself onwards, in which he has shown that the core conditions do work.] The guidelines have arisen directly from the requirements of the core conditions. Thus we can say that they are not just opinion but are based on real evidence, in real life.

I think ideas about contracting derive from the notion of **congruence**, as the worker explores what they have to give, etc., there is every reason to accord them the right (make space for their need) to place certain essential limits on the relationship. Most obviously though congruence translates into the value of honesty. It probably is not respectful to deal with clients dishonestly, it certainly is not congruent. Again I think the justification for this is pragmatic as much as moral or ethical. In complex relationships it is difficult to maintain falsehood, without adding further fictional elements to the account. These actions make you more and more prone to being caught either by self-contradiction or through the increasing non-verbal signals of discomfort. How can a client feel you are being real for them if they also experience you as lying?

The honesty criterion also affects the issue of trust which is an essential part of **empathy**. A client who finds it really hard to trust finds it hard to give much of their inner world, so it is difficult to get into an active empathic frame with them; and without that, the evidence shows that the chances of helping are diminished. If clients are to trust us then they must know that we will not abuse our power, and this in my view is where sanctions against workers meeting their own needs through the vulnerability of clients comes from.

If a worker may exploit a client financially, sexually, emotionally, then how can the client (even one for whom trust is not the big issue) begin to be open and vulnerable enough to move towards change? Thus even though it's not a guarantee, any ethical code needs to consider a non-exploitation clause.

The other ethical constraint that arises from the need for empathy and therefore trust in helping relationships is the need for confidentiality. This can be seen as a way of ensuring that the protection afforded to a client's vulnerability by prohibiting the worker from exploiting the client for sexual, financial or other gain, is extended as widely as possible. The requirement for respect also provides a source for a norm of confidentiality, because talking about people tends to objectify them, and as they become potential for discussion and gossip to diminish them (and the person gossiping). If we are to maintain our positive position in relation to our clients - to continue to 'prize' them, then a confidentiality and no gossip rule will help us to do so.

You may have noticed that my original lists on p 189 didn't really touch on issues concerned with oppression and equal opportunities etc. It really should have done. As we have seen earlier, it's really important to consider issues of difference (in power, expectations etc.) in all helping situations because these concerns are derived from the core conditions too. Thus we can list topics that any ethical system for any level of helping based on the counselling approach needs to include:

- the right to clear information

- a contract   • self-determination
- help-seekers valued not criticised
- awareness of issues of oppression
- honesty   • non-exploitation
- confidentiality

> *Activity*
> • *Read the Code of Ethics & Practice for Counselling Skills on the next two pages, either by yourself or with others.*
> • *If you are already bound by a professional code or organisation guidelines find copies of these and see how it differs from the above.*
> • *Write a list of your own personal ethical priorities as a helper. Share it with somebody else.*
>
> **Note:** *If you are thinking of going on to train further to become a counsellor (or if you're just curious) get a copy of the Code of Ethics & Practice for Counsellors from BAC and compare it with the above tasks.*

Whether you develop as what BAC calls a 'counselling skills practitioner' or use the counselling approach as a parent or a friend, or if you go on into training for professional practice as a therapeutic or problem-solving counsellor, issues raised in this chapter will keep coming back to you. No matter how experienced you are, how thoroughly you have considered the sociological and ethical issues touched on here, life and real relationships are more complex still and will constantly throw up new dilemmas to test your integrity and understanding. I suspect that this chapter has been just a few relatively early paces on a long journey.

British Association for Counselling Code of Ethics and Practice:
Guidelines for those using Counselling Skills in their Work

In response to members of BAC, this Code is a revision of the 1989 Code of Ethics and Practice for Counselling Skills. All members of this Association are required to abide by the existing Codes appropriate to their work until such time as a new Code is adopted by the membership.

A. Introduction
The purpose of this Code is to outline the ethical principles involved in the use of Counselling Skills.

The attached practice guidelines which relate to this Code (Section D) are primarily intended for those who are trained in the use of Counselling Skills within another role. For those working within an explicitly contracted counselling relationship, the Code of Ethics and Practice for Counsellors applies.

The user of Counselling Skills will hereafter be known as 'the practitioner' and the recipient of Counselling Skills will be known as 'the client'.

Counselling Skills Users, their organisations, their managers and their clients should have access to this Code.

All BAC members abide by its Equal Opportunities Policy Statement. The full statement can be found at the end of this Code.

B. Counselling Skills
For the purpose of this Code and the Practice Guidelines:
The **practitioner** respects the client's values, experience, thoughts, feelings and their capacity for self-determination. The practitioner aims to serve the best interests of the **client**.

Counselling Skills are being used:
- **when** there is intentional use of specific interpersonal skills which reflect the values of counselling,
- **and** when the practitioner's primary role (e.g. nurse, tutor, line manager, social worker, personnel officer, helper) is enhanced without being changed;
- **and** when the client perceives the practitioner as acting with in their primary professional or/caring role which is **not** that of being a counsellor.

C. Code of Ethics
C.1 Values
The practitioner's values are those of integrity, impartiality and respect for the client. The practitioner works in a non-exploitative way.

C.2 Anti-discriminatory Practice
Practitioners must consider and address their own prejudices and how they stereotype others. They must ensure that anti-discriminatory practice is integral to their work when using Counselling Skills.

C.3 Confidentiality
C.3.1 Practitioners offer the highest possible levels of confidentiality consistent with their primary professional or work role.
C.3.2 Any limits to confidentiality must be made explicit.

C.4 Competence
C.4.1 Practitioners are responsible for ensuring that they have training in the use of Counselling Skills and that this training is appropriate and sufficient for the Counselling Skills work they undertake.
C.4.2 Practitioners are responsible for working within the limits of their competence.
C.4.3 Both practitioners and the organisations for whom they work have a responsibility for monitoring and developing the practitioner's competence in the use of Counselling Skills. Non-managerial supervision is recognised as one of the best methods for achieving this.
C.4.4 Both practitioners and their organisations have a responsibility for addressing those aspects of an organisation which impede the ethical use of Counselling Skills.

C.5 Integration of Codes of Ethics and Practice
Many of those who use Counselling Skills in their work are also bound by another Code of Ethics and Practice relating to their primary professional or work role. Practitioners therefore have responsibility for managing the integration of this Code with any other Code and for resolving difficulties or conflicts which may arise. It is important to recognise any way in which the primary role limits the use of Counselling Skills.

D. Practice Guidelines
These guidelines apply the values and ethical principles outlined in this Code of Ethics for use in practice. Within another role the Counselling Skills user may help someone to recognise feelings, thoughts and behaviours and, when appropriate, to explore them in greater depth. The guidelines address issues of competence relating to these skills in practice.

D.1 Confidentiality
Confidentiality is crucial to the working relationship. For this reason any limits to the degree of confidentiality offered must be

carefully considered. As the use of Counselling Skills often takes place within a network of overlapping accountabilities the following clauses need to be understood within the context of the network.

Practitioners must therefore:

D.1.1 have clarified for themselves the extent of confidentiality which is consistent with any other roles they hold whilst using Counselling Skills

D.1.2 when appropriate, reach an agreement with the client at the outset about the extent of confidentiality

D.1.3 take great care not to disclose, either inadvertently or under pressure, information given in confidence

D.1.4 wherever possible, negotiate any change in the agreement with the client.

D.1.5 ensure confidentiality of material relating to the use of Counselling Skills which is used either for research purposes or in presenting cases for supervision or training. *Practitioners using such material must therefore:*

D.1.6 where appropriate, obtain the consent of the client for such use

D.1.7 effectively disguise the client's identity.

D.1.8 ensure that discussion about such material is respectful and purposeful and is not trivialising.

D.2 Competent Practice

Practitioners should consider:

D.2.1 whether it is appropriate to use Counselling Skills within their other role

D.2.2 whether their level of training in the use of Counselling Skills is adequate for the work in each individual instance or setting

D.2.3 how any other relevant professional Codes might affect their use of Counselling Skills within the work and whether any specific limits to confidentiality arise

D.2.4 how any emerging areas of potential role conflict could be resolved

D.2.5 whether the purpose of using Counselling Skills within a given context is clear to the client

D.2.6 whether the necessary arrangements have been made with colleagues to ensure that an environment offering safety and privacy can be provided

D.2.7 the power aspect of relationships within the work and any consequent need to address this

D.2.8 the significance of their own and the client's social and cultural contexts in the work undertaken

D.2.9 establishing an appropriate referral network

and should:

D.2.10 value and facilitate the expression of thoughts and feelings

D.2.11 acknowledge the client's thoughts and feelings and consider whether further exploration is appropriate or not at that moment

D.2.12 be aware of their responsibility to resolve conflicts between ethical priorities

D.2.13 be respectful of the client's world

D.2.14 ensure non-discriminatory practice in their Counselling Skills work

D.2.15 recognise when it is appropriate to refer a client elsewhere

D.2.16 recognise and work with the client's reactions to the referral process

D.2.17 wherever possible, make an appropriate closure of any Counselling Skills work

D.2.18 consider any responsibilities there may be for follow up.

D.3 Supervision

Regular and formalised non-managerial supervision for practitioners is widely recognised as good practice and is highly recommended. It should be an adjunct to managerial supervision of the total work.

Supervision offers practitioners a regular opportunity, outside the line management system, to discuss and monitor their Counselling Skills work whilst still maintaining client confidentiality. It is a formal, collaborative process which is primarily concerned with the well being of the client and secondarily with that of the practitioner.

The supervisor will have knowledge and experience in using Counselling Skills and will also be familiar with the Code of Ethics and Practice.

Supervision can:

• help practitioners to maintain ethical and professional standards of practice

• enhance confidence, clarity and competence in the work

• develop constructive thinking about the effectiveness of the work

• acknowledge and help to recognise and manage the emotional impact of the work in order to enhance effectiveness and prevent burnout.

Further guidance on the ethics and practice of supervision can be obtained from BAC's Code of Ethics and Practice for Supervisors.

D.4 Accountability

Practitioners are accountable for their work to the client, the organisations in which they may practise and their professional bodies.

Practitioners should therefore:

D.4.1 have received adequate basic training

D.4.2 maintain ongoing skills development and relevant learning

D.4.3 monitor their personal functioning and seek help or withdraw from using Counselling Skills, temporarily or permanently, if their personal resources become sufficiently depleted to require this

D.4.4 take all reasonable steps to ensure their own safety

D.4.5 evaluate their practice, drawing where appropriate on feedback from clients, colleagues and managers

D.4.6 recognise the impact of their own beliefs and prejudices on the work they do

D.4.7 monitor their work to ensure that they are not discriminating against or disadvantaging their clients

D.4.8 exercise caution before engaging in a different type of relationship with those who are or have been clients (e.g. to a business, social, sexual, training, therapeutic or other relationship) and consult with a supervisor or manager whether such a change is appropriate.

Equal Opportunities Satement

'The British Association for Counselling' (BAC) is committed to promoting Equality of Opportunity of access and participation for all its members in all of its structures and their workings. BAC has due regard for those groups of people with identifiable characteristics which can lead to visible and invisible barriers thus inhibiting their joining and full participation in BAC. Barriers can include age, colour, creed, culture, disability, education, ethnicity, gender, information, knowledge, mobility, money, nationality, race, religion, exual orientation, social class and status.

The work of BAC aims to reflect this commitment in all areas including services to members, employer responsibilities, the recruitment of and working with volunteers, setting, assessing, monitoring and evaluating standards and the implementation of the complaints procedures. This is particularly important as BAC is the 'Voice of Counselling' in the wider world.

BAC will promote and encourage commitment to Equality of Opportunity by its members.

Chapter 15 Summary

1. It is clear that in order to be respectful, authentic and empathic there are a set of behaviours, beliefs and values that must be held and put into action.

2. The codes of ethics for helpers using counselling skills link closely with the values and practical applications of the core conditions.

3. If, however, you are using counselling skills as an addition to your main job, e.g. if you are already a teacher or nurse, you will already have a set of rules that govern your professional behaviour. Your task is to find some way of making sure that these two codes of conduct can be worked together.

Helper Support

16

What is support and how is it different from supervision?

Although everybody seems to be talking about support and supervision in counselling circles, it would appear that in my experience, few share the same definitions. 'Out there' people have very different personal support needs and very different visions of what helper support and counsellor supervision could, and should, be.

The British Association for Counselling (BAC) publish a Code of Ethics and Practice for the Supervisors of Counsellors - this establishes one benchmark. Unfortunately for those using counselling skills, this benchmark lies outside the territory we have marked out for counselling skills helpers. We may take the BAC Code to tell us some things that counselling skills helper support is not, but it doesn't really tell us what it is.

This is both good news and bad news. Whilst we (counselling skills helpers) have no clear guidance, we can make it up as we go along. If we proceed with awareness and care, we can take the opportunity of developing something that is of real use in an area (looking after ourselves as helpers) that we may otherwise be guilty of neglecting. There can be no doubt that this is an important personal and ethical issue, since there will be nothing that detracts more from our helping abilities than ignoring our own need for support.

This chapter will be a whistle-stop look at helper support to give you a flavour of the issues involved in support for counselling skills helping. We will be comparing support to other similar relationships, like supervision. We will be looking at helper burnout and how support might help us avoid it. We will examine the sort of backup a helper using counselling skills might need. And finally we will be considering support from both sides - being supported and being a supporter.

> *Activity*
> • *Take a moment or two to brainstorm words, images, sounds, situations etc., that you associate with support.*
> • *Make a note of your brainstormed ideas.*

Rather than do this exercise again myself, I looked in the dictionary to give me some idea of the range of words that might be associated with support. I was surprised to find that my years of being a counsellor and supervisor had narrowed my own range of vision. I was reminded that support included, e.g.

- being actively interested in something (like a football supporter),
- taking a secondary (but involved) part - like a supporting actor,
- being an advocate, and
- providing the necessities of life (supporting a family).

How do these ideas mesh with your notions of support from the brainstorming activity? In counselling circles, support and supervision are often used together, sometimes they appear to mean the same thing. We have quite deliberately called this chapter *Support* rather than *Supervision* to emphasise the important differences between the two concepts, for example:

Supervision

• The term supervision is associated with being overseen, judged, evaluated, sacked etc. It has hierarchical connotations.

• Supervision is something we associate more with counselling and counsellors rather than helpers using counselling skills in a wider range of settings.

• Supervision mainly aims to look after the client's interests (only one way of doing this is to help the helper).

Support

• Support suggests more of a peer relationship.

• Support sounds less formal, more everyday.

• Support aims to look after the helper's interests (and in the process make us better helpers).

We would like to suggest that although the activities of helper support and counsellor supervision overlap, they *are* different. Not least because in this chapter we will consistently put those words together, i.e. counsellor - supervision, and helper - support. So, the first difference we wish to emphasise is that:

• *Supervision* is essentially a *professional service,* and is seen as a requirement.

• *Support* is essentially an act of *personal attention* and is currently seen as desirable.

In order to find out what we, as helpers using counselling skills might use support for, it helps to look at what we already do to get the support we need in our everyday lives. The next activity might help clarify this.

Activity

• *Take a piece of paper and draw yourself or put your name in the middle. This paper is going to be your personal support map.*

• *Draw or write the names of the places, people and things where you currently get your personal support.*

• *Draw connecting lines and write in what sort of support you get from each source.*

• *If you want to complete your personal support map, you could write in those people you give support to.*

• *Some might be the same people as in the first part of the exercise, so the support arrows will be two-way.*

When I first tried this exercise, I was surprised by the rich variety of places, things, people and experiences in my life that I find supportive. Before doing the exercise, I had thought that my support map would be small and well-defined. It turned out to sprawl across most of my life. What can you learn from your support map?

• Try grouping the support into types or categories; what sort of categories can you come up with?

• Try looking for gaps in your map - like holes in a net - where or what sort of support are you not getting, or getting too little of?

• Look for things that you reach for to comfort you when you need support that might do you more harm than good in the long run.. (In my case, I identified food and 'comfort eating').

One final question relating to the above exercise; did it occur to you that you could put yourself on the map as someone who gives support to yourself?

Most personal support maps have a mixture of support sources, from partners, close friends and relatives, through to professionals who may charge you for their services. This spread of support in our personal lives helps us better understand how we might put together a support network for ourselves as helpers.

Stress and burnout in helpers

If support is something we all need in order to be good helpers, but never do much about it, then *burnout* is something that always happens to someone else, never to us. Much has been written on the subject of stress and burnout amongst helpers, both professional and voluntary. Using counselling skills in our helping work is no protection against stress and its effects.

Some people have even argued that some training in counselling makes people even more prone to stress. In their poignantly entitled *'The Ultimate Disappointment: The Burnedout Counsellor,'* Warnath and Shelton (1976) suggested that trainees are frequently caught in a double bind between being told that they must be honest, open, transparent and congruent; but afraid to do so in case they are not seen as a good student. Later Pines (1982) reckoned that people are given unrealistic expectations in training because all the case examples end up as

successful and the work experience on courses gives no idea of the real pressures of helping.

My own experience of training on counselling skills courses is that trainees suffer badly from role conflict back at work. There can be clashes of values between, for example, counselling and nursing or between counselling and teaching which do nothing to lower stress levels at work. At times like these, learning about counselling skills and how to integrate them into our working and personal lives is more like a curse than any help at all.

If these accounts ring true then at least you have been warned. Support is needed even when you are training to use counselling skills. Fortunately, support is usually not in short supply on counselling skills courses. You are all, after all, being trained to provide better helping relationships and the tendency is to be more supportive to each other, if only to practice your skills! If training sometimes unwittingly sows the seeds of future stress, then let it also sow the seeds to undo the stress. Getting used to support on your course is no bad thing. When the course finishes, don't leave a gap in your support net, look around for ways of getting the support you need to continue to offer and develop your helping skills.

Backup

In Chapter 14 on pages 166 & 167 we looked very briefly at just how important it is to feel safe when you are using counselling skills to help someone. We suggested that there were three kinds of confidence you need:
  • Confidence in your competence,
  • Confidence in your physical safety and
  • Confidence in your backup and support.

Being confident in all three areas requires hard work on your part and sometimes it will involve other people. It is difficult to imagine any definition of backup that didn't ask something of other people.

The definition of backup we are using here is
'All the resources you need, physical, human and information in order to continue to help someone safely and competently, excluding your own personal resources of knowledge and skills.'

The degree to which you feel you need backup will depend upon the setting in which you choose to practise your counselling skills. Some professional settings such as nursing, teaching, social work and youth work will already have backup systems in place. However, these backup systems are likely to be geared towards providing continuing *medical* help, or continuing *educational* support, rather than continuing *counselling skills* helping. So it may be that even in the best organised helping set-up, there may be elements of the backup system for counselling skills missing.

Physical backup - a place for helping

We have stressed throughout this book that there is a difference between counselling and helping using counselling skills. One of the differences between the two types of helping is the setting in which the activity takes place (although this is by no means a hard and fast distinction). We might want our ideal counselling setting to be comfortable, private and quiet. Whilst we might also see the ideal counselling skills setting as being private and quiet, the reality is that counselling skills helpers are expected to do it (according to the joke) standing up, lying down, on the move, in a corridor, in a ward, in a classroom; in fact just about anywhere and in any position.

We have seen from the vignettes that settings can be formal and informal, private and less private, but what happens in all of them is that the counselling skills helper has enough physical backup to provide a safe space in which to do the counselling skills helping. There are some minimal general requirements for this:
- No interruptions.
- Feeling safe, not working alone in a building.
- An environment quiet enough so that you can hear and be heard.
- Any discomfort must not be distracting.

And there are some situation-specific requirements:
- Privacy is sometimes important (drawing curtains round a hospital bed).
- Feeling safe (keeping the address secret, e.g. for a women's refuge).
- Having a cover story (making sure that a young person has another reason for seeing you in a youth club, so that their friends don't find out they're seeking help).

Activity
- *What general physical requirements do you think are necessary?*
  - *How could you make them happen where you practise counselling skills?*

- *What minimum requirements are necessary in special settings, such as making home visits, working in a youth club or on a busy hospital ward for example?*
  - *How could you make them happen where you practise counselling skills?*

Human backup - networks for support

Whenever we are offering counselling skills we must acknowledge the human resources we need including any professional backup we might need. We can think of human backup as coming in two sorts; first there is the everyday servicing of our needs as a helper - we might call this support, and second there is emergency backup when we get out of our depth or sense that the helping required is beyond our limits. I think of this as the sort of help that arrives when the police radio back to base *'We need backup!'*

Sometimes we might refer the person we are helping on to another helper, but sometimes this is not the best thing to do since the help-seeker may have already formed a trusting relationship with you. On such occasions we might need to get our helping backed up almost on the spot, for example, we might need to turn to someone after a helping session and call on them to give us advice on what to do next.

Many organisations and agencies have backup systems so that a helper on the ground can phone for immediate backup from a day leader or shift supervisor. Sometimes this person is more experienced or skilled, but sometimes all it takes is to have someone not involved to offer another view on the situation. Some agencies keep the phone number of a doctor, psychiatrist, clinical psychologist or professional counsellor who have offered their services to give some assistance and advice in those situations when the problem is beyond your limit.

Activity
- *If you are working for an organisation, are you confident that your helping is backed up?*
  - *Do you have on-line backup or are you left to fend for yourself?*
  - *What are you supposed to do if the counselling skills element of your helping takes you out of your depth?*

- *If you are working alone, does your counselling skills work require backup?*
  - *What arrangements have you made to back up your counselling skills helping?*

Information backup - data for helping

Information for help-seekers. When we are asked for help and we think that counselling skills will be useful in the 'helping mix', it is sometimes the case that the person we are helping requires information of some kind. Such a requirement is on the border between practical and personal support, and it falls into the realms of counselling skills helping because information is more often than not asked for and given through a relationship. It is clearly impracticable to assemble and maintain a comprehensive library of information, but you may find it useful to keep some basic information that has themes associated with the type of people you help most often. For example, if you work with young people, keeping a list of youth counselling agencies in your area, where to go to get advice on accommodation, money problems, safe sex and contraception, drugs etc., will come in handy.

The purpose of keeping this information is not so that you can dispense advice, but rather so that you can refer someone on to an agency or person who can give them more specialised information and help. Being a counselling skills helper does not mean that you have to know everything about everything. Although you may have areas of expertise yourself, you should know where these begin and end. (You may, after all, be on *other people's* information list as someone to whom *their* client's can be referred for advice on drugs, accommodation or whatever.)

The purpose of carrying information to give to those you are helping is to increase the range of options they have for helping themselves. Information is power and people are empowered by knowing what is available and where to find out more.

When giving information you should remember that counselling skills are delivered through a relationship. We have explained that people are most open to change when they are offered the core conditions. It makes sense, then, that if we wish them to take in some information, they will be most open and receptive when we also provide the core conditions. The core conditions also ensure that we do not foist unwanted information on them against their wishes, since if we are being empathic we will have discovered just what information they want and if we are being respectful, we will let them take it on at their own pace without us forcing it down their throats.

Information for help-givers
Counselling skills helpers will need information for a variety of purposes including making constructive referrals, keeping up to date with local services, keeping up to date with counselling skills developments and on-going training opportunities.

There is no need to catalogue the types of information you might wish to keep here, save to say that it is important that you consider the information you will want to keep for your own purposes. Do not think that being a counselling skills helper is a state of rest; you will be continuing to develop your knowledge, skills and self-awareness, and information will play a part in this process. You may also need to be able to make quick and sure contact with other professional or voluntary helpers, services and agencies in your area.

Activity
If you work on your own, you may think that you do not need all of the information suggested here. If you practise your counselling skills via work or a voluntary agency, you may well have some or all of this information to hand.

• Do you know what training opportunities for counselling skills exist in your area?
• Do you know how to contact social services and what they offer?
• Do you know where to go to get legal advice?
• Do you know where to refer help-seekers to get special help on, for example, sexuality, HIV, spiritual concerns, educational opportunities, equal opportunities, race and issues of ethnicity, support for health problems, e.g. palliative care, etc?
• What other sorts of information might be important to you in your work?

Organising support
Self-support
Support is, in some senses, just as much a frame of mind as an act of assistance from another. It would serve us well if we could cultivate the attitude which puts support at the top of our list of priorities. One way we can do this is to develop our self-support skills. This involves:

- Taking general care of ourselves. (Elsewhere, (Sanders 1996) I have likened this to getting a car ready for a long journey - what essential maintenance do we need as helpers?)
- Having a sense of when we need to stop and say, *'Enough,'* or, *'Help'*.
- Developing self-monitoring and self-evaluation skills.
- Using your confidence in your self-evaluation to get what you need.

Your counselling skills course will help you develop self-monitoring and self-evaluation skills. Many courses will ask you to look at your own practice and give an opinion of what you are doing well and what you can improve on. Even though you will get support and encouragement when you are developing these skills, most people find that it is very hard to not deal in extremes. We tend to jump to the extreme of thinking that we are brilliant and defending ourselves when feedback to the contrary is offered, or we think we are useless and can't listen to the positive points that others make about our performance. Even given these difficulties, most people find that they have a feeling of general discomfort when things aren't going right in a helping session. Learn to cultivate this early warning signal and to trust it.

Don't ignore the signals you send to yourself that say, *'Stop! Enough! I'm doing too much!'* You must learn to look out for these signals and act upon them. If you do not you will exhaust yourself and eventually burn out. Burnout is very unpleasant, don't underestimate your own tendency to stress by overestimating your capacity to help without breaks and support.

Peer support
This is the sort of support that we give to each other, usually unpaid but covering an assortment of arrangements. These can range from workers at the same agency getting together in groups to support each other, to pairing up with a fellow student after the course to review and support each other's counselling skills practice.

Peer support is often favoured when employers and agencies either can't or won't provide helper support as part of the job. You should always strive to get your employer or agency manager(s) to provide adequate support for helping staff. This is increasingly being recognised in some areas such as social work and nursing, where caseload and clinical supervision are slowly gaining in popularity.

Whatever the circumstances of peer supervision are, it is likely to offer the following benefits:
- learning through exposure to different ways of doing things,
- getting a sense of belonging to a group which has some common experience,
- feedback on practice,
- increased opportunities to network with other helpers.

You will have to think about how frequently you meet, how long for and where. If you don't think these issues are important, try organising your peer support in the pub for as long as you can, whenever you can make it every other Friday night. Whenever you set up peer support opportunities, do remember that the aim of the meeting is helping work-related and that it will not be helpful to socialise, chat or gossip even though the temptation may be great.

Consultative support

If at all possible, counselling skills helpers should have access to independent consultative support. The word *consultative* indicates that a person is specifically employed in a consultative capacity. They are usually paid and should be *independent* of the organisation, its management and its staff. This enables the consultant support to make recommendations that are neither influenced by management needs, nor by workers custom and practice. Both can occasionally operate against the interests of helpers and clients.

The best known model for this kind of support is counsellor supervision. BAC publishes a Code of Ethics and Practice for the Supervision of Counsellors and should be used as a reference if you wish to develop or implement a consultative support system. It is debatable whether counselling skills helpers share the same requirement for supervision as professional counsellors. Indeed, it is a debate that we would encourage *you* to have in your workplace and voluntary agency and include those responsible for managing the helping service you offer. Best practice will only develop through active involvement of helpers' and commitment of the managers and organisers.

Training

Keeping abreast of the latest developments in helping, both in general and in particular, is a good way of increasing your confidence through meeting others, exchanging views and of course developing further skills and knowledge. Take advantage of seminars, training days and courses in your area, e.g:
- local colleges, universities,
- independent training organisations,
- hospitals,
- national organisations such as BAC have local groups which meet regularly.

You may even find that your employers or agency provide an on-going training programme. Take advantage of opportunities wherever and whenever possible. Development both personal and professional as a helper is a life-long process. I thoroughly enjoyed reading Brigid Proctor's chapter in Dryden and Thorne (1991) where she charts her life as a helper, trainer and supervisor. Although the chapter is entitled *'On Being a Trainer'* I was struck by the amount of learning that went on, and I can certainly identify with the idea of being perpetually open to new experiences and new learning.

Receiving support

The use we make of support says much about us as helpers. If we think that support is just for emergencies or when things begin to actually break down, it says something about the value we put on maintaining high quality helping. Maybe we simply think that support is for only those that need it, not for us. Although these may appear to be extreme views they are widely held. Less extreme is the way we might routinely fail to make the best use of support opportunities because we do not prepare well enough of because we approach support sessions with an offhand attitude. Francesca Inskipp and Brigid Proctor (1993), in their publication *The Art, Craft and Tasks of Supervision'* explain the purpose of counsellor supervision and suggest exercises to help prepare for supervision so that counsellors can make the most of it. Whilst the jury is still out on whether *counselling skills* helpers require *supervision,* we can say that if you have gone to the trouble of getting support, the least you can do is use it to best effect:

- Prepare; don't go to a support session 'cold'.
  - Spend some time (up to around an hour, although ten minutes will do) thinking about why you want support and what particular issues you would like to work on in that session.
  - Take any notes or materials you need to make best use of the time.
- Be creative - its OK to draw pictures or act out a scene to explain something better.
- Watch out for any defensive reactions you might have to feedback from others - be as open as you can be.
- Take responsibility for your side of any support contract you might have made. Suggest a contract if your support-giver doesn't offer negotiation unprompted.

Giving support

When someone offers a helper support, it is done through a relationship. It is a helping relationship just like other helping relationships we have been looking at in this book. At risk of sounding like a broken record, we'll say it one last time:

The best tools you have to give support to another helper are the core conditions.

Brigid Proctor, in an undated National Youth Bureau publication, introduced the idea that supervision has three functions; that it is *formative, restorative* and *normative.* We have been suggesting that the best way to facilitate the *restorative* or supportive function is to provide the helper with a threat-free environment by offering the core conditions.

Although the core conditions are the foundation of helper support, I have suggested (Sanders 1993) the following additional guidelines to help provide a more focused approach to support for counselling skills helpers:

- Start with the intention of creating a safe environment in which your partner can learn from their experience.
- Look for links or connections between the issues and concerns that they might have.
- Look for patterns of thoughts, feelings, behaviours and events in what they are saying and in their work.
- Ask them if what they are saying or feeling sounds familiar to them or has echoes in other areas of their lives.

I would also now add to these suggestions:

- Do not be afraid to give honest feedback - if the core conditions are in place, this will be OK since it is simply an extension of congruence.
- Be ready to help them deal with their feelings. Do not think that supporting a helper is just about *figuring out what happened* as if it were a mental puzzle.
- Concentrate on the helper; their thoughts, feelings and behaviour *not* the help-seeker or client. Do not gossip or start a diagnosing game to 'sort out' the client in their absence.

Debriefing

When a helper has been involved with a particularly distressing event, they may well need a special on-the-spot support session, sometimes referred to as *debriefing*. Debriefing can be tailored to suit the environment and it might involve not only support for the helper, but also statement-taking and medical attention. If debriefing is not available, helpers may become inefficient, forgetful, anxious, distracted, withdrawn or show any of the many symptoms of post-traumatic stress and shock.

Debriefing is used in a variety of settings and for a number of events or occasions. It is probably most sensible to have a policy whereby the service or agency both lets individual helpers ask for it when they feel they need it, and lets management insist on it if they feel the helper is suffering from shock. Such situations might include:

• When a helper has to listen to a story that they find particularly distressing.
• When a helper is threatened, abused or attacked.
• When a help-seeker attacks themselves or commits suicide.
• When a helper is working at the scene of a disaster or horrific event.

The exact procedure for debriefing is best worked out by the service or agency concerned. The following guidelines may help when considering debriefing:

• Make sure the staff doing the debriefing are properly trained. This should include an understanding of post-traumatic shock and the typical symptoms.

• Make sure the debriefing is in no way connected with appraisal or evaluation of performance.
• Look into the legal aspects of statement-taking if debriefing is to include any preparation for this.
• Make sure that there is some space for confidential disclosure during the debriefing session.
• Ensure sufficient time for debriefing. Ten minutes will not do.
• Provide appropriate space for debriefing and recovery.
• Ensure continued support - e.g. transport home, follow-up next day.
• Give the debriefers some clout - if they recommend a day off work or a week off duty, make sure it happens.
• Make sure you give someone the responsibility for deciding when someone is fit to resume helping. This is not a medical decision, it's a decision about a helper's competence.
• If a helper is badly affected - make sure there is continued support available. Don't make the mistake of caring for your clients more than you care for your staff. This mistake is sometimes thought of as a virtue by agencies and employers, and practised widely.

On a final note, picking up on the last point, it is so important that helpers are neither trapped by nor become victims of their caring for others. As more help-seekers become *customers* and helpers become *service providers*, there may be a tendency to forget that helpers are *people*. People can be worn out, and the responsibility for preventing this is shared by us all.

Chapter 16 Summary

1. *Supervision* and support are different; supervision is a mixture of personal, professional and developmental monitoring and boundary keeping activities, required by professional counsellors. *Support* is the part of that mixture that Brigid Proctor has called *restorative.*

2. Stress in helpers can eventually lead to burnout. The seeds of stress may be sown on counsellor training courses where unrealistically high expectations can be set, or trainees feel they are in 'double-binds'.

3. Counselling skills helpers may need to get both backup and support. Backup can be physical, human or informational.

4. Four ways of organising support are offered; self-support, peer support, consultative support and training.

5. The skills involved in giving support are again the core conditions. Particular ways of delivering these skills include highly structured *debriefing.*

Endpiece

Alan and Pete: At the outset we said that we would say something about the process of writing this book together. It also seems to us that this is the best place to record our thanks to those who have directly or indirectly assisted us in getting the writing done and keeping the whole thing together.   Alan is writing this in Nottingham, Pete is putting finishing touches to other sections on his word processor in Manchester. Since this conclusion really is being written as we finish the book, we really do know who we have to say thanks to! The book is already a summary of ideas and concepts that we think will probably be helpful, so we will not be attempting to summarise them further here, but this chapter will offer you ways to review where you are now and to consider your next steps beyond *Next Steps*.

Alan: We have been living with this book, as an idea, as a project, as a part-formed product for a long time now. It is quite hard to believe that we are very nearly at the end of it: that within a few weeks of me writing this endpiece in my study/counselling room on a wet morning in January ('95) some of our first readers may be working through the text: finding the ideas puzzling or delightful, meeting our characters and our ways of exploring key concepts and skills and deciding whether they like our work or not. We very much hope that this book will have proved to be enjoyable, that you will feel that it has supported and developed your understanding of counselling, assisted in your development of skills and your personal growth, and been a useful companion on this part of your journey.

Alan and Pete: At one point in our excited explorations of what we could put into this book we came up with the idea of recording some of our discussions about key concepts and skills and then editing them so that our readers would be offered dialogue and difference (within a broadly agreed framework) rather than a more singular, *'take it or leave it'* approach to our material. We thought (for a moment or two before we abandoned the idea as entirely unmanageable) that such an approach would open up to you the process of writing this book as well as offering lively diversity. Even though we abandoned the idea of recorded dialogue the notion of being open about how we have worked, of being unmysterious about the process, stayed with us since it mirrors the habits of the helper who takes a person-centred *approach* to helping. You may not be particularly interested in how we got this book together, but if you are the following paragraphs say a little about how we have worked and how we have felt and changed as a result.

We have already said something in the 'Introductions' chapter about the origins of this book and how we knew each other. Beginning to get it together at that early stage was very exciting, although it was only one of many things happening for both of us at the time, and it is quite difficult now to disentangle some of the events and discussions. Often quite late at night, sometimes over a meal after other work was completed, occasionally over breakfast, our conversations were partly about this book, partly about other actual or potential texts for PCCS, partly about course developments in Manchester and at Nottingham Trent. Often we talked about each other and what we believed or thought or felt, and what experiences we had had that shaped our understanding of a concept or the way we thought it might be offered in this book. We guess that these explorations and negotiations, part intellectual, part practical (*'You do this by then and I'll do that'*) and, sometimes about feelings and experiences, mirror quite closely aspects of your development through your course and as you have read this book.

Alan: I wish I had thought from the outset how good it would be to keep a journal of this process in the way that we have suggested to you that you might keep a journal of your progression through this part of your training. At least it would have made it easier to write this review of what we did and what we learned, and at best we might have captured and retained more of the important elements of our individual development through this period and what we have learned about collaboration.

Alan and Pete: Although, as we come to the end, we both feel that we own and are responsible for the book as a whole, the overall concept and shape being the outcome of agreement (by direct negotiation and by trial and response) we have written very little actually together (no more that a few sentences and the wording of the back cover). Nearly all of the text was written first by one of us then sent to the other for comment/editing sometimes going round more than once, eventually ending up with Pete who put it in final form onto the PC. I think it took us both quite a lot of courage and trust both to send each-other our 'creations' and to comment boldly and directly on what each had written.

Alan: I certainly found both parts of this process quite a challenge and at times had to work hard not to be defensive, but to remain assertive where it did matter.

Pete: I commented at the end of our last face to face session (most has been 'phone, and post or fax) that on overall balance I have found a formal collaboration more difficult that writing on my own. This says something about me I guess. I find writing a challenge anyway; an almost daily stream of crises of confidence *'No one will want to read this,'* or, *'Everyone knows this already.'* interspersed with equally ridiculous highs of the, *'This is the best thing ever written'* type.

Alan and Pete: One of the unexpected challenges for both of us was the gradual realisation that although we apparently agreed quite quickly on the sort of 'voice' we wanted for *Next Steps*, actually creating it was more difficult because there are profound differences in how we think and write that have needed to be interwoven. It's possible that these differences reflect the ways in which we get from an idea to a page of type, as well as our teaching experiences in slightly different sectors of education. (Pete worked in Further Education, and Alan got a lot of his experience either in the private sector or in Higher Education).

Although most chapters have something of each of us, you may recognise that the fairly discursive approach of this chapter so far is Alan's way, whilst you may have noticed that Pete:

- prefers to leave the discussion to you
- tends towards shorter and punchier sentences
- breaks up his text into bullet points
- sometimes leaves the ideas hanging for you to round off.

(It's hard to tell whether this really reflects how we *think*, but it seems significant at *some* level.)

Pete: I will usually have ideas in my head for a long time, and a sense that they are gradually shaping themselves into the chapter I am writing, so that when I eventually sits down with the keyboard it often comes out fluently and almost complete. (At least that's what I tell myself!) I write straight to the disc quite late (very late by most people's standards) and almost never revise it. Maybe that's why I find collaboration difficult, since I have had to consider revising my work.

Alan: I work quite differently. Initially I have some ideas and hopefully a sense of the shape of the piece (which have to be written down otherwise they will escape), but then I sit down at the keyboard and write a first draft rather laboriously and often uncertainly, not really knowing until I read it whether it works at all. Then that draft is edited and edited, chunks are rewritten, false starts eventually identified and discarded and quite slowly the piece emerges. I think if we were literally working side by side the difference would be alarming for both of us, a bit like being driven by someone who handles the car in a very different way from your style of driving: you may trust them to get you there in one piece because their no-claims bonus is intact, but you itch for them to change gear seconds before they reach for the gear lever, and there is a dent in the floor where you have been breaking when they still have their foot on the accelerator.

Alan and Pete: The struggle to write together has been compulsively interesting and engaging for both of us at times. We have both learned a lot; sometimes from what each of us produced for the book and often from the dialogue that surrounded our work.   What we were often sharing was how we approached things as *teachers*, and we realised that we were writing as teachers. We had lots of discussion about whether any of this would work, because we expect most readers will have a face to face tutor (perhaps several) and we knew that we needed to be careful to support the work of those colleagues, and try to make sure that if they too are working from a counselling approach to helping, that we do nothing to undermine them.

Clearly not everything has come out quite as we expected - for instance although we still hope that it will have been possible for you to track certain themes or ideas through the text our original conception was that such themes would emerge as pretty clear alternative pathways through the thicket rather than the fainter tracks with the odd signpost that have emerged. The material that we intended is all there, it is still possible to track it through (don't forget to use the index) but the way through the woods, the connections between the concepts, is less well defined than we thought it might be. The good news is that even if you wandered from the path you aren't likely to have been lost for long, and are probably not going to have come to any harm! You may even have found some things you might otherwise have missed.

Pete: As the book progressed, I got a sense of real learning for myself, a sense of understandings shifting and broadening making real differences to how I *think* even if I might not end up *acting* very differently. I think I have learned by the process of doing it, that full contact with people or ideas at both a thinking and feeling level leads to change.

Alan: For me, the learning and discovery has been at lots of levels, for example further clarification of some of Rogers concepts and underlying theories, a better understanding of elements of the craft of writing, more knowledge about some aspects of my critical and defensive self, greater insight into what it takes to get from an idea to a text in your hands, and warmth and friendship shared with Pete and Maggie (the two halves of PCCS publishing- between them co-author, editor, business manager, typist, typesetter, layout artist, proof reader, print manager, PR and advertising executive and general dogsbodies as well).

Alan and Pete: Both of us want to put on record the really important part that Maggie has played in the creation of this text: not only as a partner in PCCS, and in Pete's life, but quite directly as editor, helping us to cut out gobbledegook and obstructive jargon and helping us to recognise when we have not been clear with ideas, or too florid in our use of metaphor and analogy. Maggie has also taken responsibility for indexing, and some of the chapter summaries. Heartfelt thanks then, from both of us. Both of us also want to acknowledge that other family members, colleagues and friends have been affected by our absences, abstraction tiredness or moodiness throughout the construction of this book. For their (usual) tolerance and forbearance we thank them all.

It may sound like the soft of thing all authors say but the biggest debts we owe are to people too numerous or private to mention by name. Those who shared in our development and taught us theory and skills, those with whom we have shared our learning when they were our counsellors, our students, our clients, our supervisors and supervisees. Often when we have been writing, we have imagined individuals and groups we have worked with, and thought how they might understand the idea that we were trying to convey, or how they might have been helped by an approach or way of working that we were seeking to explore. Without that crowd of people to recall none of this would have worked, and without you our readers now none of it would have any point - so our thanks are definitely to you too.

Pete: When writing the chapter on *Support*, I remembered some forgotten home truths about how I sustain myself through each day and how important other people are to me. I would like to particularly thank Barbara Cordwell for willingly bearing not only her part of our shared training load, but also my bit as well on a number of occasions. I would not have got through the more fraught writing days without the music of New Order, The Lemonheads and the Levellers, so thanks are due to them for their unwitting assistance with this project.

Alan: I have already mentioned in *Introductions* the assistance of my colleagues at work in the earliest stages of the project, without the initial stimulus it would not have happened like this at all. On a day to day basis I have been greatly supported by my partner's patience and forbearance when I was locked away writing late, absent at weekends or just too tired to make much sense at the end of the day. By sometimes taking on some of my tasks she made space for me to fit in all this alongside my other work, and she did that whilst herself engaged in demanding professional work as a Health Visitor and finishing an OU History degree with a 2.1. Thank you Sarah it's been a staggering twelve months.

Alan and Pete: The last part of this endpiece concerns you the reader; where have you got to, and where are you going next? Education and training in Counselling at every level is becoming more and more widely available, but at this stage in the development of the discipline and practice it is pretty chaotic. It's difficult to know about the levels of training being offered, the competence and experience of the trainers who offer them in both the public and private sectors and in both Further and Higher education. It seems to us that there are beginning to be four or five levels at which counselling training is being offered.

[a] Introductory Courses: 25 to 60 or so contact hours introducing the field of counselling and allowing an appreciation of some basic skills (The kind of course for which *First Steps* was written as a companion).
[b] Foundation/Certificate/Counselling Skills Courses: 75 to 150 contact hours or so, providing both a firmer grounding in the central concepts of counselling, perhaps some theoretical diversity, and almost universally, practical skills training. Such courses commonly cater both for those who wish to acquire some knowledge and skills from the counselling approach as a forerunner to professional training and those who wish to use their learning to enhance their functioning in other professional and operational roles (The kind of course for which *Next Steps* has been written as a companion.)
[c] Advanced Certificate/Diploma/Professional Training: 300 to 500 contact hours or so, providing a full professional training, both at a conceptual and skills level, setting counselling in an intellectual and social context and requiring supervised professional practice (and often personal experience as a client) as an essential part of professional development. (No doubt *Further Steps,* or some such title, will appear as the companion for this level course in the not-too-distant future.)
[d] Master's Level: a year or so of additional study making more academic demands than Diploma or Professional training, perhaps requiring a higher level of academic achievement alongside professional competence, sometimes allowing for more specialised training in a particular approach or area of work often including a greater understanding of , and doing some, relevant research etc.
[e] BAC Accredited Counsellor/Independent Registration: not itself a *course*, but arguably the end point of initial training for those who aspire to professional counselling. This level requires Diploma level training and marks the logical goal of professional development: acceptance by one's peers as a mature professional practitioner. Find out more from BAC about requirements for Individual Accreditation.

One of the shortcomings of the way of thinking about counselling that is inherent in this model is the implication that the use of counselling skills within an informal setting or another occupational role is inferior and simpler activities than professional counselling. As this view begins to be challenged maybe we will begin to see courses which recognise the complexity of using counselling in this way and allow such practitioners access to Diplomas in Counselling Skills. Some would argue that NVQ's may be helpful in this regard. We disagree fairly vehemently about the validity and inevitability of the whole NVQ structure so we will leave you to explore that elsewhere.

Anyone with a serious commitment to counselling (within a profession or as a profession) would do well to join the BAC and thus be able to benefit from the knowledge and expertise located within its central organisation and its membership. If you plan to be a professional it's never to early to begin to think about registration and accreditation because then you will know what you are aiming for right from the outset. Even if it takes many years to get there. Many counsellors in the making prefer to take the local stopping train rather than the inter-city express because they find the time and the scenery more serene and edifying: nevertheless knowing your destination from early on in the journey makes it more likely that your side trips down branch lines will be chosen and fruitful, rather than accidental and frustrating.

As we draw to a close we really are interested in how have you received this book and how have you used it, what you have found most helpful and what has tended to obstruct or irritate you. We hope that you have enjoyed our work, but even if on balance you wish you hadn't spent your money and time on this text we would like to hear your feedback. So here is a last exercise for you to help you to summarise your responses:

> • *Make a note of the three things that you have most enjoyed about this text.*
> • *Next make a note of the three things that you consider the most important pieces of learning for you as you used the text.*
> • *Next make a note of three things that left you confused or were unclear in the text.*
> • *Then three other things that you would have liked to see done differently (maybe we missed things out, or included things you felt unnecessary).*
> • *Finally make a note of three things that you found unhelpful.*

If you were to make a copy of the results of this summary and feedback exercise and send it to us at PCCS it would really make our day and be helpful to us when we come to revise the text for future editions. Like your face to face tutors and your peers on your course, we are real people who need real feedback; so if you have the time we really would like to hear from you.

References

Carkhuff, R.R., (1969a) *Helping and Human Relations; Vol. I* , New York: Holt, Rinehart and Winston.

Carkhuff, R.R., (1969b) *Helping and Human Relations; Vol. II* , New York: Holt, Rinehart and Winston.

Sue Culley, (1991) *Integrative Counselling Skills in Action,* London: Sage

Windy Dryden, (1990) *Rational-Emotive Counselling in Action,* London: Sage.

Dryden, W. and Thorne, B., (1991) *Training and Supervision for Counselling in Action,* London: Sage.

Gerard Egan, (1981) *The Skilled Helper, New Edition*, Brooks/Cole.

Gerard Egan, (1994) *The Skilled Helper - A Problem Management Approach to Helping*, Brooks/Cole.

Heron, J., (1990) *Helping the Client,* London: Sage.

Francesca Inskipp and Brigid Proctor, (1993) *The Art, Craft and Tasks of Supervision, Part 1. Making the Most of Supervision.* Cascade Publications.

Mearns, D. and Thorne, B., (1988) *Person Centred Counselling in Action,* London: Sage.

Michael Jacobs, (1988) *Psychodynamic Counselling in Action,* London: Sage.

McLeod, J., (1993) *An Introduction to Counselling*, Buckingham: Open University Press.

Richard Nelson-Jones, (1993) *Practical Counselling and helping Skills (3rd Edn),* London: Cassell.

Pines, A., (1982) 'Helpers' Motivation and the Burnout Syndrome.' In Willis, T.A. (ed) *Basic Processes in Helping Relationships*, New York: Academic Press.

Proctor, B., (undated) 'Supervision: A co-operative exercise in accountability', In Marken, M and Payne, M. (eds) *Enabling and Ensuring.* NYB and Council for Education and Training in Youth and Community Work.

Carl Rogers, (1951) *Client-Centered Therapy,* London: Constable.

Rogers, C.R. (1957) 'The Necessary and Sufficient Conditions of Therapeutic Personality Change.' *Journal of Consulting Psychology,* Vol.21, No.2, pp 95-103.

Rogers, C.R., (1986) 'A Client-Centered/Person-Centered Approach to Therapy.' In Kutash, I.L. and Wolf, A. (eds), *Psychotherapists Casebook,* San Francisco: Jossey-Bass.

Rowan, J., (1983) *The Reality Game*, London: Routledge.

Pete Sanders, (1996) *An Incomplete Guide to Using Counselling Skills on the Telephone, revised 2nd edition*, Manchester: PCCS.

Pete Sanders, (1996) *First Steps in Counselling,* 2nd edition, Ross-onWye: PCCS.

Julius Seeman, (1983) *Personality Integration: Studies and Reflections,* New York: Human Sciences Press.

John Southgate and Rosemary Randall, illustrated by Frances Tomlinson, (1978) *The Barefoot Psychoanalyst, 2nd revised edition,* Assoc. Karen Horney Psychoanalytic Counsellors.

Peter Trower, Andrew Casey and Windy Dryden, (1988) *Cognitive Behavioural Counselling in Action.* London: Sage.

Warnath, C.F. and Shelton, J.L., (1976) 'The Ultimate Disappointment: The Burnedout Counsellor.' *Personnel and Guidance Journal,* 55, 172-175

Steve Williams, (1993) *An Incomplete Guide to Referral Issues for Counsellors,* Manchester: PCCS.

Further Reading

If you wish to pursue your interest in counselling approaches, either in general or in particular, perhaps in preparation for further training; we can recommend the following books. They are all written in an approachable style.

Sue Culley, (1991) *Integrative Counselling Skills in Action,* London: Sage

Windy Dryden, (1990) *Rational-Emotive Counselling in Action,* London: Sage.

Michael Jacobs, (1988) *Psychodynamic Counselling in Action*, London: Sage.

Tony Merry, (1999) *Learning and Being in Person-Centred Counselling,* Ross-on-Wye: PCCS Books.

Tony Merry, (1995) *Invitation to Person-Centred Psychology*, Whurr.

Peter Trower, Andrew Casey and Windy Dryden, (1988) *Cognitive Behavioural Counselling in Action.* London: Sage.

If you are on a counselling training course and you are returning to study after a long break, or not feeling to confident and having difficulty with your assignments, the following book may help:

Pete Sanders, (1998) *Step in to* Study *Counselling - A Students' Guide to Tackling Diploma and Certificate Course Assignments* 2nd edition*,* Ross-on-Wye: PCCS Books.

If you use counselling skills on the telephone in the course of your job, or do telephone helpline work, either paid or as a volunteer:

Pete Sanders, (1996) *An Incomplete Guide to Using Counselling Skills on the Telephone -revised 2nd Edition,* Manchester: PCCS Books.

Useful Addresses

Advice, Guidance, Counselling and Psychotherapy Lead Body Secretariat: 40A High St, Welwyn, Herts, AL6 9EQ

British Association for Counselling: 1 Regent Place, Rugby, Warwickshire, CV21 2PJ

Index

Subjects

ABC (of RET), 76, 79
Action, 147-150
    as client movement, 148
    as the helper's agenda, 147
    skills, 149
    two views of, 147
    what action?, 147
Activating event, 76
Active listening, 91, 108, 109
    non-judgemental, 110
    authentic, 112
Aggression, 182, 183
Authenticity, 50-55
    and questions, 129
    in real life, 55
Authentic responses, 113
Awfulizing, 77

Backup, 169, 197
    human, 199
    information, 199
    physical, 198
British Association for Counselling, 34, 38, 59, 191, 192, 195, 211, 212
    Code of Ethics and Practice for Counselling Skills, 192-193
Burnout, 197

Challenge, 143-146
    as a response, 145
    as a skill, 144
Clarifying, 28, 109
Client-centred, 91
Communication, 46, 107
Competence, 120
    confidence in your, 166
    conscious, 120
    unconscious, 120
Concreteness, 62, 64
Congruence, 35, 50-55, 103
Coping strategies, 140

Core conditions, 35, 41-46, 128, 150
    necessary and sufficient, 61, 62
Conscious, 71
Consequence, 76
Content, 115
    feelings, 116
    thoughts, 115
Contracts, 103
Core self, 80

Debriefing, 204
Defence mechanisms, 71
Denial, 82
Dependence, 176
Developmental support, 37, 38, 59
Difference, 175
Difficult situations, 165-184
    learning about, 165
Discrimination, 46, 107
Distortion, 82
Distress,
    helping someone in great, 169
Disturbing,
    helping someone who is very, 171
Drug abuse, 189
Dynamic equilibrium, 70, 71

Eclectic approaches, 86
Ego, 70
Empathy, 35, 41-46, 103, 150, 175
    and questions, 128
Ending, 151-154
    in real life, 152
Ethics, 177, 178, 185-194
    and congruence, 190
    and counselling, 187
    and culture, 186
    and empathy, 190
    and respect, 190
    BAC Code of, 192-193

Feedback, 121
Feelings, 139
    acknowledging, 108
    content, 116
    identifying, 108, 116
Frame of reference,
    internal, 42, 43, 44, 107, 114
    external, 44

Groundrules, 5

Helping event,
    content of, 25, 28
    focus of, 25, 28
    structure of, 25, 27
Humanism, 90
Humanistic approaches, 80-85

Immediacy, 62, 64
Integrative approaches, 86-88
Intoxication, 188, 189
Introjected values, 81
Introjection, 81

Journal, personal, 10
Judgement,
    and self-development, 48

Learning grid, 8 & 9
Learning
    making a record of your, 10
Limits,
    helping someone within your, 167
Listening
    active, 91, 108, 109
    to content, 115
    to feelings, 116
    to process, 118
    to thoughts, 115
    to person's whole world, 119

Musturbation, 76

New perspectives, 133-142
    skills for developing, 135
    What are?, 136

Oppression, 18, 20, 175
Overgeneralisation, 77

Paraphrasing, 109
Patterns, 137
Personalisation, 77
Personal support, 37, 38, 59
Person-Centred, 16
    Approach, 69, 80-85, 91, 144
        and human personality, 80
        and mental life, 81
        view of the helper and helping process, 83
Phenomenology, 80, 90
Practical support, 38
Problems,
    individual, 22
    personal, 17
    practical, 17
Problem-solving, 37, 58, 59, 133
    strategies, 138
Process, 115, 118
Projection, 72
Psychoanalysis, 70
    and human personality, 70
    and mental life, 81
    view of the helper and helping process, 73
Psychodynamic Approaches, 70-74

Questions, 123-132
    and core conditions, 128
    arguments against the use of, 123
    closed, 126
    leading and loaded, 126
    open, 127
    sensitive use of, 123

Reaction formation, 72
Reading log, 11
Reality testing, 138
Reassurance, 62, 64
REBT, 75-79, 87, 138
    and human personality, 75
    and mental life, 76
    view of the helper and helping process, 78
Referral, 168, 169
Relationships, 20

Repression, 71
Resources, 140
Respect, 35, 46-50
        the challenge of, 47

Safety,
        confidence in your physical, 166
Self concept, 81
Self harm, 165, 172
Silence, 174
Skills directory, 11
Stress, 197
Structuring, 95, 178
        before the relationship starts, 98
        during the helping relationship, 100
        for helping, 96
        in the first few moments, 99
        how, 97
        when, 97
        when the relationship changes, 101
Sublimation, 71
Supervision, 195, 196
Support, 167, 195-206
        consultative, 202
        giving, 203
        organising, 201
        peer, 201
        receiving, 202
        self, 201
Systemic issues, 17

Therapeutic counselling, 38, 59
Thinking, 139
Third party, 178, 179
Thoughts, 115
        content, 115
Training, 202
Turning against self, 72

Unconscious, 71
UPR, 35, 46-50, 103
        and questions, 129

Names

Berne, E. 74

Carkhuff, R.R. 50, 52, 62, 64, 147
Culley, S. 87, 88, 89, 90, 127, 147

Deaux, 88
Dryden, W. 127, 202

Egan, G. 61, 86, 87, 88, 89, 133, 135, 147
Ellis, A. 75, 76, 77, 78, 79, 86, 139

Freud, S. 70, 71, 73, 83, 86

Heron, J. 89

Inskipp, F. 203

Jacobs, M. 73

McLeod, J. 60
Mearns, D. 42, 46

Nelson-Jones, R. 89, 127, 147

Pines, A. 197
Proctor, B. 202, 203

Randall, R. 73
Rogers, C.R. 4, 35, 41, 42, 44, 47, 61, 62, 69, 80, 81, 82, 83, 86, 90, 91, 95, 140
Rowan, J. 52

Sanders, P. 108, 120, 203
Shelton, J.L. 197
Southgate, J. 73

Thorne, B. 42, 46, 202
Trower, P. 127

Warnath, C.F. 197
Williams, S. 168
Wrightsman, 88

If you are enjoying *Next Steps in Counselling,* try this companion book to help you tackle your certificate and diploma assignments

Step in to *Study* Counselling
A Students' Guide to Tackling Diploma and Certificate Course Assignments 2nd edition
Pete Sanders
ISBN 1 898059 19 5 £12.00

This book has become an essential study guide to students on certificate and diploma courses. It covers just about every type of assignment imaginable from how to improve your essay-writing through to the traumas of tape-transcribing. Journal writing, peer assessment, how to give feedback on fellow students' skills work, self-evaluation and making client notes are just a few more of the many topics explored.

An Incomplete Guide to Using Counselling Skills on the Telephone
Revised 2nd Edition
Pete Sanders
ISBN 1 898059 12 8 £11.50

After the overwhelming success of the first edition of this book, we are pleased to publish a revised and updated edition taking into account the latest developments in this fast-growing field. With two new chapters and other new material, this book contains 198 pages of essential information for anyone wishing to offer helping relationships over the telephone.

An Incomplete Guide to Referral Issues for Counsellors
Steve Williams
ISBN 1 898059 01 2 £9.00

A book to help practitioners develop an informed, ethical, principled framework for responsible referral decisions. The book has been received enthusiastically by trainers and trainees at all levels of counselling training.

Order all books direct from PCCS Books Ltd, postage and packing free.
Orders delivered within five working days.
Telephone (01989) 77 07 07 with your credit card details.

The new introduction to person-centred counselling from its origins to current developments in theory and practice

LEARNING AND BEING IN PERSON-CENTRED COUNSELLING
A TEXTBOOK FOR DISCOVERING THEORY AND DEVELOPING PRACTICE

Tony Merry *with additional material by Bob Lusty*
ISBN 1 898059 24 1   156x234   pp approx 180+iv   £13.00

THIS BOOK IS a complete rewrite and extended version of the successful *What is Person-Centred Therapy* by Tony Merry and Bob Lusty previously published by the Gale Centre. At almost twice the size of the original, it contains new, up-to-date material and offers in-depth discussion of all aspects of person-centred counselling in theory and practice.

The coverage of the topics is innovative, comprehensive and thorough. Tony Merry is renowned for his straightforward and accessible writing style, making *Learning and Being in Person-Centred Counselling* suitable for a wide variety of readers.

Augmenting the clear presentation, the book is brought to life by many suggestions for exploring and developing person-centred values, qualities, attitudes and skills.

LEARNING AND BEING IN PERSON-CENTRED COUNSELLING is recommended for:
- certificate and diploma in counselling trainees and tutors;
- undergraduate psychology students and lecturers;
- nurses and social workers in training;
- those on vocational and professional helping professions-related courses;
- trainees on integrative, cognitive or psychodynamic courses;
- anyone seeking input on contemporary person-centred theory and practice.

CHAPTERS INCLUDE
- Human nature, actualisation and the development of the person;
- A theory of counselling;
- Developing person-centred values, skills, qualities and attitudes;
- Training issues: client work and personal development;
- Supervision;
- Working and being in groups;
- Resources;

TONY MERRY teaches at the University of East London on postgraduate and undergraduate courses in counselling and counselling psychology. He is author of several books and articles on counselling. He co-founded the British Association for the Person-Centred Approach in 1989 and is currently editor of *Person-Centred Practice* and the *Universities Psychotherapy Association Review.* He has contributed to workshops and other person-centred events in Europe, including several with Carl Rogers in England, Ireland and Hungary in the 1980s.

Bob Lusty *worked closely with Tony Merry at the University of East London for over 20 years. He is now in private practice as a counsellor and supervisor.*

Books to help you in continuing your counselling studies

Emerging Woman
Natalie Rogers
ISBN 1 898059 11 X £12.50

'My daughter has written a personal, sensitive and moving book about her own journey as a woman...This book confirms what I have long believed: what is most personal is most general. Women in general will respond precisely because it is so revealing of the intensely private story of one woman.' Carl R Rogers

This absorbing book is for everyone, whether your interest is in womens' issues, personal change and self discovery, sex roles, mid-life as a new beginning or living alone.

Counselling, Class & Politics: Undeclared Influences in Therapy
Anne Kearney
ISBN 1 898059 09 8 £10.50

'Anne Kearney's book...does not make for comfortable reading, but if we value our integrity, we should make it obligatory reading.' Professor Brian Thorne.

'...this is a respectful demolition of the view that counselling is apolitical and that counsellors can take up a position which is not political...I have been waiting for this text since I began training counsellors... Almost like a programmed text it will take you into your hidden agenda about class and politics in counselling.' Alan Frankland.

Person-Centred Approaches in Schools
Jackie Hill
ISBN 1 898059 07 1 £10.50

This text suggests a blueprint for a way of being in schools that values and respects the individual, helping staff and pupils tackle the long-standing problems affecting secondary education including bullying, poor motivation, truancy and aggression.

Childhood Sexual Abuse, Sexuality, Pregnancy and Birthing: *A Life History Study*
Patrica Smith
ISBN 1 898059 10 1 £8.50

This monograph is based on a research project undertaken by the author. The content, a consideration of the relationship between sexual abuse, pregnancy and motherhood, breaks new ground. As such, the study is of importance to women who have experienced childhood sexual abuse, to their partners and to all people working in the health professions, helping services and counselling.

Order all books direct from PCCS Books Ltd, postage and packing free.
Orders delivered within five working days.
Telephone (01989) 77 07 07 with your credit card details.